The Architect's Brain

Other Wiley-Blackwell titles by Harry Francis Mallgrave

An Introduction to Architectural Theory: 1968 to the Present
Harry Francis Mallgrave and David Goodman

A sharp and lively text that offers a substantive yet accessible narrative history of this period, *An Introduction* charts the veritable revolution in architectural thinking that has taken place, as well as the implications of this intellectual upheaval for the field.

Paperback isbn 978-1-4051-8062-7

Architectural Theory Volume 1: An Anthology from Vitruvius to 1870
Edited by Harry Francis Mallgrave

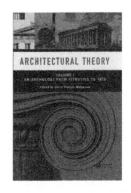

Architectural Theory: Vitruvius to 1870 surveys the development of the field of architecture from its earliest days to the year 1870. The first truly comprehensive anthology that brings together the classic essays in the field, the volume chronicles the major developments and trends in architecture from Vitruvius to Gottfried Semper.

Paperback isbn 978-1-4051-0258-2

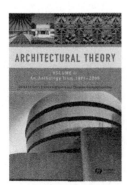

Architectural Theory Volume II: An Anthology from 1871 to 2005
Edited by Harry Francis Mallgrave, Christina Contandriopoulos

This second volume of the landmark *Architectural Theory* anthology surveys the development of architectural theory from the Franco-Prussian war of 1871 until the end of the twentieth century. The entire two volume anthology follows the full range of architectural literature from classical times to present transformations.

Paperback isbn 978-1-4051-0260-5

The Architect's Brain

Neuroscience, Creativity, and Architecture

Harry Francis Mallgrave

WILEY-BLACKWELL

A John Wiley & Sons, Ltd., Publication

This paperback edition first published 2011
© 2011 Harry Francis Mallgrave

Edition history: Blackwell Publishing Ltd (hardback, 2010)

Blackwell Publishing was acquired by John Wiley & Sons in February 2007. Blackwell's publishing program has been merged with Wiley's global Scientific, Technical, and Medical business to form Wiley-Blackwell.

Registered Office
John Wiley & Sons Ltd, The Atrium, Southern Gate, Chichester, West Sussex, PO19 8SQ, UK

Editorial Offices
350 Main Street, Malden, MA 02148-5020, USA
9600 Garsington Road, Oxford, OX4 2DQ, UK
The Atrium, Southern Gate, Chichester, West Sussex, PO19 8SQ, UK

For details of our global editorial offices, for customer services, and for information about how to apply for permission to reuse the copyright material in this book please see our website at www.wiley.com/wiley-blackwell.

The right of Harry M. Mallgrave to be identified as the author of this work has been asserted in accordance with the UK Copyright, Designs and Patents Act 1988.

Wiley also publishes its books in a variety of electronic formats. Some content that appears in print may not be available in electronic books.

Designations used by companies to distinguish their products are often claimed as trademarks. All brand names and product names used in this book are trade names, service marks, trademarks or registered trademarks of their respective owners. The publisher is not associated with any product or vendor mentioned in this book. This publication is designed to provide accurate and authoritative information in regard to the subject matter covered. It is sold on the understanding that the publisher is not engaged in rendering professional services. If professional advice or other expert assistance is required, the services of a competent professional should be sought.

Library of Congress Cataloging-in-Publication Data
Mallgrave, Harry Francis.
  The architect's brain : neuroscience, creativity, and architecture / Harry Francis Mallgrave.
    p. cm.
  Includes bibliographical references and index.
  ISBN 978-1-4051-9585-0 (hardcover : alk. paper) ISBN 978-0-4706-5825-3 (paperback: alk. Paper)
1. Cognitive neuroscience.   2. Architects.   3. Architecture and philosophy.   4. Architecture and science.   5. Creative ability.   I. Title.   II. Title: Neuroscience, creativity, and architecture.
  QP360.5.M35 2010
  612.8′233–dc22

                                               2009036208
A catalogue record for this book is available from the British Library.

This book is published in the following electronic formats: ePDFs 9781444317282; Wiley Online Library 9781444317275; ePub 9781118078679

Set in 10.5/13 pt Galliard by SPi Publisher Services, Pondicherry, India

2 2012

Contents

Illustrations

Introduction

My intentions in writing this book are twofold: first to look at the remarkable strides currently being made in neuroscience, and second to begin the lengthy process of discerning what this new knowledge might have to say to architects and many others involved in fields of design.

In the first regard, one can scarcely be disappointed. Even a cursory glance at what has taken place in scientific laboratories over the last decade – from leaps of knowledge along a neurobiological front to sophisticated imaging devices recording the activities of the working brain – reveals that we are living in the midst of monumental discoveries. For, in gaining an increasingly detailed understanding of the human brain, we are not only achieving major insights into the nature of what has historically been called the "mind" but also exploring such piquant issues as memory, consciousness, feelings, thinking, and creativity. This understanding is radically reshaping the image of who we are and where we come from, biologically speaking, and at the same time it is allowing us for the first time to ponder answers to some questions that have been posed over thousands of years of metaphysical speculation.

Certainly one of the more pivotal insights of our day, one that is particularly germane to our digital age, is that we are not machines, or more specifically, our brains are not computers. In fact, the nonlinear way in which the brain gathers and actively structures information could not be more different from the manufactured logic of a computer. The brain, to put it in more graphic terms, is a living, throbbing organ, one that over millennia (with its ever increasing consumption of the body's fuel) has gone to extreme lengths to guard our essential well-being and enhance the propagation of the species. Taking into account its totality – from the thin mantle of gray matter scrunched along the inside cavity of the cranial vault to the nerve cells in our feet – the brain is a fully embodied entity. It is a physical entity but at the same time its whole is greater than the sum of it electrical and chemical events.

Such an understanding is not only reconfiguring the image of our-selves but also casting a distinctly archaic air on that long-standing distinction between body and mind. The brain comes equipped with approximately 100 billion neurons and with a DNA complex of 30,000 genes, which were fully sequenced only in 2006. Oddly, though, the brain arrives at birth with only about half of its nerve cells, or neurons, wired together, and this again is a fact of great importance. If indeed it is we who do much of the neural wiring through the postnatal experi-ences with which we invest this palpitating entity then we should assume the same responsibility for the brain's development. We, in fact, have the power to alter much of our neural circuitry (for better or worse and within limits of course) until the day we die. As architects this means one thing: we can always become better designers by adding to the complexity of our synaptic maps, and thereby create a better or more interesting environment in which the human species can thrive.

Moving beyond such generalities, however, the issue of what the recent advances of neuroscience says to architects becomes more dif-ficult. Historically, one of the problems has been that, until the last decade or so, few instruments of science were trained on healthy brains. Today the problem has become the opposite; with the prolif-eration of the new imagining devices beginning in the late 1980s, we now have a prodigious amount of experimental literature being gath-ered on a daily basis, so much so that it is difficult to see the proverbial forest from the trees. With the still accelerating pace of investigation, we have also seen a broadening of areas to which this research is being applied. In 1999, for instance, the London microneurologist Semir Zeki, who had devoted more than 30 years to mapping the brain's visual processing, shifted the direction of his research by proposing a field of "neuroaesthetics" to explore the brain's interaction with art.[1] Parallel with his efforts, the art historian John Onians, who too has long been interested in the biological foundation of artistic perception, has proposed a "neuroarthistory," following the lead of one of his mentors, Ernst Gombrich.[2] Another researcher at University College London, Hugo Spiers, has recently collaborated with an architect and held workshops at London's Architectural Association.[3] In the spring of 2008 the artist Olafur Eliasson joined others in Berlin in forming the Association of Neuroesthetics, which promises to serve as "a Platform for Art and Neuroscience."[4] Meanwhile, in San Diego, a group of architects and scientists, led by the architect John P. Eberhard, have founded the Academy of Neuroscience for Architecture (ANFA), with the explicit mission of promoting and advancing "knowledge that links research to a growing understanding of human responses to the built environment."[5] Such interdisciplinary alliances will no doubt continue to multiply and expand their range of interests over the next few decades.

The question, then, is where these collaborations may lead. The interests of Zeki, Onians, and Eliasson are grounded in aesthetics and therefore ponder such questions as the neurological basis for experiencing art, while the ANFA proposes experimental research that can be applied directly to design. In this last respect, one is reminded of the promises of some of the behavioral sciences of the 1960s, when the studies of anthropologists, sociologists, and psychologists held out the prospect of working models that could improve the human condition. There is, however, one crucial difference to be found in these activities in the 2000s, which is that we now have quite different tools and a growing bounty of biological knowledge at our command. These new instruments are giving us a more insightful and, in some cases, a quite specific picture of how we engage the world.

Having said this, I want to stress that my approach is slightly different. My interest lies principally with the creative process itself, that is, with the elusive issues of ambiguity and metaphoric thinking that seem to lie at our very core. And what I see neuroscience offering designers today, quite simply, is a sketch of the enormous intricacy of our intellectual and sensory-emotive existence. I say this with no trepidation, even if it also means that this research will not as yet offer us any neat or easy answers and, in fact, will rather quickly be overtaken by its own progress. If, today, we are for the first time taking images of the working brain in all of its complexity, we are still a few years away from constructing the final genetic and epigenetic models of this involved process. For this reason, this newly forming terrain of investigation should be of especial importance to younger designers, whose careers will no doubt unfold within the continuing advancement of such knowledge.

Nevertheless, the portrait that is emerging of the seemingly infinite diversity or multiformity of human existence is not a strikingly new figure. Scientists, psychologists, religious leaders, philosophers, and artists of every bent have been telling us the same thing since the beginning of recorded time. And architects, if I might borrow an analogy from Zeki, have always been neuroscientists – in the sense that the human brain is the wellspring of every creative endeavor, and the outcome of every good design is whether the architect enriches or diminishes the private world of the individual experiencing it.

To provide some historical background on this matter, I have, in Part One of the study, attached a series of short essays, mostly about architects who earlier considered the issue of how we view and ponder the built world. They depict insights that, when seen within the present context, stand out as exceptional for their time. The sketches are purposely piecemeal and incomplete, and the idea that there is something like a "humanist brain" or a "picturesque brain" will strike some as odd. My point in employing such a strategy is not to defend the thesis in a strict sense (although there is increasing evidence with our new understanding of plasticity that this is in fact the case), but rather to suggest how "old" some of these newer ideas of today can be judged to be. While not intending to narrow the arc of architectural design or invention, I offer these intellectual moments – from Leon Battista Alberti to Juhani Pallasmaa – because some of these ideas are indeed finding affinities, if not validation, in today's research.

Similarly, the neurological chapters of the second part of the study, which can be read separately from these essays, are little more than gestures offered tentatively, as the work of the next few years will no doubt shed much more light on them. What is already becoming clear today, however, is that the model of the human brain that is emerging is not a reductive or mechanistic one. The labyrinthine character of this sinuous organ is not only deeper or more profound in its involved metabolisms than we previously imagined but it is also open-ended in its future possibilities, or the course that humanity and human culture will eventually take. Therefore our knowledge of its workings will never suggest a theoretical program for architecture, a new "-ism" to be captured as the latest fad. I say this in full view of the course of architectural theory over the past 40 years – the short-lived parabolic trajectories of the postmodern and poststructural movements and their evolution into digital and green design.

If neuroscience will not suggest a theory, it may offer something else, which is a theoretical route or the ability to reformulate a few basic questions about the person for whom the architect designs. In the early 1950s the architect Richard Neutra made a precocious plea for the designer to become a biologist – in the sense that the architect should center his or her concern not on formal abstractions but on the flesh-and-blood and psychological needs of those who inhabit the built world. One might echo similar sentiments today by suggesting that the notion of "ecology" could be recast in grander biological terms as a field of "human ecology," in which the idea of sustainability extends a theoretical arm to embrace the complexities of the human organism and its community. Arguably, the neurological outline for such an approach is now taking shape, and the prospects, even when considering such enigmatic issues as the designer's creativity, are intriguing. Becoming more fully aware of the extent of our biological complication, whose underpinnings reach deeply into the sensory-emotive world that we daily inhabit, is simply a first step in this process.

I want to thank several people who have assisted me, first of all John Onians, who first raised the artistic importance of neuroscience in a most compelling way. An invitation to a workshop from the University of British Columbia on "Varieties of Empathy in Science, Art and Culture," deepened my interest because it allowed me not only to return to some old themes but also to see that these themes had been enjoying resurgence in psychological and philosophical circles today – largely through the impetus of neuroscience. A graduate seminar at Illinois Institute of Technology with a highly energetic and talented group of students further advanced my thinking, and I want to credit the efforts of Matthew Blewitt, Thomas Boerman, Linda Chlimoun, Jeremiah Collatz, Ahmad Fakhra, Frederick Grier, Kyle Hopkins, Henry Jarzabkowski, Michael Jividen, Alexander Koenadi, Christine Marriott, Bryan May, Lorin Murariu, Ronny Schuler, Gideon Searle, Albin Spangler, Ben Spicer, and Jennifer Stanovich.

Several people have been gracious to read parts of this manuscript. I would like to thank Marco Frascari, David Goodman, Sean Keller, Kevin Harrington, Tim Brown, Eric Ellingsen, and Peter Lykos for their constructive advice. I am most grateful to Amjad Alkoud for his work on all of the scientific illustrations. I would also like to thank many others at IIT who have been of assistance, among them Romina Canna, Peter Osler, Rodolfo Barragan, Steve Brubaker, Tim Brown, Kathy Nagle, Matt Cook, Nasir Mirza, Thomas Gleason, Rich Harkin, and Stuart MacRae. Above all I would like to express my gratitude to my lovely wife Susan, who not only offers expert editing and advice, but who has always supported my extended work habits in so many ways.

Part I
Historical Essays

1

The Humanist Brain

Alberti, Vitruvius, and Leonardo

first we observed that the building is a form of body (Leon Battista Alberti)[1]

In most architectural accounts, Renaissance humanism refers to the period in Italy that commences in the early fifteenth century and coincides with a new interest in classical theory. The ethos of humanism was not one-dimensional, for it infused all of the arts and humanities, including philosophy, rhetoric, poetry, art, architecture, law, and grammar. Generally, it entailed a new appreciation of classical Greek writers (now being diffused by the printing press), whose ideas had to be squared with late-antique and medieval sources as well as with the teachings of Christianity. In this respect, Leon Battista Alberti epitomized the humanist brain.

In the case of architecture, humanism often had a slightly different connotation. It has not only entailed the belief that the human being, by virtue of his divine creation, occupies a privileged place within the cosmos but also the fact that the human body holds a special fascination for architects. I am referring to the double analogy that views architecture as a metaphor for the human body, and the human body as a metaphor for architectural design. In this sense too Alberti was a humanist, for when his architectural treatise of the early-1450s appeared in print in 1486 (alongside the "ten books" of the classical Roman architect Vitruvius) he promulgated a way of thinking about architecture that would largely hold fast until the eighteenth century. In this way Alberti became perhaps the first architect in history to construct a unified body of theory – what historians have referred to as the theoretical basis for a new style.

Born a "natural," or illegitimate, child into a wealthy family of merchants and bankers, Alberti came to this task with mixed blessings.[2] If his illegitimacy deprived him of legal inheritance, his family purse at least insured him of a good classical education at the University of Bologna, where he took his doctorate in canon law in 1428. By this date he had already begun to disclose his literary talent (his writings on a variety of subjects are prodigious) and interest in mathematics. Like many well educated men of the time, he gravitated into the service of the church, first as a secretary to the cardinal of Bologna. Four years after taking his doctorate, in 1432, he was living in Rome as a secretary to the head of the papal chancery, and therefore working indirectly for the pope. In 1434, however, civil unrest forced the papal court to leave Rome for Florence. It was here, where a new approach to architecture, sculpture, and painting was already taking hold, that Alberti formed a friendship with Filippo Brunelleschi and Donato Donatello, both of whom he may have met a few years earlier. Their shared interests were added to when Alberti began to paint, and within a year he wrote the first of his three artistic treatises, *De pictura* (On Painting, 1435). The date of his second artistic tract – *De statua* (On Sculpture) – is unknown, although it was quite possibly composed in the late 1440s. Meanwhile, around 1438, Alberti journeyed with the papal court to Ferrara, where he cultivated his interest in architecture. This pursuit intensified when Alberti and the papacy returned to Rome in 1443 and the scholar, once again following in the footsteps of Brunelleschi, began his investigation of Roman classical monuments. Out of these labors, and with his growing assurance, came his third and final artistic treatise, *De re aedificatoria* (On Building), which he presented in 10 books to Pope Nicholas V in 1452. With this task completed, Alberti devoted the next 20 years of his life to the practice of architecture, for which his fame surpassed that of his many literary endeavors.

De Pictura and *De Statura*

Although his treatise on architecture remains his largest theoretical undertaking, the two smaller studies on painting and sculpture already tell us much about his artistic outlook. *De pictura* is, first of all, a highly original work attempting to delineate the principles of linear perspective.

Its aim is to elevate painting above the status of artisanship, and it provides several useful pointers about how painters can curry the favor of generous patrons by cultivating good manners and practicing high morals.[3] In its dedication, Alberti exalts the inspired work of Renaissance artists by equating their efforts with the "distinguished and remarkable intellects" of classical times.[4] Chief among them is Brunelleschi, who had recently completed the dome for the Florentine cathedral – that "enormous construction towering above the skies, vast enough to cover the entire Tuscan population with its shadow, and done without the aid of beams or elaborate wooden supports."[5]

De pictura has two broad themes. One is Alberti's attempt to supply this new 'fine art' with the theoretical underpinnings of geometry, which for him is not a mathematical issue but rather a divine ideal that brings an imperfect human being into closer harmony with the divinely created order of the universe. Geometry, for Alberti, is the humanization of space, and in fact the treatise opens with his apology for invoking geometry "as the product not of a pure mathematician but only of a painter."[6] Alberti also bases the measure of his perspectival geometry on three *braccia* – "the average height of a man's body."[7] Thus the rules of perspective are corporeally embodied in human form.

The second theme is the concept of *historia*, the elaboration of which encompasses nearly half of the book. It does not mean "story," as Alberti makes clear, and he devotes page after page to discussing how to achieve "this most important part of the painter's work."[8] Collectively, this vital artistic quality resides in achieving grace and beauty in a work by displaying people with beautifully proportioned faces and members, possessing free will and appropriate movements, depicting a variety of bodies (young and old, male and female), abundant color, dignity and modesty, decorum, drama, monumentality, but above all, the animate display of emotion. *Historia* commands the artist, through his creativity, to produce a work "so charming and attractive as to hold the eye of the learned and unlearned spectator for a long while with a certain sense of pleasure and emotion."[9] It has therefore been said that just as Alberti's theory of perspective provides a visual link between the painter's eye and the objects within the spatial field, his notion of *historia* supplies an emotional link that should move the spectator to experience empathy. Quite naturally, he believed it to be an attribute favored in antiquity, and thus it is entirely logical for Alberti to open the third book of his treatise by encouraging painters to become familiar with classical poetry and rhetoric.[10]

This humanist slant is also very apparent in his tract on sculpture, in which he provides an individuated proportional system based on the variable measure of six human feet (therefore fixed according to the person and not to a standard, differing for persons of different height or foot length). Vitruvius, of course, had opened the third book of *De architectura* with a similar proportional system, albeit with some notable differences.[11] Vitruvius's system of proportion, closely related to his notion of symmetry (*symmetria*), was based on a series of fractional relations of the body parts to the whole (the head, for instance is 1/10 of the body's height), whereas Alberti divides each foot into ten inches and each inch into ten minutes in order to give very precise measurements. Vitruvius had also presented his proportional system just before he described the human figure lying on his back with outstretched arms and feet, contained within a circle and square. Alberti, however, presents his system without metaphysical fanfare. His numbers are purely measurements, even if also derived from the human body.

De Re Aedificatoria

But this does not mean that Alberti did not have his rationale. We can see this by turning to his much lengthier treatise on architecture, *De re aedificatoria*, where his artistic ideas find their logical conclusion. And if there is one compelling metaphor that appears consistently throughout the exposition of his theory it is the idea of corporeality – architecture as the re-creation of the human body. "The Great experts of antiquity," as he informs us in one passage, "have instructed us that a building is very like an animal, and that Nature must be imitated when we delineate it."[12] Again,

> the physicians have noticed that Nature was so thorough in forming the bodies of animals, that she left no bone separate or disjointed from the rest. Likewise, we should link the bones and bind them fast with muscles and ligaments, so that their frame and structure is complete and rigid enough to ensure that its fabric will still stand on its own, even if all else is removed.[13]

This corporeal metaphor determines terminology. Columns and fortified areas of the wall are the "bones" of a building, the infill walls and paneling serve as muscles and ligaments, the finish of a building is its skin.[14] The roof, too, has its "bones, muscles, infill paneling, skin, and crust," while walls should not be too thick, "for who would not criticize a body for having excessively swollen limbs?"[15] Every house, moreover, should have its large and welcoming "bosom."[16]

Architecture for Alberti, more specifically, is not to be formed in the manner of just any human body, and thus his standard, or canon, demands a cosmological foundation. His opus on theory begins with the definition of a building as a "form of body," which "consists of lineaments and matter, the one the product of thought, the other of Nature."[17] In this duality, we have the raw materials of nature at human disposal, upon which the architect impresses a design, like the divine creator, through the power of reason. Book One is entirely given over to the issue of lineaments, which Alberti defines as "the precise and correct outline, conceived in the mind, made up of lines and angles, and perfected in the learned intellect and imagination."[18] Lineaments, as his larger text makes clear, are more than simple lines or the composition of a building's outline; they form the building's rational organization that is open to analysis through the six building categories of locality, area, compartition, walls, roofs, and openings. Area, the immediate site of a building, is where Alberti brings in his discussion of geometry, but compartition seems to be the essential term for him. It calls upon the architect's greatest skill and experience for it "divides up the whole building into the parts by which it is articulated, and integrates its every part by composing all the lines and angles into a single, harmonious work that respects utility, dignity, and delight."[19] It also encompasses the element of decorum in mandating that nothing about a building should be inappropriate or unseemly.[20]

Little that we have discussed so far departs from classical Vitruvian theory, which too is founded upon the belief that every composition of the architect should have "an exact system of correspondence to the likeness of a well-formed human being."[21] Neither is it especially at odds with the Stoic inclinations of Vitruvius, which allowed him to emphasize, above all, the primacy of sensory experience.

But Alberti will not be content with this resolution because he believed that Vitruvius never clearly disclosed how one could achieve this higher harmony of parts. Therefore he introduces a second duality that mirrors his earlier one of lineaments and nature, which is the dialectic of "beauty" and "ornament." He introduces both concepts in Book Six, a point at which he resumes his treatise after a lapse of some time, in part, as Alberti himself acknowledges, because of the extreme difficulty of the task. In truth, he probably used his literary hiatus to consult a number of other classical sources.

We can surmise this, at least, when he proffers his first tentative definitions of his new duality: "Beauty is that reasoned harmony of all the parts within a body, so that nothing may be added, taken away, or altered, but for the worse."[22] This "great and holy matter" is rarely found in nature, which Alberti reports (with a typical corporeal metaphor) by citing a dialogue from Cicero's *De natura deorum* in which a protagonist notes that on a recent visit to Athens he rarely found one beautiful youth in each platoon of military trainees.[23] Alberti seeks to repair this general deficiency of nature by offering the idea of ornament, which, in a cosmetic sense, can mask the defect of someone's body, or groom or polish another part to make it more attractive. Thus, beauty is an "inherent property" of something, while ornament is "a form of auxiliary light and complement to beauty."[24]

But this tentative definition, as the reader soon learns, is entirely misleading. Ornament, in particular, is for Alberti a much broader concept. It, along with beauty, can be found in the nature of the material, in its intellectual fashioning, and in the craftsmanship of the human hand.[25] The notion of ornament can also be applied to many other things. For example, the main ornament of a wall or roof, especially where vaulted, is its revetment.[26] The principal ornament of architecture is the column with its grace and conference of dignity.[27] The chief ornament of a library is its collection of rare books (especially if ancient sources).[28] And the ornaments of a city can reside in its situation, layout, composition, roads, squares, parks, and individual buildings.[29] A statue, he notes on one occasion, is the greatest ornament of all.[30] If there would be one way to summarize Alberti's view of ornament, then, one might say that ornament is the material of building or design, either in its natural condition or with human labor applied to it – that is, it is material intrinsically attractive or impressed in some way by the human hand and brain. Such a definition is vaguely similar to but not coincidental with Vitruvius's conception of ornament as a formal vocabulary, a system of *ornamenta* or rules of detailing applied to architectural *membra* (members).[31]

Nevertheless, this is not all that Alberti has to say on the subject, for three books later (in Book Nine) he returns to this "extremely difficult inquiry," now armed with new terminology. Once again a corporeal analogy precedes his discussion, as Alberti considers the relative merits of slender versus "more buxom" female beauty. His objective is not to answer this human question, which smacks too much of subjectivity, but rather to provide beauty with a more solid or absolute underpinning. Hence beauty cannot be founded "on fancy," but only in "the workings of a reasoning faculty that is inborn in the mind."[32] And because reason is a human privilege specifically endowed by God, the brain and its reasoning power is invested with divine authority. This duality of beauty and ornament is then superseded by a new idea, the third mediating concept of *concinnitas*.

Deriving from the Latin, the English "concinnity" still perfectly expresses the concept that Alberti defined as "the spouse of the soul and of reason," and it has as its task "to compose parts that are quite separate from each other by their nature, according to some precise rule, so that they correspond to one another in appearance."[33] It is not a term that appears in Vitruvius, and Alberti seems to have taken it from the rhetorical theory of Cicero, where, under the attribute of ornament, the classical author defines it this way:

> Words when connected together embellish a style [*habent ornatum*] if they produce a certain symmetry [*aliquid concinnitatis*] which disappears when the words are changed, though the thought remains the same.[34]

Such a definition of classical rhetoric is concerned with oratorical style, but Alberti's thought demands a more absolute grounding and thus he offers a revised definition of beauty:

> Beauty is a form of sympathy and consonance of the parts within a body, according to definite number, outline, and position, as dictated by *concinnitas*, the absolute and fundamental rule in Nature. This is the main object of the art of building, and the source of her dignity, charm, authority, and worth.[35]

The translator's choice of the English term "symmetry" in the passage from Cicero underscores how close in meaning this term is to Vitruvian *symmetria*, the most important of his six principles of architecture.

Vitruvius defines symmetry as "the proportioned correspondence of the elements of the work itself, a response, in any given part of the separate parts to the appearance of the entire figure as a whole."[36] However, he uses a different word for beauty from Alberti. Whereas the latter employs the more traditional term *pulchritudo* (beauty as a high ideal of excellence), Vitruvius prefers the word *venustas*, which, on a more corporeal level, suggests a beauty known to the senses. As Cicero informs us, the Latin word was derived from the goddess Venus.[37]

For Alberti, however, beauty is imbued with a higher necessity as defined by the importance of number, outline, and position. These three requisites of good architecture, of course, allow him to raise the issue of harmonic proportions, which govern all things within the universe, including the parallel numerical harmonies of music and architecture. Alberti's discussion of these ratios is somewhat involved, but in general he prefers simple ratios such as 2:2, 2:3, 3:4, and 4:9, which apply both to music and architecture. These ratios are not arbitrarily conceived but are inherently in concordance with the unique reasoning powers of the human brain:

> For about the appearance and configuration of a building there is a natural excellence and perfection that stimulates the mind; it is immediately recognized if present, but if absent is even more desired. The eyes are by their nature greedy for beauty and *concinnitas*, and are particularly fastidious and critical in this matter.[38]

This biological nourishment, as it were, again shares a certain affinity with another passage of Vitruvius, which notes that "our vision always pursues beauty," and that if a building is badly proportioned for what the eye expects then it "presents the viewer with an ungainly, graceless appearance."[39] There is, however, one crucial distinction between these two viewpoints. For Vitruvius the matter of bringing proportions in line with the mechanics of the eye allows the architect to make "optical adjustments" where needed.[40] For Alberti the prescribed ratios rise to the level of cosmic necessity, and thus he at least implies that the architect has no leeway to adjust them. If there were to be one exception, it would be the three orders, which, metaphorically speaking, are based on the corporeal proportions of three different body types: the Doric male, the Ionic female, and the Corinthian daughter.

Alberti's theory of the brain can thus only be characterized as one of embodiment. Just as the body is the house for the human mind or soul, so is a building a house for the human body. Unlike a body, however, a building can elude the infelicities of imperfect nature, provided that it is invested with ornament and with that essential element of *concinnitas* that endows it with proportional harmony through the divine powers of reason. Such is the embodied perspective of a humanist architect.

Filarete and Francesco di Giorgio

The linkage of architecture to the well proportioned body by Alberti fixed this image for the Renaissance, but not without a few somatic explications before the end of the fifteenth century. Certainly one of the more enchanting Renaissance treatises equating building with the body was that of Filarete, who quite explicitly informed his fictional interlocutors "by means of a simile that a building is derived from man, that is, from his form, members, and measure."[41] Filarete, who was eight years older than Alberti, never acquired the educational background of a classical humanist. His treatise of the early 1460s nevertheless takes the form of a Socratic dialogue in Milan, in which he – the architect – convinces the resident prince and a few other proponents of the superiority of the new architecture (Florentine Renaissance) over the older Gothic style still employed in Lombardy. He does so by laying out his vision for the ideal city of Sforizinda.

The body/building analogy for Filarete goes beyond literary trope to frame a complete philosophy of architecture. A building should be based on the most beautiful part of the human anatomy, the head, and thus be divided into three parts. Its entrance is its mouth and the windows above are the eyes.[42] The building needs to be nourished regularly with maintenance, or else it will fall into sickness and disease. The most inventive part of this analogy is a building's design or initial conception. Because the patron of the future enterprise cannot conceive the building alone, he must follow the course of nature and hire an architect to conceive and bear the child:

> As it cannot be done without a woman, so he who wishes to build needs an architect. He conceives it with him and then the architect carries it out. When the architect has given birth, he becomes the mother of the

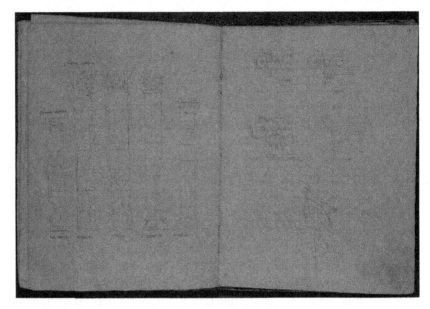

Figure 1.1 After Francesco di Giorgio Martini, *Opera di Architettura* (c.1479–80). Courtesy of Spencer Collection, The New York Public Library, Astor, Lenox and Tilden Foundations, Ms. 129, fol. 18v

building. Before the architect gives birth, he should dream about his conception, think about it, and turn it over in his mind in many ways for seven to nine months, just as a woman carries her child in her body for seven to nine months.[43]

Just as, after labor, the good mother sees that her new son or daughter is properly attended to, so the architect goes out and finds the best tutors, that is, the most skilled carpenters and masons, to erect the edifice. Invoking another carnal metaphor that quite possibly might have offended Alberti's sense of decorum, Filarete concludes that "building is nothing more than a voluptuous pleasure, like that of a man in love."[44]

Filarete was of course familiar with the treatise of Vitruvius, as well as the writings of Alberti, and he may have met the latter when they both lived in Rome. His ideas seem to derive from both. Not only is the shaft of a Doric column – following Vitruvius – based on the proportions of a nude male (therefore "fuller in the middle" before tapering toward the top), but the fluting of the Corinthian column modestly emulates the pleated dress of the maiden.[45] Similarly, when the first humans of the post-Edenic world felt the need to construct shelter, they took their proportions from Adam himself, who, indeed, had been created by God and therefore had a perfect body.[46]

The corporeal metaphors of Filarete's treatise are in some ways surpassed by those of his contemporary Francesco di Giorgio Martini, the Sienese architect, painter, sculptor, and engineer. Two codices of his treatise have survived – one in Turin (*Saluzzianus*, before 1476) and one in Florence (*Magliabecchianus*, 1489–91), as well as an intermediate manuscript (*Spencer*) relating to Vitruvius that Richard J. Betts assigns to the years 1479–80.[47] All three rely heavily on the Latin text of Vitruvius (although less in the case of the third one), and in fact the former two, as Betts also suggests, might be seen as the earliest attempt to translate the Roman author. What makes all three manuscripts especially appealing is the fact that they are profusely illustrated with dozens and dozens of drawings in which the human face or body are superimposed over measured capitals and cornices, columns, building plans, sections, and elevations. All point to his belief in the profound correlation between human proportions and architecture, which is evidently all-encompassing:

> And this [an order] has more beautiful appearance if, as has been said, the columns, bases, capitals, and cornices, and all other measures and proportions … [originate] from the members and bones of the human body. First we see that the column is of seven or nine parts according to the division of this body, the capital one thickness of the column, and the height of the foot half the height of the head, the base half of the thickness of the column. The flutes of the column, or channels, twenty-four as the human body has twenty-four ribs. And wanting to show the rules of columns or cornices, capitals, it is necessary to describe and demonstrate the measures of this body. And, as has been said, the compositions of temples and buildings is in commensuration, which architects must understand most diligently.[48]

Leonardo

One of the people impressed with Francesco di Giorgio's treatise was Leonardo da Vinci, who, in 1490, met his senior of 13 years in Milan. In June of that year, in fact, the two men traveled to Pavia to consult on the rebuilding of the cathedral there. One of the surviving Martini manuscripts was owned by Leonardo (possibly a gift from Martini himself), and its various annotations attest to how carefully Leonardo studied the work.

Born in 1452, Leonardo, it must be stressed, was as much a scientist as an artist.[49] He was trained as a painter in the Florentine studio of Andrea del Verrocchio and was a mature, if still uncelebrated artist when he left the city in 1481 for an 18-year stay in Milan. Why he moved from the center of the Renaissance to the prosperous Lombard capital (at that time the third largest city in Europe) remains a mystery, but obviously he felt his economic prospects would be better served at the wealthy court of Ludovico Sforza – to whom he originally applied for a position as a military engineer. In any event, it was in Milan that he developed his interests in proportions, geometry, and architecture. In 1499, the arrival of French troops forced him to flee to Florence, but after several years of unsettled activities he returned to Milan in 1506 to work for the French court. When civil turmoil revisited the city in 1513 Leonardo shifted his base to Rome. In 1516 he moved once again, this time to France, to be the First Painter to the French king François I. He died in the Château de Cloux, at Ambroise, in 1519.

The key to understanding the brain of Leonardo is his own life-long interest in human anatomy and the brain. On a visit to Florence in 1507 he famously dissected a corpse at the hospital of Santa Maria Nuova (a practice strictly frowned upon by the church), but his interest in the human body and its operation is clearly evident during his first residence in Florence, when he was instructed in drawing human forms. This interest thrived even more in Milan, and by 1489 Leonardo had prepared an outline for an anatomical study to be entitled "Of the Human Body." For this venture he seems to have prepared hundreds of anatomical studies, perhaps the more interesting of which were several of the brain itself. He was the first artist to do so, and since knowledge of this organ at this time was miniscule, Leonardo followed the medieval tradition of assigning its activities to three pouches or ventricles aligned in a row behind the eyes: the first the receptor for sensory impressions; the second the seat of the intellect, imagination, and judgment; and the third that of memory. Later sketches, from around 1508, after his dissection in Florence, show the same ventricles in an ever so slightly more accurate rendering of the brain's organic complexity, but the gray matter of the cortex remained for Leonardo little more than

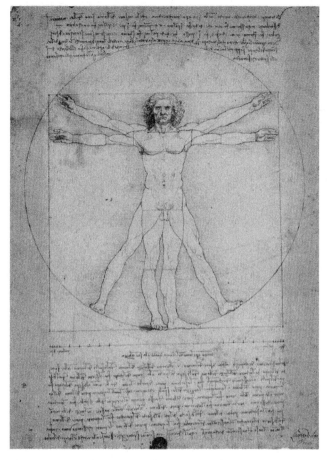

Figure 1.2 Leonardo da Vinci, Vitruvian Man (c.1490).

a wrapping for the essential areas below. Medieval anatomical notions stressed that all thinking took place in the *sensus communis* or "common sense," located in the very center of the brain.

These studies are also interesting because it was during these same years – the second half of the 1480s – that Leonardo developed his interest in architecture and its dependence on human proportions. His study and sketches of this time were probably inspired, at least in part, by the publication of the treatises of Vitruvius and Alberti, as well as by his access in Milan to the local manuscripts of Filarete and Martini. His well-known image of the Vitruvian man within a circle and square

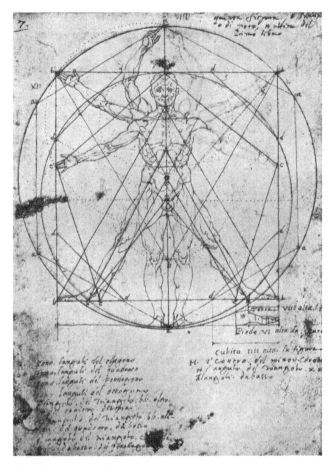

Figure 1.3   Carlo Urbini (after Leonardo da Vinci), from the *Codex Huygens.*
Courtesy of The Pierpont Morgan Library. Manuscript 2006.14, fol. 7

(now residing in Venice) dates from around 1490 and it – as we can surmise from the tracings found in the Codex Huygens – was not an isolated drawing but part of larger group of anatomical studies.[50] The tracings of this codex, which were made in the sixteenth century by the Milanese artist Carlo Urbino, were presumably copied from original sketches of Leonardo (some known, some lost), although some may also derive from sketches of his disciples.

Perhaps the most fascinating are those based on the Vitruvian man, which exploit the movements implied in the Venice drawing but with other geometries. One, for instance, records a three-fold movement of a male within a series of circles, polygons, triangles, and a square.[51] Leonardo was evidently searching for geometrical validations to support the divine connection between the human figure and the macrocosmos, and this hypothesis is supported by the fact that, as Martin Kemp notes, the centerline of the Venice drawing is pockmarked with compass points, especially around the face.[52] Kemp refers to these images as the quintessential "Ptolemaic vision of the cosmos," by which he means that the navel and penis of man (the differing center points of the circle and the square) remain the constant around which the universe and its motion revolves.[53] Leonardo apparently said the same thing, as we find translated in an early eighteenth-century set of engravings made from the Codex Huygens:

> So it happens in our Scheme, that y^c Motion which is attributed to the *Members*, will be found to be y^c first Cause & its proper Center, which turning in y^c form of a *Circle*, the *Compas* will trace y^c Stability of what Actions one will, of Natural Motion, alloting to several one and diversified Lines in one, turning its Center according to our first Order of y^c Heavenly *Bodies*, constituting this Body formed upon y^c Natural Plan of our Great *Masterpiece*, whereby we rayse up & turn our selves: this is Demonstrated upon y^c first *Figure*, and the Whole Scheme with all its variety by a single *Line*.[54]

It should also be noted that many of Leonardo's architectural sketches, such as his design for a centralized temple, also date from this period. His muscular sketches of interior domes and apses, which won the approbation of his fellow engineer in Milan, Donato Bramante, are from this time too.[55] The latter, of course, would, within a few years, become the architect for Saint Peter's in Rome.

Certainly contributing to Leonardo's fascination with proportional ratios and geometry at this time was his friendship with the mathematician and Franciscan monk Luca Pacioli, who arrived at the Sforza court in 1496. Two years earlier, Pacioli had published his *Summa de arithmetica, geometria, proportioni et proportionalità*, which exalted the divine creative spark behind the mathematically perfect universe. In 1498 Pacioli had completed his manuscript for *De Divina Proportione* (published in 1509), for which Leonardo had contributed a number of geometric drawings. Pacioli was quite explicit on his cosmic view of things: "First we shall talk of the proportions of man, because from the human body derive all measures and their denominations and in it is to be found all and every ratio and proportion by which God reveals the innermost secrets of nature."[56]

Perhaps the first artistic demonstration of this interest for Leonardo was his mural for the Refectory of Sta Maria delle Grazie, *The Last Supper*, which he completed in 1497. The painting was apparently laid out on a grid of mathematical intervals that differ from the rules of perspective. Speaking of the tapestries along the two side walls, Kemp makes the following observation: "The tapestries appear to diminish in size according to the ratios 1:½ :1/3:¼ or to express it in whole numbers, 12:6:3. In musical terms 3:4 is the tonal interval of a fourth, 4:6 is a fifth and 6:12 is an octave. The consequence of these ratios is that the tapestries would actually have been different in width if this were a real room."[57]

Such interests did not diminish when Leonardo returned to Florence in 1500, where he was soon joined by Pacioli. Among his new interests were the geometrical transformations first explored by Archimedes. Patrons and admirers of his paintings, in fact, were dismayed that "mathematical experiments had so distracted" him to the point that he was no longer painting.[58] Again, it was also during this period in Florence that his scientific pursuit of human anatomy intensified. Leonardo was obviously obsessed with solving what he believed to be the ageless problem that lay at the heart of the humanist worldview. In a way similar to Alberti, he had reinstated classical antiquity's anthropomorphic understanding of the universe, albeit with much greater empirical or scientific rigor. And he did so with a seriousness that would not allow the next generation of Renaissance architects to operate outside of the theoretical framework of this metaphor. Even his arch-rival Michelangelo, who returned to Florence in 1501 to work on *David*, could not break the seductive hold of this legacy. In a letter written to an unnamed cardinal in 1550, Michelangelo matter-of-factly reported that "it is therefore indisputable that the limbs of architecture are derived from the limbs of man. No one who has not been or is not a good master of the human figure, particularly of anatomy, can comprehend this."[59] Twenty years later, the great Andrea Palladio expressed the same position when he defined beauty in terms strikingly similar to Alberti's notion of *concinnitas*:

Beauty will result from the form and correspondence of the whole, with respect to the several parts, and the parts with regard to each other, and of these again to the whole; that the structure may appear an entire and compleat body, wherein each member agrees with the other, and all necessary to compose what you intend to form.[60]

It is such a compelling vision that it is difficult to believe that the eyes of Renaissance architects did not actually see these harmonic relations in their buildings with equal certainty. Palladio's cultural cognition (the configuration of his brain's visual circuitry) was arguably informed and conditioned by what he deemed to be divine ratios, and his brain – as his "body" of architecture makes clear – could not conceive of design outside of them. He perceived the essential beauty of such proportions, even if our brains, in the twenty-first century, are in most cases no longer able to do so.

2

The Enlightened Brain

Perrault, Laugier, and Le Roy

The taste of our century, or at least of our nation, is different from that of the Ancients (Claude Perrault)[1]

The artistic sway of the humanist brain, the touchstone of Italian artistic culture in the fifteenth century, began to spread northward in the following century, aided, of course, by the new invention of the printing press. The first French translation of Alberti appeared in Paris in 1512, and Jean Martin's French edition of Vitruvius followed in 1547. The fourth book of Sebastiano Serlio's *Architettura*, which came out in Venice in 1537, was published in Antwerp in a Flemish and German translation in 1539, while Books One and Two were first published in Lyons in 1545. The first German edition of Vitruvius – Walther Ryff's *Vitruvius Teutsch* – appeared in Nuremberg in 1548. This trek of Renaissance and classical ideas steadily makes its way northward over the course of the sixteenth and seventeenth centuries and culminates in Scandinavia with Laurids Lauridsen de Thurah's Danish translation of Vitruvius, *Den danske Vitruvius*, in 1746.

Meanwhile, artistic sensitivities were already shifting in Italy, in large part because of a religious crisis. The Reformation in northern Europe in the first half of the sixteenth century posed a serious challenge to the authority of the Church of Rome, and the papacy responded by promoting a new order of reformers, the Jesuits, who were charged with mounting a Counter-Reformation. Architecture was destined to play a very important role in this campaign and, indeed, what is often considered to be the first church in the baroque style, the Church of Gesù in

Figure 2.1 Francesco Borromini, San Carlo alle Quattro Fontane, begun in 1638. Photograph by the author

Rome, was started in 1568, or two years before Palladio's classical treatise appeared. By the middle years of the seventeenth century – through the high talents of such architects as Gianlorenzo Bernini, Francesco Borromini, and Guarino Guarini – this new style had evolved into visually complex, geometric, and highly ornate compositions of fleshy mass, often with spectacular effects of spatial dexterity and plays of light. Some of its early masterpieces in Rome, such as Borromini's San Carlo alle Quattro Fontane, were still unfinished at the time of his death in 1667.

The latter date is important, as we shall see, for if we focus on just this year we can already find a stark contrast of artistic directions being defined between the more sensuous forms of the South and the more rational interpretations of classicism taking place in France. Such a divide also points to another interesting feature of the human brain, which is the cultural lens through which it looks at things. If seventeenth-century France possessed its Descartes, Holland had its Spinoza, Germany its Leibniz, and Britain its Locke – all with very different ways of understanding the world. Nowhere do we find this contrast more vividly described in France than in looking at the architect who would attempt to halt the spread of Italian baroque into his country.

Claude Perrault was born in Paris in 1613, 14 years before his younger brother Charles, who would later become the celebrated author of fairy tales.[2] Claude was trained as a physician, received his doctorate from the Ecole de Médecine in 1642, and shortly thereafter joined the faculty of the University of Paris as a professor of physiology. Over the next 46 years he amassed a large body of research in physiology, comparative anatomy, mechanics, physics, and mathematics. On different occasions he collaborated with Leibniz and with the renowned Dutch physicist Christiaan Huygens, whose brother Constantine, in 1690, would in fact purchase the codex of drawings believed to be by the hand of Leonardo. In 1666 Perrault was elected alongside Huygens to the inaugural class of the Académie des Sciences, the new scientific institute sponsored by the young and ambitious Louis XIV. It was from the Academy's Paris observatory, a design generally attributed to Perrault, that Huygens made important planetary observations in the first half of the 1670s.

Perrault, in his outlook, was above all a Cartesian and this too deserves a few comments. The French philosopher René Descartes (1596–1650) had ushered in a new era of science and philosophy in France with a doctrine generally known as 'Cartesian doubt,' which promised to cleanse the sciences of many of their speculative confusions by limiting investigation to "what we can clearly and evidently intuit or deduce with certainty, and not what other people have thought or what we ourselves conjecture."[3] For Descartes this tool implied a more rigorous use of the quantitative methods for science, as well as an open skepticism toward the remnants of the Aristotelian scientific tradition. It also allowed Descartes to disengage the body from the soul with his famous dualism of a *res extensa* (corporeal substance) and *res cognitans* (thinking substance). The former is the material world that operates in a mechanical fashion and is therefore the object of science, whereas the latter – what Descartes also called consciousness – is immaterial, indivisible, and therefore separate from the body. Neuroscience today has much to say about the long-standing residual effects of this metaphysical duality, but for Perrault Cartesian doubt allowed him to approach architecture with a similar skepticism toward both classical and Renaissance theory.

Perrault's two initiations into Parisian architectural circles, both momentous in their outcome, took place in 1667. The first was a decision by the crown to fund a new French translation of Vitruvius, which was intended to serve as a textbook for the planned Royal Academy of Architecture, which in fact opened in 1671. In many respects the decision was a French declaration of independence from the baroque turn of Italian architecture – that is, an attempt to define French national classicism more rigorously by reverting to the original authority of Vitruvius. Perrault probably received the commission for two reasons. One was that he, by virtue of his medical schooling, was one of the few interested individuals in Paris with knowledge of both Latin and Greek. The second was the fact that his brother Charles was then serving as the secretary to Jean-Baptiste Colbert, the chief minister to Louis XIV and the driving force behind the new academy. Perrault thus had an inside track, but this advantage should not diminish the fact that he would produce not only a superb translation but also a set of critical annotations that far excelled earlier editions of Vitruvius.

Perrault's second architectural venture of 1667 was not unrelated and grew out of the dispute over the Louvre, which was intended in the 1660s to be the primary palace for Louis XIV.[4] A turreted medieval castle originally occupied the site on the northern (or Right Bank) of the Seine, but it was dismantled in two building campaigns of 1546 and 1624 that replaced it with a long rectangular building oriented north and south with a monumental central pavilion. In 1659, two years before the ascension of the Sun King, a third building campaign was begun to extend this building at each end with two wings running to the east, which would then be enclosed by another monumental building along the east side, defining the large square courtyard that still exists today. The new eastern wing was to serve as the king's palace.

Construction was halted in 1662, as Colbert, who had just been appointed, was unhappy with the design. A limited competition ensued in which Claude and Charles Perrault jointly submitted an unsolicited design proposal, but the prize was taken by the renowned Bernini, who was invited to Paris in 1665 to prepare a final design. His summer stay in that city, however, was filled with acrimony over his baroque design, and when he returned to Rome in October, work on the wing was once again halted. Finally, in 1667, the king appointed a three-person committee to prepare a new design, a panel consisting of the king's first architect Louis Le Vau, the king's first painter Charles Le Brun, and Claude Perrault. How or why Claude, who had little or no architectural experience, was selected remains something of a mystery. His choice may have been an attempt by Colbert to exercise (through Charles) some control over the outcome. Then again, Perrault had just received or was about to receive the commission to translate Vitruvius, and thus Colbert may have felt that Claude could bring his expertise in classical theory to the team.

Notwithstanding, the East Wing turned out to be a masterpiece of French classicism, although it would take another century for the architectural establishment in France to recognize this fact. The very large building broke entirely with the more massive, masonry-and-pilaster walls of Italian palaces. Its principal motif was the large colonnade across the main story of the facade, which lacked any Renaissance or classical precedent. The grouping of these columns in pairs also violated classical canons. Again, the large flat entablature between these paired columns, almost 20 feet in span, required the invention of an entirely new structural principle – the reinforcing of masonry with a complex framework of iron bars. In principle, it was an invention akin to that of reinforced concrete several centuries later. The question of who authored this committee design remains unanswered to this day. Claude Perrault, however, was more than happy to claim full credit, even if others involved with the project contested his claim.

The question is irrelevant for our purpose because of what happened next. In 1673 Perrault published his translation of Vitruvius, a little over a year after the French Academy of Architecture officially opened. In a footnote to the third chapter of Book Three, he explained the idea behind the revolutionary design with the following remark:

> The taste of our century, or at least of our nation, is different from that of the ancients and perhaps it has a little of the Gothic in it, because we love the air, the daylight, and openness [*dégagemens*]. Thus we have

Figure 2.2   The Louvre, East Wing. Engraving by Sébastien Le Clerc, Lifting of the Louvre Pediment Stones (1674)

invented a sixth manner of disposing of columns, which is to group them in pairs and separate each pair with two intercolumniations.[5]

The seemingly innocent statement has at least three revolutionary facets to it. The first is the simple declaration that the culture of the French nation (and therefore its architecture) can differ from that of Italy and classical antiquity and can in fact pursue new inventions – the first blow in what later would be termed the "Quarrel of the Ancients and the Moderns."[6] The comments were also a none too subtle swipe at the newly appointed director of the Royal Academy of Architecture, François Blondel, a defender of the ancients who was implementing a program based on classical and Renaissance precedents.[7]

The second revolutionary element is the reference to Gothic architecture, which was universally seen within classical culture as a "bizarre," if not a barbaric pile of architectural forms without antique sanction. In 1669, however, Perrault had made an architectural tour of southern France on which he was impressed not so much with the forms of Gothic architecture as with the structural ingenuity displayed by the style.[8] His invocation of the Gothic in this passage is thus suggesting a lighter or better engineered interpretation of classicism, one more in keeping with French "taste."

The third unusual aspect to this passage is his reference to "open-ness," the French word *dégagemens*. The term, in modern French *dégagement*, has the same root as the English word "disengagement," although in French it generally means "clearing" something away. Perrault is arguing that by using his newly invented colonnade on the Louvre he is clearing the structure from the wall behind, and thereby lightening the wall's load and mass. This clearance in turn allows larger openings in the wall behind, and therefore better ventilation, daylight, and (thanks to the high relief) the appearance of openness. Once again this was a criticism aimed at the corporeal or sensuous character of the baroque style.

There is, however, a fourth – and most important – revolutionary element to this passage, which is the text of Vitruvius to which it refers. The footnote is attached to a passage in which Vitruvius praises the Hellenistic architect Hermogenes for departing from earlier precedents by removing an inner row of columns of a double colonnade and thereby adding majesty to his temple with its outer colonnade now set in high relief.[9] The Latin word that Vitruvius used to describe this novel effect was *asperitas*, which Perrault rendered with the French term *aspreté* (now *âpreté*). The equivalent English word is "asperity," which a dictionary today defines as "severity" or "roughness of sur-face." Within its seventeenth-century context, however, Perrault is referring to the 'lively aspect' or 'visual tension' induced by his colon-nade with its deep shadows in relief – that is, by the positive severity of effects it has on the retina of the eye. He is therefore sanctioning Hermogenes's innovation to classicism and at the same time justifying it with an anatomical or physiological explanation of its aesthetic effect – the first such defense in architectural theory.

Blondel, who surely felt his efforts at the Academy being under-mined by Perrault's willingness to sanction innovation, eventually responded to this footnote with no less than three chapters of the sec-ond volume of his *Cours d'architecture* (1683). Perrault, in turn, coun-tered with a much expanded footnote to the second edition of his translation of Vitruvius, in which he defended the right of his era to create new inventions. Yet the full extent of his argument was put forth in another book that appeared in 1683, his *Ordonnance for the Five Kinds of Columns after the Method of the Ancients*.[10]

The book's theme centers on the nagging proportional issue sur-rounding the use of the architectural orders. Vitruvius had presented his proportions for the orders, all the while admitting that these proportions had changed over time.[11] Alberti, of course, had insisted that certain proportions, the same as those employed in musical harmonies, were privileged and therefore absolute. The problem in 1683 was actually twofold. Measurements of classical Roman monuments had since shown that no buildings in antiquity had followed the prescriptions of Vitruvius or any other discernible proportional canon. Second, no two Renaissance architects and authors writing on this issue agreed as to what these numerical proportions should be for the orders. Thus, if columns should be based on absolute or harmonic values, there was as yet no known system for them. Perrault resolved the problem in a coolly scientific way. He took the different proportions found on all of the approved examples of column orders and calculated the arithmetic mean for each part. He justified this approach, moreover, with two arguments that would eventually prove devastating to humanist theory.

First, on the basis of his medical studies, he denounced the premise that harmonic values should be the same for both music and architecture, because physiologically the eye and the ear process their perceptions in two different ways. Musical harmonies, he reasoned, are perceived by the auditory sense directly without the assistance of the intellect, while visual harmonies are understood only through the mental operations of the brain. In his words, "the eye, which can convey knowledge of the proportion it makes us appreciate, makes the mind experience its effect through the knowledge it conveys of this proportion and only through this knowledge. From this it follows that what pleases the eye cannot be due to a proportion of which the eye is unaware, as is usually the case."[12]

The second argument was equally interesting. Seeing the insoluble dilemma to the problem of absolute proportions, he divided beauty into two types. Positive beauty relies on the empirical evidence of "convincing reasons" and concerns such things as the richness of the materials and the exhibited craftsmanship. Arbitrary beauty, by contrast, is "determined by our wish to give a definite proportion, shape, or form to things that might well have a different form without being misshapen and that appear agreeable not by reasons within everyone's grasp but merely by custom and the association the mind makes between two things of a different nature."[13] Hence, the whole question of proportions is now consigned to the realm of arbitrary beauty, that is, to the ever-changing fashions of human culture. It must also be emphasized that Perrault upended this essential premise of humanist theory entirely on the basis of his knowledge of human anatomy. As would have been much appreciated by Leonardo, Perrault had been dissecting corpses since his early days in medical school.

Humanist theory, however, did not go gently into that good night. Blondel died in 1686, just as the quarrel between the ancients and the moderns was rising to the level of a clamor. Perrault followed him two years later – quite understandably, of an infection incurred while dissecting a camel. The classical curriculum of the school that Blondel established remained relatively intact for much of the next century, while Perrault languished in relative obscurity, in part because of the slow pace of building activity on the Louvre. After having decided to move his throne to Versailles, Louis XIV put all of his resources there, and the overly ornate baroque style of Versailles, which came to be known as the rococo, launched a new architectural fashion that in the first decades of the eighteenth century would become the rage across Europe.

Laugier

What ultimately led to Perrault's rehabilitation was something of an intellectual upheaval, better known as the French Enlightenment. This is not the place to go into the nuances of this cultural transformation in both Europe and North America, except to note that in France it was a time of intense intellectual excitement and curiosity, as well as one with an increasing disdain for the vested interests of the king, the aristocracy, religion, and the censorious power of the state – therefore fittingly culminating in 1789 with the French Revolution.

A good architectural representative of the Enlightenment was the theorist Marc-Antoine Laugier, a native of Provence who in his youth became a Jesuit priest and therefore enjoyed a superb classical education.[14] In 1744 he moved to Paris and was assigned to the church of Saint Suplice, where he first became famed for his oratory skills. His talent attracted sufficient attention by 1749 for him to be invited out to Versailles on occasions to sermonize before the king. This honor eventually proved to be less than a blessing, for in one sermon given at Versailles, on Easter Sunday in 1753, he railed a little too pointedly against the king's personal and political indiscretions. His order that night sent him out of sight and harm's way – to Lyons.

The outcome of his sermon, however, seems to have been anticipated by the priest in advance. For in the early 1750s Laugier had become active in salon circles of Paris, especially those surrounding Denis Diderot, and Laugier had apparently already decided to leave the Jesuit Order. This decision presented a tricky legal problem because it required the signature of the pope. Thus it was not until 1756 that his transfer to the Benedictines was finalized. Freed of his obligation to preach, Laugier returned to Paris on his own and resumed his interest in the arts and letters. He was by that date at least mildly feted as the author of the well-received *Essay on Architecture*, the second edition of which, bearing his name, appeared in 1755. The first edition of 1753 was published anonymously and had been written during his earlier stay in Paris.

Laugier's tract on architecture, with its great antipathy toward the excesses of the rococo, broke radically with the immediate past. Vitruvius – who "has in effect taught us only what was practiced in his time" – is now viewed as altogether irrelevant, and his counsel is to be replaced with the supreme criterion of "reason."[15] Laugier's description of his own brain's burst of creative insight with regard to architecture – his Eureka! moment – is striking:

> Suddenly a bright light appeared before my eyes. I saw objects distinctly where before I had only caught a glimpse of haze and clouds. I took hold of these objects eagerly and saw by their lights my uncertainties gradually disappear and my difficulties vanish. Finally, I reached a stage where I could, through principles and conclusions, prove to myself the inevitability of these effects without knowing the cause.[16]

The book opens with a bow to the first *Discourse* of Jean-Jacques Rousseau – with an early human being residing in a rustic condition (prior to the corrupting influences of society and culture) and relying only on his instincts.[17] Inclement weather forces him to consider the need for shelter and, instead of moving into a damp cave, he spies some fallen branches and plants four into the ground, connects them with some horizontal limbs, and then adds inclined branches with leaves to form a gabled canopy. These three inventions of reason (columns, entablature, and roof) constitute all that is essential to architecture, and such other contingencies as walls, doors, and windows are allowed, but only as unfortunate necessities. All forms of ornament, however, are disallowed as license, as are arches, piers, pilasters, engaged columns, and a host of other elements that cannot be supported by the enlightened stricture of reason.

The second principle of Laugier's architectural theory is Perrault's notion of *dégagement* or "openness," certainly the most frequently repeated technical term throughout the text. Laugier uses it in a variety of senses, but especially for the appearance of openness that is found in a building when free-standing columns are used, either outside or inside. Laugier insists that columns should never be engaged in the wall, and with respect to church interiors the preferred use of columns in the nave (instead of more massive piers) is insisted upon – despite the obvious structural limitations of columns. Perrault's colonnade for the Louvre, as well as the interior of Jules Hardouin-Mansart's chapel at Versailles, are each cited more than a half-dozen times in the text as exemplary models to be followed. By contrast, Perrault's conception of *âpreté* or "visual tension" appears only once in the book, but in a way that underscores how well Laugier understood Perrault's interpretation of this word.

> On entering the nave of the Chapel of Versailles everybody is struck by the beauty of its columns, by the picturesque vista (*âpreté*) through its intercolumniations; but as soon as one approaches the apse, there is not a person who does not notice with regard the stupid interruption of the beautiful row of columns by a depressing pilaster.[18]

The rendering of Laugier's term *âpreté* here as "picturesque vista" by the translator Wolfgang Herrman, I think, comes very close to the visual–physiological sense of the word intended by Perrault. It was also a concept that – now that it had been reintroduced into architectural theory – would soon be developed in a still more interesting way.

Le Roy's "Successive Sensations"

The impetus to this further development was the startling rediscovery of classical Greek architecture during the 1750s. For several centuries, Athens had been under Ottoman control and was therefore relatively inaccessible to European travelers. Most of those who had ventured to the city, either on diplomatic missions or as individuals, took no notice of its classical buildings, many of which had been partially embedded in later construction. The cella of the Parthenon, for instance, had been transformed over the centuries into both a church and mosque. In 1674, 13 years before the Parthenon was struck by a Venetian cannonball, a French diplomatic team lead by Marquis de Nointel made a stop in Athens on a return from a mid-East tour. The team included the noted artist Jacques Carrey and the team was surprised to be allowed access to the Acropolis – surprised because the Turkish ruler of the city was housed in the propylaeum, and his harem in the Erechteum. For two weeks, Carrey scrupulously recorded the frieze and pedimental sculptures of the Parthenon but, remarkably, took no notice of the (still intact) colonnade on which they stood.

This caesura in European cultural history was beginning to be felt by the middle of the eighteenth century, as several teams of travelers, mostly wealthy dilettantes, were making archaeological explorations of classical sites around the eastern Mediterranean. The work inspired two English painters living in Rome, James Stuart and Nicholas Revett, to announce their intention in 1748 to travel to Athens and record its classical monuments. Funded by subscribers and by the London Society of Dilettanti, they left Rome in March of 1750, but they did not arrive in Athens until March of the following year. Once there, though, they remained for two years and returned to London in 1754 with trunk loads of drawings, which they decided, for various reasons, not to publish immediately. Moreover, when the first volume of their long-anticipated study did appear in 1762, it contained mostly secondary Roman works and none of the major Athenian monuments.

This situation, in the meantime, had been remedied by Julien-David Le Roy, a student who had been living at the French Academy in Rome in the early 1750s. He had been moved by the excitement surrounding Stuart and Revett's trip and decided to venture to Athens on his own. He boarded a French warship in Venice in the spring of 1754 and by the following February had arrived in Athens, by way of Constantinople. He spent only three months there, but was able to sketch many of the original Greek monuments. Back in Paris, in the fall of 1755, Le Roy received both financial backing and the assistance of several talented engravers, and in 1758 his *Ruins of the Most Beautiful Monuments of Greece* shook the artistic sensibilities of the European

Figure 2.3   Julien-David Le Roy, View of the Temple of Minerva (Parthenon).
From *Les Ruines des plus beaux monuments de la Grece* (1758)

artistic community.[19] Here were the first accurate views of classical
Greek architecture and here was a style of classicism noticeably different in its proportions from Roman architecture, which for almost a
century had been the only approved model of the French Academy.
These engravings thus provided the seed for a fierce international
debate between connoisseurs of classical art – over the question of
whether Greece or Rome had the superior artistic culture.

Le Roy led the charge in France on behalf of the Greeks. In his book
he praises their "ideas of grandeur, nobleness, majesty, and beauty," seeming a reworking of J. J. Winckelmann's phrase of three years earlier –
"noble simplicity and quiet grandeur."[20] Le Roy's engravings not only
rendered the phrase more graphic but they also demonstrated that
Greek architecture was simpler in style, more massive in its profiles and
proportions, and therefore more plastic in character. The heavier proportions of the Greek orders also rekindled the issue of whether there
were absolute proportions, a debate that had been resting since the
Blondel and Perrault dispute of a century earlier. Le Roy, almost alone
among his contemporaries in 1758, sided with Perrault and argued
that the Greeks had indeed varied their proportions over time and thus

proportions were inessential to the beauty of Greek monuments. With regard to the Greco-Roman debate that was just taking shape, he pleaded for a "path of reconciliation" between the two competing camps on the matter of proportions.[21]

But if proportions were inessential for the Parthenon's overall aesthetic impression, as Le Roy asserted, the monument needed some other basis by which one might judge its beauty. Le Roy had not solved the problem in 1758, but by the time of his next publication in 1764 he had come up with a rather ingenious solution. The subject of this book – the evolution of Christian churches since the time of Constantine – would seem an odd place to offer an insight into the source of the Parthenon's beauty, but it was entirely logical within the intellectual context of Perrault and Laugier. If the Parthenon's beauty could not be defined strictly by the proportions of its columns, he reasons, then it must be defined by the visual and therefore neurological impression that the colonnade makes on the brain. Underlying his argument is, in fact, an early exposition of the notion of the sublime:

> All grand spectacles impress the human race. The immensity of the sky, and the vast expanse of land and sea, which we discover from the peaks of mountains or from the middle of the ocean, seem to elevate our souls and expand our thoughts. The grandest of our own works impress us in the same way: on seeing them, we receive powerful sensations, far superior to those – pleasing, at best – that we receive from small buildings.[22]

Therefore, the size or scale of a building makes a vivid impression on the brain, and for the Frenchman a large building with a colonnade makes a much stronger one than one without a colonnade or one with engaged columns. But this still is not an entirely satisfactory explanation for the colonnade's beauty, and he thus probes further for the reason for a colonnade's great beauty. A great painter, he goes on to argue, limits the number of figures in a painting because too much activity confuses the viewer and distracts attention from the main theme. In a contrary way, a poet is able to proffer a stream of images precisely because these images are experienced sequentially in time. "The architect's art," Le Roy then reasons, "like the poet's, lies in multiplying these sensations by making them successive – rather than in restricting them, as the painter does, to those that a picture can give in a single instant."[23] In other words, the three-dimensional nature of the architectural colonnade, which requires a person to walk around it in order to examine it, offers the occasion for multiple vantage points, and moreover vantage points that can be varied both by angle and distance as the spectator moves around the building. These are the paramount aesthetic qualities that a colonnade offers the spectator, and to demonstrate this point Le Roy turns to a well-known example:

> Run your eye along the full extent of the colonnade of the Louvre while walking the length of the row of houses opposite; stand back to take in the whole, then come close enough to discern the richness of the soffit, its niches, its medallions; catch the moment when the Sun's rays add the most striking effects by picking out certain parts while plunging others in shadow; how many enchanting views are supplied by the magnificence of the back wall of this colonnade combined in a thousand different ways with the pleasing outline of the columns in front of it and with the fall of the light.[24]

Its compelling beauty must then lie in its visual or physiological experience. And the beauty of a colonnade more specifically resides in the secession of always changing vistas, that is, not in the columns themselves but in the physiological experience one takes in by moving around the deeply silhouetted colonnade with its play of light and shadow. Le Roy goes to great rhetorical lengths to emphasize this point:

> In short, so universal is the beauty derived from such colonnades that it would remain apparent even if their constituent pillars were not superb Corinthian columns but mere trunks of trees, cut off above the roots and below the spring of the boughs; or if they were copied from those of the Egyptians or the Chinese; or even if they represented no more than a confused cluster of diminutive Gothic shafts or the massive, square piers of our porticoes.[25]

Le Roy was so certain that he had opened a new door for architecture that he did not hesitate to borrow this chapter – word for word – from his book on church design and incorporate it into the second edition of his book on Greece as his new explanatory centerpiece: "Essay on the Theory of Architecture."[26] And he was correct in the sense that theory had shifted ground during the Enlightenment, although, as we will see, not uniquely so to France. For following Le Roy's logic, architecture now becomes a constructed form of neurological exploitation.

3

The Sensational Brain

Burke, Price, and Knight

I mean, likewise, that when any organ of sense is for some time affected in some one manner, if it be suddenly affected otherwise, there ensues a convulsive motion. (Edmund Burke)[1]

What Descartes had given to French intellectual thinking, John Locke would provide for the Anglo-Saxon world – a definitive philosophical foundation for scientific and aesthetic thought. His major treatise, *An Essay Concerning Human Understanding*, appeared in 1690, and it distinguishes itself from French philosophy on one critical issue. If Descartes had hypothesized that we are born with a few innate ideas (such as the certitude of mathematical ideas) from which we can deduce other truths, Locke argued that we are born with a *tabula rasa* or 'blank slate.'[2] All our knowledge about the world is therefore empirical, that is, it comes to us after birth through our perceptual sensations or experiences in the world. The strict dependence of mental understanding on sensations is called sensationalism, although Locke in this regard would not go as far as some of his followers.

In the first edition of his book, Locke did not speak to the issue of beauty and proportions, but in his second edition, of 1700, he added an essay that established a basis for such aesthetic issues.[3] He suggested that we form our ideas of beauty and proportions by the manner in which the brain works. When we perceive an object, these sensations elicit memories and associative ideas within the brain. If the shape of a specific Greek urn, for instance, evokes the memory of other curved forms that we once found pleasing, we might judge this particular urn to be beautiful. The judgment of beauty and good proportions are thus relative and based on custom, which of course had been Perrault's formulation.

Lockean empiricism went through extensive development in the eighteenth century at the hands of several British philosophers, but the most important for our theme was that of David Hume. In 1754 he and a group of like-minded intellectuals in Edinburgh – a group today known as the Scottish Enlightenment – formed a debating club called the Select Society, which in the following year offered a prize for the best essay on the issue of "taste." Allan Ramsay, a close friend of Hume who had been living in Rome, responded at once with an essay in *The Investigator*, entitled "Dialogue on Taste." He argued that not only was "taste" relative (and therefore largely determined by the individual or culture), but that there is no "reason why a Corinthian capital clapt upon its shaft upside-down should not become, by custom, as pleasing a spectacle as in the manner it commonly stands."[4] Hume, for whom the only knowable world was found inside the brain, was not so certain, for he believed that the sentiments of pleasure that we associate with a beautiful object are cultivated and strengthened by mental habits. He thus responded to Ramsay in 1757 with his own essay, "On the Standard of Taste," in which he followed the empirical conception of aesthetic judgment, but only to a point. "Beauty," he argues, "is not a quality in things themselves: it exists merely in the mind which contemplates them; and each mind perceives a different beauty."[5] And if each brain perceives a different beauty it is because each brain has different experiences on which to base the judgment. What prevents judgments of beauty from collapsing into solipsism or extreme subjectivity for Hume, however, is another quality of the brain, which is its uniformity of operation. If two individuals cultivate the brain's aesthetic sensibilities to the same extent they should always find agreement on the matter of what is beautiful, and if they disagree the reason must lie elsewhere. As Hume summarizes his position, "some particular forms or qualities, from the original structure of the internal fabric, are calculated to please, and others to displease; and if they fail of their effect in any particular instance, it is from some apparent defect or imperfection in the organ."[6] Phrasing it in this way, he therefore suggests that the particular structure of the brain is also amenable to particular forms and proportions.

Burke and the Physiology of Emotion

One very interested party to this debate was the Irishman Edmund Burke, who also in 1757 published *A Philosophical Inquiry into the Origin of Our Ideas of the Sublime and Beautiful.* On seeing Hume's essay in print, just before his own book was finished, Burke held back his introductory essay, "On Taste," until the second edition of 1759 in order to respond more fully to the Scotsman. Burke had in fact penned one of the great books of the eighteenth century. It is not a lengthy study, or one that is especially difficult to read, but beneath the apparent simplicity of ideas, which often invoke architecture for their examples, lay a number of insights that would not only change the course of aesthetic theory but still retain some relevance today. His simple description of the passions as "organs of the mind" has a decidedly modern ring to it, as does – following Perrault – his attempts to draw physiology into the problem of finding "some invariable and certain laws" for this whole matter of taste.[7]

One of Burke's goals is to raise the idea of the "sublime" as an aesthetic category equal to and alongside that of beauty. The word "sublime" goes back to classical rhetorical theory, but its later conceptualization is already found in Joseph Addison's essays for the *Spectator* in the second decade of the eighteenth century, where he first distinguishes the "Beautiful" from the "Great."[8] Burke's initial concern is with the emotions or passions produced by the brain in our experiences with the world, and thus the first part of his study is largely psychological. If beauty is the emotion inspired by objects that are small, smooth, delicate, with gradual variations and clear and bright colors, the emotion of the sublime is much stronger and is found in "whatever is fitted in any sort to excite the ideas of pain and danger, that is to say, whatever is in any sort terrible, or is conversant about terrible objects, or operates in a manner analogous to terror."[9] Burke is not talking about real pain or danger, but the hint of such when we come across sensory experiences that shock us out of our day-to-day tedium, the exercise of which, he argues, is necessary to the health of our biological system. Hence, some of the causes of feelings of sublimity – as opposed to those of beauty – are astonishment, terror, obscurity, power, privation, vastness, infinity, succession, magnitude, difficulty, magnificence, light and darkness, and suddenness.

His explanation of these causes is filled with many architectural observations. Because the visual force of a perpendicular is stronger than a horizontal, a tower can better arouse the sensation of the sublime than can a horizontal building, and rough and broken surfaces count more toward this feeling than smooth and polished ones.[10] The magnitude or sheer size of a building is sufficient to evoke sublimity, as is the difficulty of its erection, such as we see at Stonehedge.[11] In a building in which the sublime is intended "the materials and ornaments ought neither to be white, nor green, nor yellow, nor blue, nor of a pale red, nor violet, nor spotted, but of sad and fuscous colours, as black, or brown, or deep purple, and the like."[12] Similarly, a powerful contrast between light and darkness produces sublimity, and he even suggests that the architect exploit these effects, such as when coming from daylight into a purposely darkened entry, "as much darkness as is consistent with the uses of architecture."[13] The idea of creating a succession of visual sensations, which we shall return to momentarily, recalls Le Roy's almost contemporary discussion of the colonnade.

The other element of Burke's study that should be singled out is his great skepticism toward the aesthetic truisms of humanist theory. Thus he goes to great lengths to dispel the notion that proportion has anything to do with beauty in the vegetable, animal, or human world. Speaking of Leonardo's image of Vitruvian man with both irony and incredulity, he makes this point quite explicitly:

> But it appears very clearly to me, that the human figure never supplied the architect with any of his ideas. For, in the first place, men are very rarely seen in this strained posture; it is not natural to them, neither is it at all becoming. Secondly, the view of the human figure so disposed, does not naturally suggest the idea of a square, but rather of a cross; as that large space between the arms and ground must be filled with something before it can make anybody think of a square. Thirdly, several buildings are by no means of the form of that particular square, which are notwithstanding planned by the best architects, and produce an effect altogether as good, and perhaps better. And certainly nothing could be more unaccountably whimsical, than for an architect to model his performance by the human figure, since no two things can have less resemblance or analogy, than a man and a house, or temple: do we need to observe, that their purposes are entirely different?[14]

The most original aspect of Burke's analysis, however, is the last section of his study, in which he attempts to explain physiologically the emotions associated with feelings of the beautiful and the sublime. His main argument is that beautiful objects tend to relax the muscles of the eye and thus reduce the tension of the organ's nerve, while the sublime has the opposite effect. Fittingly, he illustrates this principle with the experience of a colonnade:

> To avoid the perplexity of general notions; let us set before our eyes a colonnade of uniform pillars planted in a right line; let us take our stand in such a manner, that the eye may shoot along this colonnade, for it has its best effect in this view. In our present situation it is plain, that the rays from the first round pillar will cause in the eye a vibration of that species; an image of the pillar itself. The pillar immediately succeeding increases it; that which follows renews and enforces the impression; each in its order as it succeeds, repeats impulse after impulse, and stroke after stroke, until the eye, long exercised in one particular way, cannot lose that object immediately; and, being violently roused by this continued agitation, it presents the mind with a grand or sublime conception.[15]

Unlike Le Roy's formulation of a few years later, the physiological process for Burke is lost when the columns are alternately round and square, because the nerve vibration of the "first round pillar perishes as soon as it is formed."[16] Again, a long bare wall cannot produce the same effect because the eye has nothing to interrupt its progress along the surface of the wall. This is not to say that a very large wall cannot be sublime – only that in this case its principle emotion must arise from the sensation of infinity, rather than of vastness. The summary principle of Burke's psycho-physiological aesthetics, which is still quite valid, is that human emotions arise out of the corporeal or neurological processing of perceptions.

Picturesque Theory

The idea of the picturesque, as it would be employed in British landscape theory in the late eighteenth-century, is another idea with a lengthy European pedigree. In England, William Temple, John Soane, the Earl of Shaftesbury, and Joseph Addison all spoke of the beauty of irregular gardens early in the century without specifically invoking the word. The advent of the revolution in English garden design began in the 1720s with the work of Alexander Pope, Lord Burlington, Batty Langley, and William Kent.[17] Yet the word "picturesque" only begins to gain acceptance around mid-century, and indeed it is not a popular expression until after 1770, the year in which Thomas Whately employed the term sparingly in his *Observations on Modern Gardening*. The word is also found in several of William Gilpin's writings, such as *An Essay on Prints: Containing Remarks on the Principles of Picturesque Beauty* (1768). Here he defines it still close to its original Italian sense as "that peculiar kind of beauty, which is agreeable in a picture," even though he was describing the beauty of nature.[18] It is not until the 1790s, however, that we can speak of picturesque theory, and this is entirely through the writings of two men: Uvedale Price and Richard Payne Knight. Neither was a gardener, but both were dilettantes in the very acceptable eighteenth-century meaning of this word.

Price's *Essays on the Picturesque* (1794) contains two main objectives. One is to follow Joshua Reynolds in elevating landscape gardening to an art, which he does by encouraging those entering the field to study the landscape paintings of Claude Lorrain, Nicolas Poussin, and Jean-Antoine Watteau.[19] In effect, he argues that painters have long been trained to see nature better than most people. This supplication to study their work, however, also contains a very explicit condemnation of the recent landscapes of Capability Brown and Humphry Repton, which he feels are too contrived and formulaic in their use of serpentines and other informalities. Above all, Price admires the intricacy of nature, which he defines as "that disposition of objects, which, by a partial and uncertain concealment, excites and nourishes curiosity."[20]

Price's second objective is to raise the notion of the picturesque to an aesthetic category alongside that of beauty and the sublime. He thus defines it entirely in Burkean terms. If beauty is found in objects that are smooth and have gradual variation, the picturesque is found in objects that are rough or have sudden variations. If beauty is associated with things that are young and fresh, the picturesque is associated with age and decay. If beauty is symmetrical, the picturesque is irregular. Thus a Greek temple in a pristine condition is beautiful, while a Greek temple in ruins is picturesque. A pavement that is overgrown with vegetation is similarly picturesque. Beech or ash trees are beautiful, whereas a gnarly oak or a knotty wych elm covered with moss is picturesque.

A woman may be beautiful, or she may be attractively piquant, that is, have that *je ne sais quoi* that has such an arresting and striking effect. A neoclassical building might be beautiful, but a Gothic one, with its variety of forms and lack of symmetry, is picturesque.

Price also follows Burke in his physiological explanation. Just as astonishment is a key emotion of the sublime with its tensioning of the nerve fibers, so beauty relaxes the nerves with its associative feeling of "melting and languor." The picturesque falls exactly in between these two in its physiological effects, that is, "wild romantic mountainous scenes" invoke our sense of curiosity to explore "every rocky promontory," which allows nerve fibers and muscles to achieve "full tone" and the brain to engage in "free play." Therefore the experience of the picturesque "when mixed with either of the other characters, corrects the languor of beauty, or the tension of sublimity." Perhaps Price's notion of the picturesque can be best summarized by his own phrase "coquetry of nature."[21]

On this issue Price would be opposed by Knight, who in 1805 published his principal work of theory, *An analytical Inquiry into the Principles of Taste*. Price and Knight were neighbors and fellow parliamentarians. Nevertheless, Knight would oppose his friend on several counts – not the least of which was his belief that his neighbor had been "misled by the brilliant, but absurd and superficial theories of the *Inquiry into the Sublime and the Beautiful*."[22]

Nevertheless, the theoretical differences between the two men were not major. Both admired the same landscape painters and both discussed the notion of the picturesque – although their differing approaches were quite important from the perspective of modern neuroscience. Knight begins his psychological study with chapters on the five senses, in which he acknowledges that all sensations are "produced by contact" of fluids, chemical compounds, sound waves, touch, and light on the various senses.[23] His first distinction, then, is his argument that these sensations in themselves do not form the final perception, only a crude organic perception. For the full perception to emerge, the brain with its associative powers ("imprinted in memory") must also become involved, and what arises from this mixture is the idea of an "improved perception," that is, rough organic perceptions are improved when mixed with associative ideas. This is a very important insight with both old and new dimensions. On the traditional side, Knight is interested in bringing judgments of beauty or the picturesque back to the associative patterns of the brain (where Hume's aesthetics had located them), and it suggests that the brain itself can be cultivated in its aesthetic sophistication. A skilled musician, he notes, has a much greater ability to discern musical sounds than a non-musician, while a vintner has a more acute refinement of his powers of taste.[24] But such an argument also suggests, from a more contemporary perspective, that the brain is rather plastic in its perceptual development – that is, one can refine and enhance one's perceptual powers over the course of a lifetime. And the greater refinement or associative sophistication that an artist brings to an act of creation, the greater the artistic value that a work of art will possess.

It is also under the heading of improved perception that Knight first broaches the idea of the picturesque. For him it is an aesthetic power cultivated by the person viewing the composition, rather than any qualities of objects themselves. Thus those "pleasing effects of colour, light, and shadow" are not accessible to all, but only "to persons conversant with the art of painting, and sufficiently skilled in it to distinguish, and be really delighted with its real excellences."[25] There can be no rules for the picturesque, and Price's essential error lay in "seeking for distinctions in external objects, which only exist in the modes and habits of viewing and considering them."[26] At one point Knight even suggests a blind man suddenly given sight could, without any mental associations, distinguish between a beautiful and unattractive woman, because "grace is, indeed, perceived by mental sympathy."[27]

This last empathetic point aside, which we will return to in a later chapter, Knight completes his study with another interesting insight: the importance of "novelty" in the workings of the human brain. Once again, his consideration of "one of the most universal passions" begins with the physiological problem of habituation, the neurological tedium that the same or repetitive sensory experience causes, so much so that "all change, not so violent as to produce a degree of irritation in the organs absolutely painful, is pleasing; and preferable to any uniform and unvaried gratification."[28] Knight argues that the brain's need for novelty is the reason for the incessant change of artistic style, and, more importantly, he identifies it as the key to aesthetic enjoyment.

The source of it is, therefore, novelty: the attainment of new ideas; the formation of new trains of thought; the renewal and extension of affections and attachments; the new circumstances and situation, in which all the objects of these affections and attachments appear by periodical or progressive change; the new lights, in which we ourselves view them, as we advanced from infancy to maturity, and from maturity to decay; the consequent new exertions and variations of pursuit adapted to every period of life; and above all, the unlimited power of fancy in multiplying and varying the objects, the results, and the gratifications of our pursuits beyond the bounds of reality, or the probable duration of existence.[29]

These are again old ideas, but very much in keeping, as we will see, with what contemporary neuroscience is documenting about the human brain.

Picturesque Architecture

Both Price and Knight applied their respective theories to architecture, but preceding them in this regard is the work of Robert and James Adam, both of whom were also part of the Edinburgh circle in the mid-century. Robert's experiences were more worldly than his close friend Hume, in that he spent nearly three years in Italy in the mid-1750s at the start of the Graeco-Roman debate, pursued archaeological investigations along the Balkan coast, and befriended Giovanni Battista Piranesi, the great defender of Italic and baroque culture. James followed his example a few years later, and, by the time the two brothers reunited in London in the early 1760s, the "Adam style" had become the new fashion of the capital. Indeed, the quality of their work stands at the pinnacle of eighteenth-century British architecture.

What lies behind it is another seminal issue of the picturesque, fashioned in part from the discussions in Scotland and Ireland regarding taste. As early as 1762 James Adam corresponded with Lord Kames about the possibility of a "sentimental" architecture, that is, one that would appeal primarily to senses and thereby evoke sentiments.[30] The substance of these remarks is again repeated in the Preface to *The Works in Architecture of Robert and James Adam*, the first volume of which appeared in 1778. Here the two architects discuss the means and objectives of their style, the use and effects of their new ornaments, but, most importantly, their desire to compose architectural

Figure 3.1   John Vanbrugh and Nicholas Hawksmoor, Blenheim Palace.
Photograph by Lisa Eaton

forms expressing "movement," which they relate to current fashion of picturesque gardens:

> Movement is meant to express, the rise and fall, the advance and recess, with other diversity of form, in the different parts of a building, so to add greatly to the picturesque of the composition. For the rising and falling, advancing and receding, with the convexity and concavity, and other forms of the great parts, have the same effect in architecture, that hill and dale, fore-ground and distance, swelling and sinking have in landscape: That is, they serve to produce an agreeable and diversified contour, that groups and contrasts like a picture, and creates a variety of light and shade, which gives great spirit, beauty and effect to the composition.[31]

In further elaborating this aesthetic concept, they also praise the architect John Vanbrugh, whose baroque designs had earlier in the century been banished by British Palladians precisely because of their compositional variety and intricate articulation of parts. Thus a change of architectural taste was taking place in the last quarter of the eighteenth century.

This change is what Price addresses in his "Essay on Architecture and Buildings," written in 1798. He, too, is very interested in salvaging the reputation of Vanbrugh, whom he calls the most eminent of Britain's "*architetti-pittori*" – especially for his design of Blenheim Palace, where he combined in one building, "the beauty and magnificence of Grecian architecture, the picturesqueness of the Gothic, and the massive grandeur of a castle."[32] Such a work – its "striking effects" and "richness and variety" – becomes a primer, for Price, as he defines a picturesque building as one that "has strong attractions as a visible object," and one that has "character."[33] Ruins, castles, and most Gothic buildings fit this bill, but what Price seems to be seeking is an architecture with visual intricacy, abruptness and irregularity of forms, varying roof lines, good views from the interior, and a lack of classical symmetry. In line with his aesthetic theory, he too prefers an emotive and sentimental architecture, one that establishes a rapport with the roughness and irregularity of a picturesque landscape. Therefore it is not surprising that the full title of his essay is "An Essay on Architecture and Buildings, as connected with Scenery."

Once again, Knight is in general sympathy with Price's views, although he will again approach the issue from a different perspective. He was intrigued by how, in the paintings of Lorrain and of Nicolas and Gaspard Poussin (1613–75) "we perpetually see a mixture of Grecian and Gothic architecture employed with the happiest effect in the same building" – stylistic contrasts that "may be employed to heighten the relish of beauty, without disturbing the enjoyment of it by any appearance of deceit or imposture."[34] He thus wonders if, then, British architecture "has been rather too cautious and timid, than too bold in its exertions."[35]

There are actually two criticisms implied in this remark. One is his opposition to the Palladian manors and classical follies that had been the mainstays of picturesque gardens throughout the eighteenth century, and which, for Knight, suffer from excessive regularity and a too strict imitation of classical forms. The other is his antagonism toward the more recent trend of imitating Gothic works, which dismisses all rules of symmetry and proportions and suffers from excessive ornamentation. His solution, therefore, and an extraordinary one at that, is to combine these styles, as he had in fact already done at his estate of Downton:

> It is now more than thirty years since the author of this inquiry ventured to build a house, ornamented with what are called Gothic towers and

battlements without, and with Grecian ceilings, columns, and entablatures within; and though his example has not been much followed, he has every reason to congratulate himself upon the success of the experiment; he having at once, the advantage of a picturesque object, and of an elegant and convenient dwelling; though less perfect in both respects than if he had executed it at a maturer age. It has, however, the advantage of being capable of receiving alterations and additions in almost any direction, without any injury to its genuine and original character.[36]

But Knight even goes one step further. One of Price's arguments on behalf of the early Gothic Revival in Britain – a point in fact stressed by him – was that its relaxation of the rules of symmetry would allow both a more convenient floor plan and rooms better situated to take advantage of the surrounding landscape. Knight, however, disagrees and essentially argues that once one is inside one's castle, literally in his case, one is not really concerned with looking outside. Thus houses should be designed for the views of it, rather than from it. And once again, the best example in this regard is the work of Vanbrugh at Blenheim and Castle Howard:

The views from the principal fronts of both are bad, and much inferior to what other parts of the grounds would have afforded; but the situations of both, as objects to the surrounding scenery, are the best that could have been chosen; and both are certainly worthy of the best situations, which, not only the respective places, but the island of Great Britain could afford.[37]

Thus, what begins for Price and Knight as an exploration of how the brain mediates this issue of taste, now ends with a full-blown theory of eclecticism for architecture, and logically so. If, as Knight argues, the rules of symmetry and proportion cannot be discerned by "organic sensation," but only by the "improved perception" involving the association of ideas, he should employ the classical elements in his "Grecian" interiors where he, the trained aesthete, can fully appreciate them.[38] Yet the prospect of Downton castle, which may be viewed from a distance by neighbors or visitors, is not necessarily bound to these rules, and its medieval character can therefore be exploited as picturesque. Both facets comply with his understanding of the brain.

4

The Transcendental Brain

Kant and Schopenhauer

Neither Price nor Knight would have a reach outside of Britain, but the same was not true for David Hume. Between 1739 and 1776, from his quiet perch in Edinburgh, he took empiricism to its skeptical conclusion by limiting the extent to which we can really know the world, and he therefore countered the deductive metaphysics of Descartes with an inductive science of human nature. Many *philosophes* of the French Enlightenment would applaud him for his sensory realism in this regard, although they would likewise do so with the belief that the perceptual world of our brains is but a relatively faithful copy of the world outside. And herein lay its Achilles heel, at least in the view of another philosopher from a similarly remote corner of Europe.

Immanuel Kant was born and lived his entire life in the university town of Königsberg, today Kaliningrad, a slice of Russian land situated between Poland and Lithuania.[1] When he published *The Critique of Pure Reason* in 1781, his book at first fell on deaf ears. His German style was difficult and the language was not widely read in Europe; the exposition of his essential insights had left something to be desired. Unperturbed, Kant amended his work in a second edition of 1787, which contained a new Introduction in which he explicitly compared his intellectual breakthrough with that achieved by Copernicus. If the latter had reversed the traditional belief that the sun revolves around the earth, Kant professes to have done the same thing for philosophy.

Hitherto it has been assumed that all our knowledge must conform to objects. But all attempts to extend our knowledge of objects by establishing something in regard to them *a priori*, by means of concepts, have, on this assumption, ended in failure. We must therefore make trial whether we may not have more success in the tasks of metaphysics, if we suppose that objects must conform to our knowledge.[2]

It is important to understand the reasoning behind this contention, as Kant, now drawing upon the rigor of Hume's analysis, offered a way out of Hume's skepticism. Realism in the eighteenth century was based on the premise that our senses are but passive recorders of the events of the world, and that it is the conceptual mind – understanding or imagination – that interprets or makes sense of these sensory experiences. But what if the senses were not passive, that is, what if the brain were already involved in structuring sensations before they become perceptions? What we would then have are not perceptions of the world, but only perceptions of the "forms of sensibility" by which the brain organizes the world. In other words, the world that we perceive is one that has already been made to conform to the way we think.

Kant used a few other terms that would set the direction of German philosophy for another century or so. If the world in itself remains noumenal or unknowable, the objects of the senses are then phenomena or "appearances" of what takes place in the world. The "form of appearance" is the perceptual process by which the brain orders or structures these appearances. And for Kant there are two very special "pure forms" that the brain imposes on events: the casting of the world into events ordered in space and time. These pure forms of phenomenal appearances do not deny the reality of the world, but Kant nevertheless describes his metaphysics as "transcendental" because, he argues, we can really only know the pre-ordered world of our active minds. His claim, as we know today, was not mere bravado, even if it would take the sciences another century or two to document the essential validity of his point.

Kantian Purposiveness

In a small way, Kant also turned his critical powers toward architecture. In the third of his critical writings, *The Critique of Judgment* (1790), he focused his analysis on the matter of how we come to form judgments, namely aesthetic judgments, regarding beauty. In a way similar to his earlier scheme related to reason, he was interested in how certain "aesthetic ideas" allow the mind to make judgments based on the mind's internal structure. He concludes that if our understanding of the sensible world requires the forms of space and time, so too our minds must bring something to the act of aesthetic judgment. And at the conclusion of his Introduction, he lays out a chart that lists the a priori principles of his three investigations. Opposite "nature," he writes "conformity to law," but opposite "art" he lists the principle of "purposiveness" (*Zweckmässigkeit*).[3]

Although Kant's use of this word had a specific context within the aesthetic theory of the 1780s, his suggestion nevertheless might have seemed as far-fetched to some of his contemporary readers as it does to us today. The German term *Zweckmässigkeit* can carry connotations of suitability, practicality, or even functionality, but Kant obviously did not intend the term in these senses.[4] Purposiveness for Kant is, first of all, a subjective and heuristic principle, that is, it resides in our brains and therefore is not something that exists within the object, and it has to be something that allows our feelings of pleasure or displeasure to take place. Again, it is a presupposition that we bring to the act of aesthetic judgment, a measuring rod as it were – a belief that works of art should exhibit some kind of formal accord, or what Stephan Körner calls "purposive wholes."[5] It is our implied trust that just as works of nature display all-encompassing formal unity and lawful regularity, whose design principles are accessible to our mental faculties, so too should works of art possess some kind of inner form that implicitly at least mirrors the principles of nature. Ernst Cassirer notes that Kant's idea of purposiveness is nothing more than a transcription of Gottfried Leibniz's notion of "harmony"[6] Therefore when we experience a work of art, we bring to this experience the mental anticipation of finding a certain harmony in the work. In fact, the similarity of Kantian purposiveness with Alberti's *concinnitas* is striking, for it implies that the beauty of a work of architecture resides in the way the brain finds some accord with the appearance of the work of art.

Kant was explicit in this regard. For in the formative arts, such as architecture, he goes on to argue that the "*delineation*," or design, is the essential thing, that is, "here it is not what gratifies in sensation but what pleases by means of its form that is fundamental for taste."[7] With this emphasis on form or a work's design, Kant was also intent on keeping architecture or the other arts from overtly representing any kind of purpose, which is a later conceptualization fundamentally alien to aesthetic contemplation, which by definition is preconceptual. The sense of purposiveness that we bring to the aesthetic act disdains such a mundane role. In fact Kant's third principle of beauty, that which Cassirer believes "circumscribes the whole ambit of the aesthetic,"[8] reduces the matter to one simple axiom:

> *Beauty* is the form of the *purposiveness* of an object, so far as this is perceived in it *without any representation of a purpose.*[9]

In stating this principle in this way, Kant at the same time raises a very serious problem for architecture. For how does this art, which is intrinsically burdened with a specific function or purpose, ascend to this higher stage of artistic harmony or design purposiveness? It is also important to stress again that this aesthetic judgment of beauty for Kant is not arrived at through conceptualization. It is rather grounded in human physiology, or what Kant calls "feeling" (*Gefühl*), "a feeling of pleasure and pain."[10] In one passage Kant even refers positively to Epicurus, who insisted that beauty was in essence a "bodily sensation" conducive to health, a feeling harmonically combined with movements "in the organs of the body."[11] Kant at the same time is intent on distinguishing feelings from mere gratification, which for him is a purely animal instinct.[12] In this way, the judgment of beauty induces both a feeling-for-life (*Lebensgefühl*) as well as the moral animation of the soul (*Geistesgefühl*). This model for the arts, which emphasizes both feelings and subjectivity over and above any rational or idealistic approach to the problem of beauty, would strongly color aesthetic theory – but, oddly, not until the second half of the nineteenth century.

The Physiological Approach of Schopenhauer

Kant's idea of purposiveness, however, was dealt with first by a cadre of Romantic philosophers who preferred to conceptualize the problem in an idealist manner. For instance, at the start of the nineteenth century August Schlegel, in his lectures on art, drew upon Kant's model of aesthetic purposiveness when he defined architecture as "the art of designing and building beautiful forms without a definite model in nature, but freely, from a suitable and original idea of the human mind."[13] For Schlegel it was architecture's need to aspire to a higher "appearance of purposiveness" that prevented it from imitating nature directly, and what was left for the architect was to emulate nature's "general methods," that is, the regular geometries and symmetries of the crystalline world as well as the proportionality and static balance of the organic world.[14] Such a formulation actually leads Schlegel to an animate and anthropocentric redefinition of architecture: "Thus architectural creations, like animal bodies, have their above and below, their heads and their feet, their right and their left sides, and most of all their fronts and backs should be different."[15]

To insure further that architecture displays no indication of a purpose, Schlegel ends his analysis by citing a passage from Cicero in which the Roman orator discusses the gable roof of the Roman capitol, a form that was originally invented to divert rain water. This roof form has since acquired such a sacerdotal value, Cicero argues, "that even if one were erecting a citadel in heaven, where no rain could fall, it would be thought certain to be entirely lacking in dignity without a pediment."[16] It is therefore in this "apparent" satisfaction of a purpose, or in what Schlegel calls "an extraordinarily happy mediation of corporeal and spiritual demands," that we find the meaning of purposiveness.[17]

Friedrich Schelling also followed Kant's lead regarding purposiveness, yet only by imposing upon architecture still another demand. For him, architecture's initial form is none other than its basic need to fulfill or display a purpose. But this condition for Schelling (what he calls subjective purposiveness) is a state that, as with Kant, must be overcome by rendering the appearance independent of need, or as he notes, "architecture can appear as free and beautiful art only insofar as it becomes the expression of *ideas*, an image of the universe and of the absolute."[18] But then the question is how does architecture pass through this door of ideality and become – to use Schelling's word – objective? One means of doing this, he says, is seen in the Greek triglyph. Originally, as a timber member, it was the protruding head of a joist, but later, as the motif was transferred to stone, the appearance was kept without the reality of the beam and it thus became a "free art form."[19] But this simple reference to itself, as it were, does not really get to the heart of the matter, as Schelling himself soon realized, for what he too wants is a grander metaphoric play between the organic laws of nature and the inorganic forms of architecture. Architectural forms must therefore approach nature allegorically, which it can do on three ascending levels.

At its lowest level, architectural forms can imitate natural forms directly, as was done with the ornamental forms of Gothic architecture. On another level of purposiveness, which occurred during the Renaissance, architecture can emulate such higher forms of nature as the human body: "*partly in the symmetry of the whole, partly in the perfection of the individual and the whole toward the top and bottom, whereby it becomes a self-enclosed world.*"[20] Finally, at the highest level, architectural forms can achieve objective purposiveness through Schelling's famous characterization of architecture as "frozen music."[21] If the formative relations of music are temporal and dynamic in their expression, those of architecture are spatial and static. Architecture thus achieves its higher purposiveness not by imitating nature directly but rather by invoking nature's higher laws.

Schelling, of course, opened the door for Hegel, who would take German idealist aesthetics to its dialectic extreme, but the latter's popularity with many twentieth-century critics obscures the efforts of one individual to resituate Kant's notion of purposiveness on more solid grounding. Arthur Schopenhauer began his philosophical career as an avid defender of Kant's pivotal insight that we read the world through the structure of our brains, but at the same time he was highly critical of Kant's epistemological grounding of this issue, that is, his failure to draw upon the new knowledge provided by physiology. In his doctoral dissertation of 1813 – *On the Fourfold Root of the Principle of Sufficient Reason* – Schopenhauer argued that Kant's failing was in fact his inability to distinguish "sensation" (a "poor, wretched thing") from the "powerful transformation" that takes place during the "perception." And this transformation is "a function not of single delicate nerve extremities but of that complex and mysterious structure the brain that weights three pounds and even five in exceptional cases."[22]

In other words, it is the neurological workings of the brain that invests sensation with form and meaning. Seeing, for instance, is no simple act for Schopenhauer. The brain must invert the image, create a single perception out of a doubly experienced sensation, construct the third dimension, and then add distance to complete the space. Therefore understanding (the collective powers of the brain to form the perception) is no mere reflective act but the active agency that first creates the "objective world."[23] And in rudely dismissing the "beloved Absolute" of those "philosophical braggarts of Germany" (in his view,

Fichte and Schelling), Schopenhauer charts an entirely new course for nineteenth-century philosophy.[24]

The outlines for this are elaborated in his major work, *The World as Will and Representation* (1818), and here again his formulation of the problem is highly innovative. Parallel to Kant's distinction between the phenomenal world (the world that appears in the human brain) and the noumenal world (the unknowable reality that stands behind appearances), Schopenhauer differentiates between "representation" and "will." The representation, for him, is the ordered human perception of events, and will is a kind of vital energy, what today we might call the biological, electromagnetic, chemical, and gravitational forces of the world. What is of interest for us, however, is how Schopenhauer in a decidedly animistic fashion – animism defined as a projection of a vital energy into the reading of form – applies these two concepts to the arts, and especially to architecture, which for him is the lowest of the arts (music, conversely, is the highest).

If the role of art in Schopenhauer's view is to communicate higher Ideas in a Platonic sense, architecture, which manipulates organic matter, lands at the bottom of the artistic scale because of the types of Ideas that it represents. These are "gravity, cohesion, rigidity, hardness, those universal qualities of stone, those first, simplest, and dullest visibilities of the will, the fundamental bass-notes of nature; and along with these, light, which is in many respects their opposite."[25] Nevertheless, architecture must still possess Kantian purposiveness, or the harmonious working together of its parts, only now in the sense that its parts must work toward the overall stability of the whole, such that if any one part was removed the whole would collapse.[26] Therefore, the "inner form" of architectural design, at its most basic level, depicts this "conflict between gravity and rigidity," which Schopenhauer terms the "sole aesthetic material of architecture."[27] By this he means that matter is dumb; gravity wants to pull matter to the ground in a heap. The task of the architect lies in prolonging or upending this conflict, that is, in depriving "these insatiable forces of their shortest path to their satisfaction," and in keeping "them in suspense through a circuitous path."[28] The architect achieves this by devising an ingenious system of columns, beams, joists, arches, vaults, and domes that thwarts gravitational forces. On top of this we can also lay the sublime psychological experience of light, considered in the sense that we saw earlier with Edmund Burke. Thus we arrive at a fully animate conception of architecture, one of which the reading of architecture is the reading of these active forces temporarily suspended in abeyance:

> All this proves that architecture affects us not only mathematically, but dynamically, and that what speaks to us through it is not mere form and symmetry, but rather those fundamental forces of nature, those primary Ideas, those lowest grades of the will's objectivity.[29]

This disregard for such traditional architectural attributes as symmetry, as we will see, will hold some significant implications for this art, but Schopenhauer was also underestimating the force of "mere form." In fact the opposite is the case. For when our brains now strip architectural forms of their historical or symbolic trappings, we can view architecture simply as a dynamic and confrontational narrative explicating this animate drama of materiality fending off gravitational forces. We, as it were, animate architectural forms through our representation of its material will.

5

The Animate Brain

Schinkel, Bötticher, and Semper

The first architect to be influenced by Schopenhauer's radical reformulation of the problem of architecture was Karl Friedrich Schinkel.[1] This humble son of a widowed mother came to the problem in a roundabout way, for, after graduating from the Berlin Architectural Academy in 1803, he traveled to the south in the midst of Napoleon's expanding military ambitions across Europe. When French troops marched into Prussia and occupied Berlin in 1806, Schinkel's architectural career was put on hold for a full decade, during which time he explored other artistic media and turned his attention to architectural theory.

Thus it was Kantian "purposiveness" that first appears in his early writings, but it is a purposiveness interpreted through the idealist lens of Johann Fichte and Friedrich Schelling. We find Schinkel's initial attempt to define purposiveness in comments made in a diary around 1804:

> Just as purposiveness is the basic principle of all building, so the greatest possible presentation of the ideal of purposiveness, that is to say the character or physiognomy of a building, defines its artistic value.[2]

Schinkel nevertheless brings a more tectonic reading of the term, for beyond the "presentation of the ideal" he delineates architectural purposiveness through the categories of "spatial distribution" (floor plan), "construction" (joining of materials in accordance with the floor plan), and its appropriate symbolization through "ornament."[3] In yet another early notebook passage from around 1810, Schinkel follows Schlegel and Schelling in rejecting the thesis that architecture should continue to emulate these prototypes as found in the Greek temple. Schinkel argues that such a belief would force the architect to become a "slave of imitation," while the potential for architectural development is in fact "endless."[4] Such a position is already an early rejection of using historical forms, although this position would also shift.

Schinkel's mature deliberations on the matter begin in the 1820s, when he was emerging as one of Europe's greatest architects. In 1819 he received his first major commission, the Berlin Playhouse, and four years later he was awarded the job of designing the most important cultural edifice of the rapidly expanding city of Berlin, the Altes Museum. Throughout the 1820s, Schinkel traveled to France, England, and Scotland and began to comprehend the full significance of the Industrial Revolution. Through his childhood friend Peter Christian Beuth, who had a high position within the Prussian Interior Ministry, Schinkel also became very much involved with reforming higher education in Prussia, which included a major restructuring of the curricula of various trade schools as well as of the Berlin Architectural Academy. These last efforts convinced him of the necessity for a textbook on architectural theory.

Although his notebooks and papers for this project were disassembled after his death (making a chronological understanding of his thought impossible), he clearly approaches the meaning of architecture from a new perspective. It is also evident that by the mid-1820s he had become familiar with the ideas of Schopenhauer, for his writings, and most particularly his sketches, display a highly animate reading of architecture – both in their absence of any historical or stylistic references and in their emphasis on the structural lines of constructional forms. It is an animistic reading of form, however, now infused with higher emotional and symbolic values. Hence, if all architecture begins with construction, it must be "construction enhanced with aesthetic feeling."[5] Feeling, in turn, arises through the "purposive construction of each part," in which "everything essential must remain visible." It arises too with "beautiful proportions" and when ornament endows form with a "higher meaning."[6] In the last regard Schinkel nearly returns to Alberti's metaphor and describes ornament "as a decoration for human life," that is, as an "expression of a beautiful life and enhanced with reason, freedom, a sense of youthfulness."[7] His understanding of proportions also carry overtones of both idealism and Schopenhauer, for they "rest on very general dynamic laws, yet they

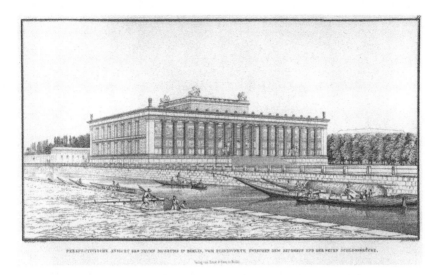

Figure 5.1 Karl Friedrich Schinkel, Altes Museum, Berlin (1823–30).
From *Sammlung architektonischer Entwürfe* (Berlin, 1819–41)

become truly meaningful only through their relation and analogy to human existence or to a similarly articulated and organized condition of nature."[8] Over and above these considerations, Schinkel endows purposiveness with a Kantian ethical character:

> Very different from sensible pleasures, forms awaken moral-spiritual pleasures, which arise partly from the pleasure of ideas evoked, partly from the delight that unmistakably arises through the mere activity of clear understanding.[9]

Schinkel's buildings from the 1820s also mirror these concerns, in that he played with the expression of a tectonics articulating a structural purpose and how it may or may not be enhanced with ethical and aesthetic values. For instance, in his designs for the customs buildings for the Packhof and Institute of Industrial Arts and Trade, he experimented with non-historical forms and a starkly tectonic style without symbolic trappings, while in the Altes Museum, with the grand allegorical narratives of the facade depicting the cultural mythology of the human race, he obviously placed his emphasis on representation. He followed these works with his design for the Berlin Architectural Academy, where, it can be argued, he combined both tendencies.

FAÇADE DES GEBÄUDES DER ALLGEMEINEN BAUSCHULE.

Figure 5.2 Karl Friedrich Schinkel, Berlin Architectural Academy (1831–6). From *Sammlung architektonischer Entwürfe* (Berlin, 1819–41)

The last building, in fact, may very well hold the key to his mature architectural outlook. It is a rather Spartan tectonic expression formed of shallow structural vaults, wrapped within a brick and terra-cotta fabric displaying no stylistic forms. Within the shallow arches and parapets of the window frames, as well as around the doors, it is articulated with terra-cotta allegories depicting moments of architectural mythology. The tectonic logic dominates, yet it is softened with poetic articulation. What makes this melding of tectonic and symbolic attributes doubly interesting is that around the time that these panels were hoisted in place Schinkel penned one of the most remarkable passages in all of architectural theory. Commenting on his lifelong struggle with the meaning or representation of architectural form – forms of construction, forms of history, forms taken from nature – Schinkel serves up what is, in essence, a correction to the purely animate reading of form by Schopenhauer:

> Very soon I fell into the error of pure radical abstraction, by which I conceived a specific architectural work entirely from utilitarian purpose

and construction. In these cases there emerged something dry and rigid, something that lacked freedom and altogether excluded two essential elements: the historic and the poetic.[10]

And herein lay the rub. To many later modernists, Schinkel's strong emphasis on tectonics and his inventive willingness to experiment with non-historical forms constituted the first explicit articulation of German modernism, a precursor to the twentieth century. But the brain of Schinkel obviously saw the matter quite differently. He was still intent on mediating Schopenhauer's vision of dynamic form within the limits of Kant's notion of purposiveness.

Bötticher's Work-Form and Art-Form

Schinkel's relatively early death in 1841 cut short his efforts, but we can see the outline of his plan by turning to the work of his chief disciple in theory, Carl Bötticher.[11] This learned architect and archaeologist arrived in Berlin in 1827 to study under Schinkel, and upon completing his studies in the early 1830s he embarked on a course of research and teaching which eventually led to his appointment to the faculty of Berlin Academy of Architecture. Bötticher remained close to Schinkel, and in 1839 he began to pursue a theme of research that had been suggested by his mentor – discerning the symbolic language of Greek tectonics.

Bötticher first raised the issue in an essay of 1840 entitled "Development of the Forms of Greek Tectonics." He defines the term "tectonics" (a term he was the first to popularize) as "the total form of an architectural body," whose parts might be considered on two levels.[12] One is the functional "work-form" of any part, by which a column, for example, in theory supports a load. The other is the articulated "art-form," which arises simultaneously as a metaphoric dressing or enhancement of the work-form – the transformation of the column into an Order. Thus the art-form "functions *neither materially nor structurally*, but only to symbolize the purpose, the function, and the nature" of the column.[13] Bötticher then goes on to argue, in a way recalling Schopenhauer, that all parts of classical Greek architecture artistically represent their mechanically-serving functions – specifically through their artistic forms. And here again we have a very animate conception of Greek architecture, one in which all of the decorative characteristics of the structural parts not only articulate their immediate purpose (the circuitous lines of gravitational forces) but also "the organism of the whole as well as of the parts" (higher Kantian purposiveness).[14]

Later in the decade Bötticher translated this thesis into a lengthy two-volume study, *Die Tektonik der Hellenen* (Greek Tectonics, 1844–52). And by expanding the range of his analysis, he again cast his ideas in idealist terms. For he would now insist that the principle of Greek tectonics was "fully identical with the principle of creative nature," that is, for the Greeks the notion of purposiveness was fully represented in the lines and ornaments of each form.[15] In his analysis of the parts of a Greek temple, Bötticher in fact insists that nothing in the detailing and decoration of the Greek temple was left to chance; every line and form spoke corporeally and metaphorically to its tectonic purpose:

> The Greek building in its design and construction shows itself in every respect to be an *ideal* organism *articulated* for the production of the *spatial need* in an *artistic* way. This space-serving organism, for the whole to the smallest of its members (*membra*), is a conceptual creation; it is an invention of the human mind and has no model in nature from which it could have been designed. Each *one* of its members proceeds only from the *whole*; for this reason, each is therefore an *imperative* and *necessary* part, an element *integrated* into the whole, which conveys and transfers its *special* function and place to the *whole*. From such a conception, the working hand of the architect [*Tektonen*] fashions each member into a corporeal *scheme*, which for the cultivation of space *most perfectly* fulfills each member's *unique* function and structural *interaction* with all *other* members. As one endows a form with an appropriate building material, and indeed with the form of an *architectural* member, as one arranges all of these members into a self-sufficient mechanism, the material's inherent life, which in a *formless* condition is *resting* and *latent*, is resolved into a dynamic expression. It is compelled into a *structural function*. It now gains a higher existence and is bestowed with an *ideal* being, because it functions as a member of an *ideal* organism.[16]

In considering the role of the cyma profile on the Doric temple, for example, Bötticher portrays it as a "symbol of conflict," either when used as an "ending" or crown molding, or when used as a "seam." In the first case, if we take the example of a cymatium atop the cornice, the vertically inclined profile becomes "a symbol for the concept of the upright, unloaded termination."[17] Yet when the same profile appears in

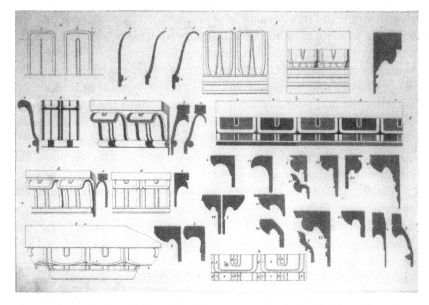

Figure 5.3   Carl Bötticher, plate from *Die Tektonic der Hellenen* (Potsdam, 1844–52)

a loaded area, such as when it becomes the echinus of a Doric column, the intense weight of the load placed on it forces the profile to fold over on itself and become a cushion with a distinct horizontal inclination. For Bötticher, the painted ornaments applied to the scheme of this profile reinforce these readings; in this case the folded leaves lead to the prototypical decoration of the egg-and-dart motif.

No one before Bötticher had read the lineaments of architecture in such an intensely animate fashion. Every line, in his analysis, became a metaphor; behind every form there was an elaborate artistic conceptualization. In this sense there was not much conceptual space between Bötticher's (or Schinkel's) corporeal and metaphorical interpretation of architecture and Alberti's embodied understanding of this art.

Semper's Metaphor of "Dressing"

Still one other architect would come forward with a theory to address this problem, but before we go forward let us retrace our steps. Kant had presented German aesthetics with the notion of purposiveness (not too distant from Alberti's concept of *concinnitas*), as the essential inherent form by which the brain reads and appreciates art. Schinkel adopted the term and interpreted it – following Schopenhauer – in a tectonic sense, eventually conceding that tectonic purposiveness could not stand alone as simple purpose and construction but had to be endowed with historic and poetic content. Bötticher applied the notions of tectonics and purposiveness to classical Greek architecture and came away with a highly animate and metaphorical interpretation of its forms. And by 1850 Gottfried Semper would take up the challenge anew, this time from a slightly different perspective.

Semper, a native of Hamburg, had by this date already lived a relatively eventful life. He received his architectural training in Paris in the late 1820s at a private school run by Franz Christian Gau.[18] After witnessing the revolutionary airs of the French political upheaval of 1830, he embarked on what would be an archaeological tour of the south: Italy, Sicily, and Greece. His discovery of extensive remnants of paint on the Parthenon put him at the center of a contentious European controversy over classical polychromy, but it warmed the heart of Schinkel when Semper, in returning home, passed through Berlin in 1833 to show him his results. The following year Semper gained a professorship at the Dresden Academy of Fine Arts, and Schinkel then assisted him in winning his first architectural commission, the Dresden Royal Theater (1838–41). The design was a great success and Semper's career flourished – that is, until 1849, when Semper, alongside his close friend Richard Wagner, participated in the failed Dresden Uprising on the side of the national parliamentary government. Banished from Germany and practice, Semper turned toward theory, but was forced to live an impoverished life as a refugee in Paris and London in the early 1850s.

Semper's first book, of 1851, *The Four Elements of Architecture*, did not specifically address the problem that Schinkel had posed, although its content was not far removed from it. Semper's underlying contention was that architecture, like nature, operates from only a few basic motives or metaphors, and that these "normal forms conditioned by an original idea" reappear continuously through infinite variations in response to specific circumstances.[19] This thesis has a strong evolutionary flavor to it, but it is evolution without the determinism of natural selection. Semper identified architecture's primary motives as four: hearth-making, mounding, roofing, and walling. All are aligned with processes of making. The hearth is the germ of tribal life around which early humans settled. Its clay gave rise to the industrial art of ceramics. Mounding raised the sacred fire off the damp earth and later became the monumental stylobate. The roof protected the flame overhead and gave rise to the notion of a tectonic structure, while the walling motive originally formed the motive for textiles and metaphorically served as a vertical spatial divider.

The most important of these motives, for Semper, was the textile one, from which he derived his "dressing" (*Bekleidung*) thesis. In German, the root word here is *kleiden*, which means "to clothe, to dress." Thus we can read it as an extension of Alberti's metaphor of "skin." Semper's argument is that original grass mats of early humans allowed the cultivation of geometric and artistic patterns that subsequently affected the artistic treatment of the wall's finishing materials. In later times, as textile motifs were applied to masonry walls for instance, they represented the wall's original meaning as a spatial divider. He pointed to the ethnological evidence that the Egyptians painted their tombs with textile-like patterns, and that the Assyrians attached alabaster panels to their walls, panels into which they chiseled images clearly influenced by textile designs. Still later, the Greeks painted their marble walls with color. The important thing to note is that these primordial motives could be transposed between both elements and materials, and thus could spawn ever more elaborate metaphors. If someone, for instance, applied a textile basketweave to a column capital, the motif represented the textile fibers in tension, restraining the outward force of the load bearing down on the capital.

It was at this point, on December 13, 1852 to be exact, that Semper came across Bötticher's book on Greek tectonics in the library of the British Museum.[20] We also know that he was deeply interested by Bötticher's analysis, because he returned to the library on several occasions over the next few weeks to take further measure of the study. Its contents obviously informed Semper, but it also left him with the chafed feeling that his own ideas, as they had been coming into focus over the last few years, had in part been preempted. For, in the draft to an archaeological article he was preparing in December 1852, he referred to his new-found rival as a "vicious little mystagogue from Berlin, the founder of a new era in architecture, the Pythagoras of the nineteenth century revealing the secrets of tectonics, and the

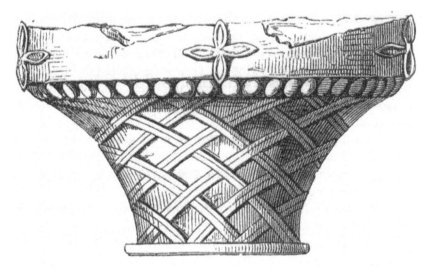

Figure 5.4   Gottfriede Semper, Basket-weave capital. From *Der Stil in technischen und tektonischen Künsten oder praktische Ästhetik* (Frankfurt, 1860–3)

rediscoverer of the 'Analogia,' before whom and his trismegistos Schinkel the world had groped in the dark and had no idea of Greek architecture or of architecture in general."[21]

Notwithstanding this initial antipathy (much the result of his humiliation over his penurious circumstances), Semper took up many of Bötticher's ideas. In a lecture given in London at Henry Cole's Department of Practical Art in 1854, in which Semper seems to have used at least one of Bötticher's drawings, the architect drew heavily upon Bötticher's analysis of the cyma and echinus and defined all such "*ornamental* parts" of a building as "those symbolical investments of the bare structure, with the aid of which we give higher significance, artistical expression and beauty to the last."[22] In another passage he referred to the double curvature of the cyma molding as a result of the "conflict between vital force and gravity. These curved leaves are representatives and symbols of a conflict between two powers and applicable in architecture, where such conflicts take place."[23]

But Semper was only rehearsing his deliberations on this theme. After moving to Zurich later in the decade, he began his two-volume

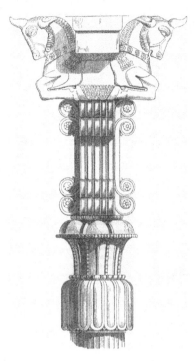

Figure 5.5 Gottfried Semper, Persian tubular column capital with Ionic volutes. From *Der Stil in technischen und tektonischen Künsten oder praktische Ästhetik* (Frankfurt, 1860–3)

theoretical masterpiece, *Style in the Technical and Tectonic Arts* (1860–3). And here such animistic thinking not only became pervasive but often takes the form of a collective or cultural psychology. In his historical survey of the textile motif, for instance, he speaks at length on Assyrian palmette motifs – their use as decorative symbols in architectural forms – referring to them somewhat disparagingly as "telluric expressions of a serving force; the organic vital principle reached here the stage of an unfree expression of the will."[24] The Ionic volutes found in many Assyrian capitals, he further argued, have their naturalistic origin in the "volute calyx of the sacred tree."[25] The "will" is again expressed without freedom because the symbols were tendentious or coded with religious meanings, whereas the Greeks later conceived such symbols purely in a metaphorical or "structural-functional sense."[26]

Figure 5.6   Ionic capitals from the East porch of the Erechtheum.
Photograph by the author

The sections of the second volume of *Style* dealing with tectonics (carpentry) and stereotomy (masonry) are rife with animistic interpretations of architectural forms. Semper was particularly interested in proving that the Greeks attempted to eliminate all thoughts of "weight" in their architectural forms (which in the spectator might raise the issue of tectonic instability), hence he interprets the structural forces acting within columns not as the transfer of gravitational load downward (as Bötticher and Schopenhauer had done), but quite the reverse. The "artistically enlivened, supporting elements become organisms" in which the load above exists "only to activate the life inherent in the column."[27] In another passage he reads the modestly sloped and self-contained, triangular form of the Attic gable (a steeply sloped gable would not work), as a strategy to activate the "life" of the supports, that is, "to engage their energy and their living, independent, intrinsic powers of resistance."[28] In this scenario, the "supple and elastic strength" of the Ionic volute, such as that found on the Athenian Erechtheum, was

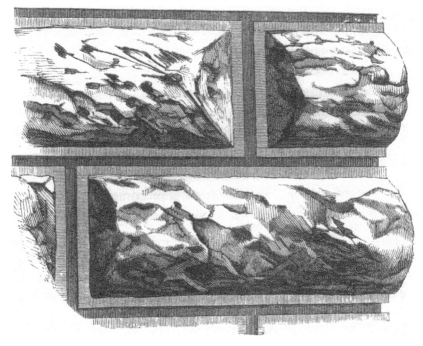

Figure 5.7 Gottfried Semper, Rusticated block from the Dresden Art Museum. From *Der Stil in den technischen und tektonischen Künsten oder praktische Ästhetik* (Frankfurt, 1860–3)

chosen as a symbol precisely because "it offers resistance without violence."[29] Collectively, the articulation of these higher symbolic forms, for Semper, represent the "finer *characteristics* or *expression* of which monumental forms are capable."[30]

Perhaps nowhere is such reasoning more incisive than in Semper's discussion of masonry rustication, where tectonic motifs once again function as grand metaphors. Historically, this "dressing" of the stonework always occurs in the lower part of a masonry bearing wall where the gravitational loads are the most severe, and the purpose of the roughened stone is to provide a secure visual base for the viewer's perception. Yet the articulation of these gravitational forces is affected by how the ashlars are detailed. If the face of the blocks traditionally bows outward under the pressure of the load, the block of stone (as Semper illustrates with a detail from his own Art Museum in Dresden) can also be edged with a flat band that in essence "frames" the bulge and thus contains the outward direction of the force. He describes the psychological reading of this joint in a manner that recalls Schelling's allegory for architecture of "frozen music":

> In the same way, the bands of joints between the bulges acquire a regular "beat," whose rhythm has both a decorative effect and emphasizes the surface of the face with its contrasting treatment. The same effect is achieved by the careful smoothing of the joint surfaces. Thus rustic coarseness can be clad in a certain manly elegance, lending it an expression similar to the symbolism of the Doric order."[31]

This musical analogy was not entirely incidental to his thinking. In one essay from the late 1850s, he placed architecture in an artistic triad with dance and music as "cosmic" arts.[32] Semper, however, relegated the most vivid of his tectonic metaphors to a single footnote in the first volume of *Style* in which he moved well beyond the limits of Kantian purposiveness. The passage to which the note is attached concerns the creation of Greek monumental architecture, which for him arose concurrently with the creation of Greek drama. Therefore the drama and the temple were born of the same artistic instinct:

> The festival apparatus – the improvised scaffold with all its splendor and frills that specifically marks the occasion for celebrating, enhances, decorates, and adorns the glorification of the feast, and is hung with tapestries, dressed with festoons and garlands, and decorated with fluttering bands and trophies – is the motive for the permanent monument, which is intended to proclaim to future generations the solemn act or event celebrated.[33]

Hence, the purpose of monumental architecture is quintessentially *theatrical* and – through an extraordinary extension of the metaphor – the painted dressings of the Greek temple are now transformed into a theatrical (Dionysian) mask, which no longer simply "dresses" but purposefully disguises both the material and thematic content:

> I think that the *dressing* and the *mask* are as old as human civilization and that the joy in both is identical to the joy in those things that led men to be sculptors, painters, architects, poets, musicians, dramatists – in short, artists. Every artistic creation, every artistic pleasure, presumes a certain

carnival spirit, or to express it in a modern way, the haze of carnival candles is the true atmosphere of art. The destruction of reality, of the material, is necessary if form is to emerge as a meaningful symbol, as an autonomous human creation.[34]

Semper extends his metaphor so far in this passage, in fact, that he leaves himself with little space for further development. It is little wonder, then, that he never completed the third volume of *Style*, which was supposed to apply his theoretical model to problems of contemporary architecture and discuss how to treat new materials and construction technologies through these primal metahpors.[35] It is also not surprising that after struggling with precisely this issue over the course of his career, Semper, in a late lecture in Zurich, politely handed off the problem to "one or the other of our younger colleagues," who would prove himself capable of endowing the new architecture "with a suitable architectural dress."[36]

Nevertheless, his labor was influential along two fronts. On the one hand, he framed the terms of the architectural debate in such a way that a clear line of theoretical development can be traced down to the first generation of modernists in both Europe and Chicago. Indeed it was in the last city, in the 1880s, where Semper's ideas were discussed within the professional community, that the "dressing" metaphor was translated into the constructional device of a "curtain wall."[37] On the other hand, his psychological analyses of how we read and metaphorically interpret artistic form effectively handed the issue of Kantian formalism back to a new generation of physiologists and psychologists, who were in fact approaching the problem from a more biological perspective. Here too Semper's insights would provide important clues for those considering the issue of just what takes place inside the human brain during the artistic activities of perception and creation.

6

The Empathetic Brain

Vischer, Wölfflin, and Göller

How is it possible that architectural forms are able to express an emotion or a mood?" (Heinrich Wölfflin)[1]

Semper's introduction into scientific circles was quite immediate. In 1855 he moved from London to Zurich to head the architectural school at the newly created Swiss Polytechnicum, now ETH or Swiss Federal Institute of Technology. There he met the fellow German refugee Friedrich Theodor Vischer, whose *Aesthetik oder Wissenschaft des Schönen* (Aesthetics, or the Science of the Beautiful) would appear in four volumes between 1846 and 1857. Vischer, whose earlier aesthetics was largely Hegelian, had been influenced by Bötticher's recent insights too, and in the third volume of his study (1851) he defined architecture as a "symbolic art," one in which the architect is charged with animating matter by infusing "buoyant life" into it through the linear and planar suspension of its parts.[2] By 1866, however, Friedrich Vischer had arrived at a new formulation of the problem – almost certainly due in part to his friendship with Semper, for the two men regularly shared drinks after the working day. Vischer now offered a physiological basis for the brain's tendency to read artistic creations emotionally and symbolically:

We will have to assume that every mental act is brought about and is at the same time reflected in certain vibrations and – who knows what – neural modifications, in such a way that the latter represent their image, that is to say, they produce a symbolic picture inside the organism. Those external phenomena that have such a particular effect on us, into which we unwittingly read our emotional moods, must relate to this internal picture as its objective representation and interpretation. The natural phenomenon accords with the related vibrations, stimulates them, strengthens and confirms them, and with the emotional state reflects itself in them.[3]

Vischer further noted that vertical lines elevate the human spirit, horizontal lines broaden it, while curves move more energetically than straight lines. He explained the brain's impulse to fashion this symbolic and emotional reconfiguration of the world as a "unifying and contractive feeling" (*Ineins- und Zusammenfühlung*) – that is, as the "pantheistic" (animistic) urge to read our emotions and ourselves in the forms of the sensuous world.[4]

Empathy and Artistic Perception

Yet it was left to Friedrich's son Robert, in a doctoral dissertation of 1873 entitled "On the Optical Sense of Form," to take the next step by introducing the concept of *Einfühlung*. Vischer's use of this term, literally "in-feeling" or "feeling-into," is an impossible one to render into English, and in fact its general translation as "empathy" has to be taken with the qualification that it is much more than the emotional transposition of our feelings into the objects of visual or artistic contemplation; it is rather a reading of these objects through our collective and personal experiences.

The younger Vischer's sources were many. For instance, he was fascinated by an early book on dream analysis by Karl Albert Scherner of 1861 – repeatedly cited by Sigmund Freud in *Interpretation of Dreams* (1900) – in which Scherner speculated that because imagination lacks a rational framework during the process of dreaming, it must translate ideas into visual impressions or metaphors. Thus a building might be an archetypal symbol for the body, while parts of it might represent specific organs. A headache, for example, might prompt a dream of spiders darting about on the ceiling.[5] Vischer was excited about the idea that so many of our empathetic processes are in fact unconscious, and thus, in a preliminary way, he defined *Einfühlung* as the unconscious projection of our "own bodily form – and with this also the soul – into the form of the object."[6]

But Vischer was, like his father, also intent in drawing out the physiological or neurological basis for such a transposition. The key concept here is his notion of "similarity," which he defines as "not so much a harmony within an object as a harmony between the object and the subject."[7] He means by this not only that we tend to relate objects to our bodily form but also that they, in turn, relate in varying degrees to the workings of our nerves, muscles, and those mysterious "neural modifications" of which his father spoke. A color might be pleasing because it conforms to one of the three primary neural groups of retinal sensitivity (a recent discovery of Hermann Helmholtz), while a compound color might be attractive if it stimulates a comfortable combination of nerve vibrations from two or all of these three groups. Again, a horizontal line might be pleasing because it conforms to the structure of our visual apparatus, whereas a diagonal line is less so because it requires an awkward movement of the eye. A line with a gentle arc is more pleasing than a jagged one because of the "congenial" nerve movements it induces, whereas a form displaying regularity is a happy one because it mimics our own corporeal regularity. Therefore – in a very modern understanding of physiology – certain sensations have an inhibitory effect on the nerves and muscles, while others enhance our vital sense of well-being.

When we elevate these sensations to the level of feelings, we also engage a score of other psychological responses. In looking at a tiny seashell on the beach, for instance, we compress ourselves into the small but intricate object, which produces a "contractive feeling" (*Zusammenfühlung*). In viewing a large building, by contrast, we experience an "expansive feeling" (*Ausfühlung*). The point of all of this is that our empathic relationship with an object is at heart "*physiognomic* or emotional."[8] We have a physiognomic understanding of the world because we have bodies, and this relationship inspires empathy when we read our emotions and our personalities into the objects of the world. Much of this engagement, once again, is unconscious. As Vischer notes, "We have the wonderful ability to project and incorporate our own physical form into an objective form, in much the same way as wild fowlers gain access to their quarry by concealing themselves in a blind."[9]

The key to this engagement, such as we experience through art, is our imagination, by which we imbue objects with our vital energy. For Vischer, this is an essential act of our humanity, a pantheistic one to be sure, but also one capable of artistic cultivation if it is to rise to the level of empathy. Thus the role of the artist or architect is to intensify sensuousness, that is, "every work of art reveals itself to us as a person harmoniously feeling himself into a kindred object, or as humanity objectifying itself in harmonious forms."[10]

Vischer calls this process "artistic reshaping," a notion that he best explains in a follow-up essay of 1874 entitled "The Aesthetic Act and Pure Form." Now more directly drawing upon Kant's idea of purposiveness, Vischer argues that a well proportioned building is beautiful, for instance, not because of its mathematical relations, but because these particular proportions "favorably induce the approach, access, and projection of my imagination, because they evoke in me a harmonious emotive process."[11] In other words, because certain works of art or architecture favorably conform with the workings of our brains, we infuse them with our emotional drama. Forms are therefore pleasing when they intensify our biological life, when they mirror or bring something to the complexity of the viewer's own neurological life.

In a curious way, Vischer's embodied notion of empathy circles around two problems that are now central to contemporary neuroscience. One is the suggestion that certain proportions can be harmonious because they are in fact innately sympathetic to the way in which the visual cortex, in a highly selective manner, breaks down and processes visual images. The other is that all forms of perception and thought, including our rich emotional life, are now described as largely associative in nature. What this means is that our artistic enjoyment is in large part conditioned by the interest that we read into the work of art, that is, by how much it enriches or challenges the associative complexity of our sensory, emotional, and intellectual (neural) patterns. In a nineteenth-century physiological sense, Vischer phrased it this way when he noted that each empathetic experience "leads to a strengthening or a weakening of the general *vital sensation*."[12]

Emotions and Architecture

The notion of *Einfühlung* would go on to enjoy huge popularity in Germanic theory in the late-nineteenth century in the hands of a number of psychologists and artists, among them, Theodor Lipps, August Endell, and Henry van de Velde.[13] In this sense, it opens up an avenue of formal abstraction (one in which forms alone, and not their historical or representational trappings, exert emotional power) that has now become synonymous with modernism. One important step along the way was taken by the art historian Heinrich Wölfflin, who in 1886 wrote a doctoral dissertation entitled "Prolegomena to a Psychology of Architecture." He opened the study with a simple question: "How is it possible that architectural forms are able to express an emotion or a mood?"[14]

The question reached to the heart of Robert Vischer's thesis in a less abstract way, but Wölfflin was also intent on avoiding the latter's pantheistic leanings as well as his emphasis on imagination. As a result, Wölfflin placed more emphasis on reading form simply as "expression," and thus his theory is less recondite in its terminology. He opens with the anthropomorphic premise that "*physical forms possess a character only because we ourselves possess a body*," that is, our bodily organization is the form, in fact the Kantian form, through which we apprehend everything physical.[15] If a building appears unbalanced in its composition, for instance, we respond intuitively with a physical sense of unease because it disrupts our own corporeal balance. The unease is not the result of the active imagination but of a more direct impression of the unbalanced condition on our muscles, or in our involuntary vestibular effort to interpret other forms through our bodily organization. Underlying this premise is another principle that is widely conceded today – which is that a degree of muscular tension corresponds to every sense impression. Two colors, for example, might have a very different effect on the body's physiology.

Wölfflin's thesis is also quite animistic, even more so than that of Schopenhauer, with whom he quibbles. If the philosopher had interpreted architecture as a gravitational play of inert masses that would otherwise collapse, save for the structural ingenuity of the architect, Wölfflin prefers to view architecture, like Semper, as the upward or energetic animation of masses, and thus the conflict becomes one "*between matter and force of form*" (*Formkraft*).[16] Hence, the essential theme of architecture is nothing less than the display of "*great vital feelings*" or expressive moods that derive from our embodied condition.[17]

Having set up this intriguing psychological base, the philosopher – arguably – does not follow through, especially within the context of the extraordinary theoretical debates of the 1880s. Instead, he chooses to turn backward to Friedrich Vischer's four moments of form (regularity, symmetry, proportion, and harmony), from which he reduces architecture's expressive elements to proportionality, horizontality, verticality, and ornament. The problem with this structure is that these notions do not offer many possibilities to pursue the theme of formal expression. Only the notion of ornament, which he defines as *"the expression of excessive force of form,"* hints at something of interest, and indeed it is here he speaks of the necessity of detailing or articulating building masses, something that allows someone experiencing architecture "to feel every muscle in one's body."[18] It is at this point, however, that Wölfflin cuts his analysis short.

The reason for such a course, which we can only surmise, is that at this point in his dissertation Wölfflin had lost interest in his theme, or at least in its limits with respect to the individual form. For in the final pages of his study, he instead turns his attention to the larger issue of architectural styles, that is, how they can be read as reflections of the collective *"attitude and movement of people."*[19] This cultural or collective "force of form" – in which every period is invested with a vital feeling and every style with a mood – in any case opens an entirely new chapter in art history. And it becomes the central thesis of Wölfflin's first book, *Renaissance and Baroque* (1888), in which the author ventures an explanation of how and why the forms of the Italian Renaissance gave way to the more complex and evolved ones of the Baroque period.[20] It turns out, however, that someone had already beat him to this issue.

The Cause of Style Change

In 1886, as he was putting the finishing touches on his dissertation, Wölfflin was probably unaware of the work of Adolf Göller, a professor of architecture at the Stuttgart Polytechnikum. He must have been surprised, then, when in the following year the little-known professor published an essay entitled "What is the Cause of Perpetual Style Change in Architecture?" Wölfflin, in fact, must have felt that the closing remarks to his dissertation had to some extent been overtaken, for in his own book of 1888, *Renaissance and Baroque*, he devoted several pages to demeaning the premises of Göller's study, although with unconvincing protestation. In fact, one can argue that Göller's rigorous formalism, by which he excluded all questions of style or symbolic content, had a profound effect on Wölfflin's subsequent methodological premises as an art historian.

Göller was formalist in the strict sense of the word. Against the perspectives of the two Vischers and the idealist aesthetics before them, he rejected the nineteenth-century's single-minded emphasis on artistic content, especially as it had been sanctioned by Hegelian theory. Like Wölfflin, he was deeply influenced by the psycho-physiological research of Johann Friedrich Herbart and Wundt, but he disagreed with both Wölfflin and Wundt in their focus on the corporeal basis for these emotions. For him, the appreciation of beauty in architecture was fundamentally a psychological act that takes place within the imagination, although there is also implied within his model some form of neurological activity.

Göller's major insight into architectural theory was his reduction of this discipline to what he called "*the art of visible pure form.*"[21] This was a property or characteristic unique to this art. In painting and sculpture, he argued, it is impossible to differentiate form from its representational content, but this is not the case in architecture, where the lines and forms in themselves compose the art. He thus defines architecture – in its first explicit non-historicist formulation – as "*an inherently pleasurable, meaningless play of lines or of light and shade.*"[22]

Underlying this definition is a psychological drama, if you will. The first moment in the formation of a style is the cultivation of a "memory image" (*Gedächnisbild*), which for Göller is the "*unconscious mental cause of the pleasure we take in that form.*"[23] It is the process whereby individuals of a particular period or a culture become increasingly accustomed to the profiles or proportions of certain forms. The sharper the memory image becomes etched into the memory patterns of individuals, the more clarity it gains, the more these particular forms become pleasurable. But there is also a limit to this process, which is the law of "jading" (*Ermüdung*). Here the mental or neurological labor that went into the cultivation of the memory image effectively becomes complete or overdone, and the spectator or creative architect no longer takes any pleasure in seeing or reproducing the same old forms. At this point the style becomes exhausted, and architects have only a few alternatives. They may seek out new arrangements of the building masses and floor plans, they may employ new combinations of conventional decorations, or they may intensify what remains of the charm of jaded forms – all of which lead to a baroque stage of a style. When all of these avenues become exhausted, the last alternative is to simplify greatly the vocabulary and offer entirely new forms in order to generate a new memory image, which will then undergo a similar dialectic process.

The simplicity of Göller's scheme belies somewhat the nuance that he also brings to his model. He is much concerned, for instance, with how the architect comes to acquire memory images of beautiful forms, with how one's exposure to both historical models and other cultures enhance this essential educational process. He emphasizes that not only do different cultures generate different memory images but also one culture is not superior to another in its particular forms (the first such leveling of national or historical styles). He also underscores the temporal limitations of a style by noting that "a master of the high Renaissance or the Baroque was incapable of enjoying a linear design of Erwin von Steinbach."[24] And he is willing to concede the fact that we, as humans, tend to derive our "sense of form" from the proportions of the human body.

Above all, Göller is concerned with style, and the great stylistic issues of his day. The Renaissance revival that had been popularized by Semper shortly before the mid-century had, by the 1880s in Germany, passed into a late-baroque phase that was nearing the end of its artistic life. Göller addresses this problem directly in a lengthy follow-up study of 1888, entitled *Die Entstehung der architektonischen Stilformen* (The origin of architectural styles). Here he struggles mightily with what the near-future would bring. Convinced that in architecture "all the simple and natural resources for the production of art-forms have already been exhausted," Göller gloomily predicts that the only option at the moment is a more learned (if eclectic) selection of forms from the existing treasury of forms.[25]

As fate would have it, however, his pessimism would be redeemed by another discerning individual. Late in 1887, the Dresden architect and historian Cornelius Gurlitt, in writing a review of Göller's two books, happily proclaimed that not only had Göller pointed the way to a viable new era for architecture by stripping form-making of its historical or stylistic guise, but also that the same model of formalist abstraction could indeed be applied to painting and sculpture, once these arts also moved beyond their overdone representational values.[26] Gurlitt's comments, derived from his reading of Göller, are really the first definitive theoretical expression of architectural modernism, and they appear on the eve of the efforts of Frank Lloyd Wright, Otto Wagner, and Hendrik Berlage, among others, to seek formal alternatives to conventional historical forms. What Göller and Gurlitt had surmised, but perhaps did not fully realize, was how close the new psycho-physiological sciences were, within the next few years, to explaining (at least in part) the nature of this perceptual transformation – which takes place in the neural patterns of the brain itself.

7

The Gestalt Brain

The Dynamics of the Sensory Field

But what a strange storehouse we find it to be! (Kurt Koffka)[1]

The aesthetic speculations of Robert Vischer, Wölfflin, and Göller, in fact, fell amid a burst of activity in the fields of physiology and psychology – the last of which was still a relatively young field. One school of formalist psychology had been started by Johann Friedrich Herbart in the first half of the century. By the 1880s it had (in addition to Göller's scheme) spun off a number of other formalist approaches to aesthetic issues, such as we find in the writings of Adolf Zeising, Eduard Hanslick, Conrad Fiedler, Robert Zimmermann, Gustav Fechner, and Hermann Lotze.[2] Even the Berlin physiologist Hermann Helmholtz was sufficiently moved by Herbart's ideas to prepare a number of experiments on musical tonality, which he published in 1863 as *Die Lehre von den Tonempfindungen als physiologische Grundlage für die Theorie der Musik* (On the Sensations of Tone as a Physiological Basis for the Theory of Music).[3]

Also following a similar scientific spirit was the work of Wilhelm Wundt. This physiologist accepted a chair in philosophy at Leipzig University in 1875, and four years later he founded his famed experimental laboratory devoted to psychological research according to strict scientific methods. Wundt, a former assistant to Helmholtz, had turned his attention to psychology in the early 1860s, and in his *Grundzüge der physiologischen Psychologie* (Principles of physiological psychology, 1874), he proclaimed what he believed to be an entirely new domain of study. Its objective was *"the investigation of conscious processes in the modes of*

connexion peculiar to them," and he saw this new field as a kind of mind–
brain parallelism in which psychological activities were deemed to be
analogous to the mechanical laws of physical bodies.[4] In his Leipzig
laboratory he trained a number of observers and conducted thousands
of experiments on consciousness, attention, spatial perception, color,
and sound. He also laid down much of the terminology used in later
research. His distinction among sensation, emotion, and feeling became
a mainstay of psychological experiments well into the twentieth century,
while his relatively minor concept of a "memory image," as we have
seen, became the keynote of Göller's thesis of style-change.

Wundt's "atomic" approach, which tended to break experience
down into discrete sensory elements or facts, was not without its critics. Foremost among these was Carl Stumpf, a student of Franz
Brentano and Lotze and the founder of his own laboratory for psychological research at the University of Berlin in 1894, although Stumpf
was active in this field well before this date. In 1873 he published his
Über den psychologischen Ursprung der Raumvorstellung (On the
Psychological Origin of Spatial Imagination), in which he first opposed
the physiological assumptions of Wundt regarding spatial perception
and argued that space was in fact immediately given to consciousness.[5]
Stumpf, however, is better known for his *Tonpsychologie* (Psychology of
Sound, 1883–90), which stressed the importance of psychological factors in musical perception – against the strictly physiological basis that
Helmholtz had sought. The suggestion that the experienced "whole"
is greater than the sum of the parts also put him at odds with the
atomic approach of Wundt, and a major argument festered for many
years between the two men. Stumpf disagreed with Wundt on another
matter by insisting that the primary subject of psychological investigation
should be the direct experience of the "phenomena" themselves – a
belief that one of Stumpf's students, Edmund Husserl, translated into
the major philosophical movement of phenomenology.

All of this activity should also be measured against the direction in
psychology being ushered in by Sigmund Freud during the 1890s.
Like Stumpf, Freud in his university studies had been strongly influenced by the lectures on psychology and philosophy of Franz Brentano,
ideas that in the 1880s melded with the physiological inclinations of
the young medical student. Once again, Freud's psychoanalysis, which
in its early years was based predominantly on physiological principles,
contrasted sharply with Wundt's experimental approach.

Wertheimer, Koffka, and Köhler

This was less the case with three other students of Stumpf – Max Wertheimer, Kurt Koffka, and Wolfgang Köhler – who established the realm of "Gestalt" psychology as one of the dominant psychological schools of the twentieth century.[6] Wertheimer, who was a few years older than his two colleagues, took the lead in defining this new field. A native of Prague, he studied under Stumpf in Berlin in the first years of the twentieth century, but then wrote his doctoral dissertation under Oswald Külpe, who had assisted Wundt for several years. In 1910, he received a position at the Psychological Institute in Frankfurt, which for the next 19 years remained his base of operations until his move to the United States.

Wertheimer's first paper of 1912, "Experimental Studies on the Perception of Movement," concerned the "phi phenomenon."[7] It dealt with the problem of "apparent motion," that is, with a particular experiment in which a light (at a certain intensity and duration) is alternately displayed behind two slits cut into a panel. The subjects (who in the original experiment were Koffka and Köhler) experience not two alternating lights, but a light that moves from one side to the other. This perceived movement demonstrated that a perception is more than what is presented by simple atomic sensations, and Wertheimer drew from it a more dramatic conclusion, as Koffka some years later related:

> But on that afternoon he said something which impressed me more than anything else, and that was his idea about the function of a physiological theory in psychology, the relation between consciousness and the underlying physiological processes, or in our new terminology, between the behavioural and the physiological field.[8]

Wertheimer in fact hypothesized that the connection between the two stimuli took place in the cerebral cortex of the brain. If the second light appeared before the neural processing of the first stimuli was completed, then the brain connects the two events and the perception becomes constructed as one of movement.

Out of this principle came the Gestalt concept of *Prägnanz*, literally "pregnant with meaning." It is perhaps the most basic principle of Gestalt psychology and it states that the brain imposes a "psychological organization" on the phenomena of experience (not entirely dissimilar to Kant's "forms of sensibility"), one that "will always be as 'good' as the prevailing conditions allow."[9] This structure not only makes it possible for the viewer to have a sense of "wholeness" about sensory events, but also "for the sensory world to appear so utterly imbued with meaning."[10] Some of these impositions are the reductive perceptual tendencies of creating forms that are regular, simple, and symmetrical, while others compose the Gestalt principles that are found in every psychology textbook – principles of closure (completing what is missing in an image), similarity (grouping similar items), proximity (grouping by location), and continuity (the continuation of lines and forms when interrupted).

Whereas such principles are often presented as the mainstays of this body of theory, what is often overlooked in so many summaries of this school are a number of novel insights found in Gestalt theory, especially in the way that it altered the predominant views regarding the human brain. One important step was simply the recognition of the great complexity of sensory experience. Already in 1927, in a paper entitled "The Unity of the Senses," Erich M. von Hornbostel, a longtime friend and colleague of Wertheimer, argued against the separation of the senses by insisting that it is only the rare perception that is limited to a single sense: "what is essential in the sensuous-perceptible is not that which separates the senses from one another, but that which unites them; unites them among themselves; unites them with the entire (even with the non-sensuous) experience in ourselves; and with all the external world that there is to be experienced."[11] Another neurologist close to Gestalt circles, Kurt Goldstein, expressed the same idea in 1934 by noting that every perception is not local but "a specific pattern of the whole organism."[12]

In Koffka's *Principles of Gestalt Psychology*, written in the following year, he devoted nearly 300 pages to developing his structural notion of an "environmental field," the perceptual medium for discerning events through which we construct such things as the visual organization, figure-and-ground, constancies of shape and color, and three-dimensional space. He defines the principal task of psychology as *"the study of behaviour in its causal connection with the psycho-physical field."*[13] In this way he attempts to link Gestalt approaches with the "field" theories of contemporary physics.

Köhler was even more specific in this regard. In his *Gestalt Psychology* (1929, 1947) he too laments the conventional assignment of local sensory stimuli to discrete independent events, and instead proffers the view that "the organism responds to the *pattern* of stimuli to which it is exposed. Perception is always a unitary process, a functional whole, which gives, in experience, a sensory scene rather than a mosaic of local sensations."[14] He likens this new perspective of psychology to William Harvey's discovery of blood circulation, which upended the mechanical interpretation of organic functions. He also emphasizes the "dynamic" factors involved in all physical processes, and therefore in psychological ones as well. In his book *Dynamics in Psychology*, based on lectures given in 1939, Köhler makes this point more explicit by noting that any "theory of perception must be a field theory," and then offers this explanation:

> By this we mean that the neural functions and processes with which the perceptual facts are associated in each case are located in a continuous medium; and that the events in one part of this medium influence the events in other regions in a way that depends directly on the properties of both in their relation to each other. This is the conception with which all physicists work. The field theory of perception applies this simple scheme to the brain correlates of perceptual facts.[15]

Both Köhler and Koffka strove to extend this notion of a field psychology beyond perception – to such areas as memory, learning, emotion, and thought. Perhaps the most interesting effort in this regard was Koffka's (seemingly lone) paper of 1928, "On the Structure of the Unconscious," in which he sought to account for how the brain produces its "many errors of memory." In speaking against what he characterized as Freud's belief that the unconscious lacks genuine creative powers, Koffka argues that "true creations of the imagination do occur as the result of processes which take place in the unconscious," by which he means that the mind continues to wrestle with unsolved problems after the matter has left consciousness.[16] In this way, he endows the Gestalt brain with remarkable powers:

> The unconscious has been likened to a store-house. But what a strange storehouse we find it to be! Things do not simply fall into those places into which they are being thrown, they arrange themselves in coming and during their time of storage according to the many ways in which they belong together. And they do more; they influence each other,

form groups of various sizes and kinds, always trying to meet the exigencies of the moment. A miraculous store-house indeed![17]

A few years later, Koffka would back away from the need for Gestalt theory to entertain the idea of the unconscious, in favor of "field properties in the physiological processes."[18] But the significance of even this mild retreat must be measured against the parallel efforts of early behavioral psychologists to confine our perceptual field solely to the activities of conscious life. In some quarters today, for instance, it is argued that at least 95 percent of all thought is carried out below the threshold of conscious awareness.[19]

Isomorphism

This early attempt to apply the idea of a dynamic field to what Köhler would characterize as "the brain correlates of perceptual facts" leads to another revolutionary concept of Gestalt theory, which is the notion of isomorphism. In its simplest definition in Gestalt theory, it means that there is a direct correlation between the perceptual event and the cortical or neurological activities of the brain. Whereas such a correlation – patterns of neurological activity (as opposed to just retinal ones) corresponding to sensory processes – might seem an obvious one today, the matter of defining precisely the nature of this correlation proved to be, and indeed remains, a difficult one. Köhler, in particular, struggled mightily with the problem. In 1920 he first notes that "any actual consciousness is in every case not only blindly coupled to its corresponding psychophysical processes, but is akin to it in essential structural properties."[20] In his book of 1929 he pushes the concept toward center stage, although still without a clear resolution. He offers examples of both spatial and temporal isomorphisms, for instance, defining the former by noting that every experienced spatial order *"is always structurally identical with a functional order in the distribution of underlying brain processes."*[21]

Yet, in two papers presented around this same time, he states this hypothesis more boldly by asserting that we must conceive "the processes underlying perception as a dynamic pattern that comes into existence in some field of the brain."[22] The caveat here is that this neurological pattern is not "a kind of geometric copy of the phenomenal body," but rather the result of a kind of "dynamic interaction" taking place, an example of what he terms "sensory dynamics."[23] Finally, in *Dynamics in Psychology* (1939, 1965), he defines isomorphism within the context of field theory most succinctly by noting that "the structural properties of experiences are at the same time the structural properties of their biological correlates."[24] Through all of these efforts to forge a definition, Köhler chastens psychology for shying away from drawing the brain's neurological structure into its models, even while lamenting the fact that neurological understanding of the brain was still in its infancy. In effect Köhler lay stranded between the fields of psychology and physiology, and one of Gestalt theory's failings, it might be argued today, resided in it viewing itself principally as a domain of psychology.

In this regard it is interesting to compare Köhler's position with the neurological work of his slightly older contemporary Kurt Goldstein. The latter, in his classic study, *The Organism* (1934), was most appreciative of the new perspective Gestalt theory had brought to the table. At the same time he was highly critical of Gestalt's emphasis on perceptual fields and its struggle with the notion of isomorphism – basically that these theories did not go far enough in defining the extent of the organism and thus confused the methodologies of biology with psychology. Goldstein sought a far more holistic approach to the issue in which the notion of a perceptual field should be extended to the whole organism, and thus far greater attention should be given to how the organism, in responding to each and every stimuli, continually struggles "to be adequate to its environmental conditions."[25] Today, neurological understanding is making rapid progress on many of these issues. In one famous experiment of 1982 on a rhesus monkey, a team of scientists demonstrated that there is in fact an isomorphic correlation between the perception of a geometric pattern and the neuronal imprint it leaves in the primary visual cortex.[26] Yet this pattern, as we now also know, dissolves into more primitive components when passing to other areas of the brain for further processing – areas engaging the much larger field of somatic, emotional, and cerebral functions. Thus in recent years the tide has clearly turned in Goldstein's direction.

Arnheim and the Rise of Gestalt Aesthetics

The Berliner Rudolf Arnheim, who in the mid-1920s had extensive contacts with both Wertheimer and Köhler, was also attracted to the idea of isomorphism, although in a different sense. It is a theme he first raises on American soil in his *Art and Visual Perception* (1954), in a chapter entitled "Expression." He defines the last term in a Gestalt manner as "*modes of organic and inorganic behavior displayed in the dynamic appearance of perceptual objects and events.*"[27] Expression is also "embedded" in structure, which leads him to his particular definition of isomorphism as "the structural kinship between the stimulus pattern and the expression it conveys."[28]

Interestingly, he chooses to illustrate this idea by considering the exterior profile of the dome of Saint Peter's, which he interprets in a physiognomic manner as a form suggesting "massive heaviness and free rising."[29] His underlying contention is that a section of a circle with a fixed radius is an inherently rigid structure, while a parabolic curve is gentler in its appearance. In taking a section through the dome, Michelangelo employed the curvature of a circle on the two sides of the dome (lending it rigidity), only he drew the circular segments from two different radii. In this way the section of the dome approaches a Gothic arch in its profile: an effect mitigated by the large cupola at the top. Hence, as a Gestalt form, it reads as a hemisphere stretched vertically, endowing it with a sense of "vertical striving."

Arnheim goes on in this chapter to introduce a principal theme of his Gestalt aesthetics, which is how the brain, in its classificatory or thought processes, tends to read perceptual events visually through the media of metaphors. This tendency is not limited to artists, he goes on to argue, but is rather our "universal and spontaneous way of approaching the world of experience."[30] This theme becomes the centerpiece of his *Visual Thinking* (1969), which is where he both summarizes the insights of Gestalt theory and breaks fresh ground. On the first front, he rejects the entrenched view of the mind as an entity with the dual functions of gathering and then processing information, and proffers instead an explicit Gestalt thesis: "cognitive operations called thinking are not the privilege of mental processes above and beyond perception but the essential ingredients of perception itself."[31] Again, in the brain there is no significant difference between thinking about an object in the world in the privacy of an armchair and going outside and directly looking at the object – a view neuroscience is now demonstrating. Moreover, for Arnheim, perception is by nature both "purposive and selective." This means that the senses did not evolve "as instruments of cognition for cognition's

Figure 7.1 Michelangelo, Dome of Saint Peters, Vatican (1546–64).
Photograph by the author

sake," but rather "as biological aids for survival."[32] Cognition, therefore, is perception and the inverse is equally true.

Another Gestalt principle that Arnheim draws out in a more conspicuous manner is that our perception of shapes comes about through the "application of form categories," or what he also calls "visual concepts or visual categories."[33] Understood in this way, visual perception is a kind of "problem solving" or a comparative distinguishing of the structure of shapes within a specific context, much of which we perform unconsciously. If, in this regard, Arnheim was generally thinking in classic Gestalt terms about such things as our geometric structuring of images, he greatly expands the range of these visual concepts later in the book by discussing the power and limits of words. What makes words so "valuable" to human thinking, he ventures to surmise, is essentially their metaphoric power, that is, their capacity to evoke visual images that are the means by which the mind categorizes things and performs its acts of thinking. It is in the "figurative" realm of visual imagery that words operate, and language, therefore, "argues loudly in favor of the contention that thinking takes place in the realm of the senses."[34] This radical contention – that language is in effect a latter-day overlay to a more primary kind of visual thinking – was almost entirely ignored at the time, but, as Merlin Donald has more recently noted, "Arnheim's view of visual metaphor and the nonsymbolic forms of representation has endured and won out; visual thinking is now seen as largely autonomous from language."[35] This linkage of metaphoric tendencies with the visual imagination and the senses, Arnheim points out, also means that thinking is fundamentally an "embodied" processing of images, a theme we will discuss more fully in Chapter 12.

Eight years after this book appeared, Arnheim published the first Gestalt study devoted exclusively to architecture, *The Dynamics of Architectural Form*. On the one hand, it is an ambitious study drawing upon sources going back to the German psychological aesthetics of the late-nineteenth century.[36] On the other hand, it is one written within the specific architectural context of the late 1970s, that is, as a defense of modernism (and especially the work of Le Corbusier), and in opposition to the recent concerns of architectural theory with "linguistics, information theory, structuralism, experimental psychology, and Marxism."[37] He dismisses such interests as tangential because they evade any discussion of architecture proper. Arnheim's contrary focus – to analyze the "visual forces" involved with architecture's perceptual field – at the same time carries with it the risk to which he on occasions falls prey, which is his reduction of building forms to abstract spaces, lines, and solids.

His study also involves ambivalence on a more interesting level when it focuses on the issue of visual complexity. For example, he is highly critical of Robert Venturi's *Complexity and Contradiction in Architecture* because he believes the author professes a liking of "disorder, confusion, the vulgar agglomeration of incompatibles, and other symptoms of modern pathology."[38] At the same time, Arnheim on other occasions is happy to praise all forms of what he terms "enriching complexity."[39] The problem is that Arnheim's principal example for the latter (a spirited defense of Michelangelo's Porta Pia) is at the same time one of Venturi's favorite examples of mannerist complexity.[40]

Arnheim nevertheless defends earlier criticisms of baroque architecture. He first cites Paul Frankl's view of the baroque – that it surrendered the coherent image of a building in favor of "a multiplicity of

Figure 7.2 Michelangelo, Porta Pia, Rome (1561–5). Photograph by the author

partial images that do not add up to the whole."[41] In an insightful way, he counters this thesis with the contention that it "is against the nature of architecture to become subservient to a momentary image or a number of such images, as happens on the stage or in a film."[42] He therefore insists that the aim of baroque architects was not to fragment the visual experience but rather "to complicate the viewer's access to the architectural theme and thereby to the fundamental meaning of a building."[43] He even likens this note of anticipation injected into the architectural experience to Shakespeare's roundabout way of leading his audience to the thematic core of his plot. Therefore, if one follows his logic, at least a semblance of ambiguity always underpins visual complexity.

The Gestalt psychologist is at his most insightful, in fact, when he considers architecture experientially, and this is especially true of his chapter "Symbols through Dynamics." Now returning to the theme of embodiment, Arnheim once again connects the issue of metaphor with the senses, from a perspective that draws near to more recent discussions. When metaphors are consciously applied in architecture, he argues, such as when we might associate a particular building with its function, they are generally superficial. He cites the particular example of Claude Ledoux's symbolization of architectural forms in the ideal town of Chaux.

Architectural metaphors, by contrast, become meaningful when they – as with visual images – are experienced as "sensory symbols":

> All genuine metaphors derive from expressive shapes and actions in the physical world. We speak of "high" hopes and "deep" thoughts, and it is only by analogy to such elementary qualities of the perceivable world that we can understand and describe non-physical properties. A work of architecture, as a whole, and in its parts, acts as a symbolic statement, which conveys, through our senses, humanly relevant qualities and situations.[44]

The "most powerful" symbols, once again, are grounded in our "perceptual sensations," such as the intensity of morning light streaming through a choir window of a cathedral or the capacity of a cupola to retain a "spontaneous affinity with the natural sky and share some of its principal expressive connotations."[45] Sensory symbols effectively intensify or enrich the architectural experience, and the most intense symbols "derive from the most elementary perceptual sensations because they refer to the basic human experiences on which all others depend."[46] In a fascinating way, it is at this junction that Arnhiem underscores his point by recalling the nineteenth-century notion of *Einfühlung*, the empathy with which we invest objects of aesthetic contemplation. In particular, he calls attention to the thesis of Wölfflin that we saw earlier – that we read architecture through our own corporeal form and muscular sensations.

But Arnheim, surprisingly, rejects this view. The muscular sensations of which Wölfflin spoke are at best secondary to the experience because, as Arnheim now insists, "the primary effect of visual expression, following Göller, is more convincingly derived from, and controlled by, formal properties of the visual shapes themselves."[47] Thus,

> I have argued that the physiological forces which organize sensory raw materials into the shapes we perceive are the same ones we experience as the dynamic components of visual images. There is no need to resort to another sensory modality, such as kinesthetic awareness, to explain this primary effect.[48]

Aside from the undue emphasis that Arnheim places on purely visual events, the problem with such a position is that it weakens his larger argument regarding the essential embodied nature and multisensory complexity of perceptual experience. Notwithstanding, Arnheim still surprises the reader today in how close he draws to some of the more recent interests of neuroscience.

8

The Neurological Brain

Hayek, Hebb, and Neutra

To be sure, this distinctly human brain harbors trouble, but it also may furnish some as yet untried survival aids. (Richard Neutra)[1]

And Arnheim was not alone in this regard. If neuroscience as a biological and cognitive discipline has largely come of age only in the last few decades, other important theoretical foundations were being laid in the immediate postwar years. One case in point is Friedrich Hayek's seemingly intuitive study, *The Sensory Order*, which appeared in 1952 and carries the subtitle "An Inquiry into the Foundations of Theoretical Psychology." Hayek, who in 1974 won the Nobel prize for his work in economics, was a product of the much heralded Viennese culture in the giddy years surrounding the collapse of the Habsburg Empire, and his book, which was started in the early 1920s, really straddles two eras.[2] In its numerical format and logical style it recalls the *Tractatus Logico Philosophicus* of his cousin Ludwig Wittgenstein, which appeared in 1921, and Hayek admits that Wittgenstein was one of his book's first readers around the time of its initial conception. But Hayek also traces its genesis to Ernst Mach's *Analysis of Sensations* (1878), in which the physicist, in a way similar to David Hume, put forth a skeptical philosophy of pure phenomenalism, in which we are forever locked into the neural monism of our own sensations. From this seemingly old-fashioned foundation, Hayek fashions a very forward-looking thesis: the neurological process of all sensory perception (and therefore all thinking) is an act of classification and therefore interpretation. These associative acts, moreover, appear on multiple levels and unfold in successive stages, all the while following specific physical laws.

It is important to see the nuance in Hayek's philosophical position. Although for reasons of practicality he is intent on retaining the concept of a mind, he denies the "ultimate dualism" of a mind operating distinctly from the forces of the physical world.[3] This duality of mind and body does not exist in reality because all mental activity is simply the brain's "transmission of impulses from neuron to neuron" – effectively a neural monism.[4] Therefore the goal of psychology is the converse of that of the physical sciences; effectively, it works back from their models to discern the "order of sensory qualities" by which the world is known to us.[5] Supporting this objective is another, somewhat convoluted tenet, which is "that mental events are of a particular order of physical events within a subsystem of the physical world that relates the larger subsystem of the world that we call an organism (and of which they are part) with the whole system so as to enable that organism to survive."[6] In simpler terms, the brain is a classificatory organ consisting of neurons whose operations have evolved over time to advance or enhance the prospects of its own biological survival.

Three hierarchical terms are primary to Hayek's sensory order. The first is the notion of "linkage," which he defines as the "most general lasting effect which groups of stimuli can impress upon the organization of the central nervous system."[7] Linkage might be seen as the process by which the primary neural circuits of the brain organize themselves in a behavioral sense in response to outside stimuli. They need not be conscious, and memory, for instance, is always a linkage between two or more such events. Neural connections formed by these linkages over time, in turn, "will evidently reproduce certain regularities in the occurrence of external stimuli acting on the organism," which Hayek calls "maps."[8] Maps are therefore the neural record of past associations that have acquired significance; they repeat what we know from experience. More specifically, a map is "the apparatus for classification or orientation, capable of being called into operation by any new impulse, but existing independently of the particular impulses proceeding in it at a given moment."[9] Finally, there is the third neurological system of the "model," which is the "pattern of impulses which is traced at any moment within the given network of semi-permanent channels."[10] If maps constitute the neural record of past classifications, models are dynamic systems and specific to the environmental event taking place, but they are at the same time limited by the structure of existing maps.

On this basis, Hayek constructs a very dynamic system for the operations of the brain – entirely in theory. Neurological models are continually informed by new impulses, and thus are constantly changing. Models of several different events can exist side by side. Maps of mental associations are not afterthoughts that later act upon phenomena, but the very classificatory networks that define these phenomena. Because this is the case, they also run ahead of the sensory world through the vehicle of expectations. All newly arriving neural impulses are always evaluated against existing maps and often modify them. Moreover, the same impulses will not always produce the same response, but sometimes new ones. More fundamentally, sensory qualities that we attribute to objects, recalling Hume, "are strictly speaking not properties of that object at all, but a set of relations by which our nervous system classifies them or, to put it differently, *all* we know about the world is of the nature of theories and all 'experience' can do is to change these theories."[11] Once again, such learning takes place on multiple levels, in that "the formation of abstract concepts thus constitutes a repetition on a higher level of the same kind of process of classification by which the differences between the sensory qualities are determined."[12] All of these ideas today have some currency.

It is interesting in this regard that Hayek chooses to apply the word "isomorphism" to his sensory system. He was well aware of the use of the term by the Gestalt school, and he even remarks that they defined it in an "ambiguous and imprecise" way.[13] But his stricter mathematical definition of the term as a "relation between the neural and the phenomenal order" is scarcely a clearer one – a point that he too eventually concedes.[14] Nevertheless, Hayek sees his work as a superstructure built over Gestalt theory. He credits the school, first of all, for destroying the myth that our sensory world is the result of atomic events, and in this regard the Gestalt emphasis on the "organization of the field" was a far superior model. He also believes his "sensory order" will take this neurological understanding one stage further, in that it will explain the brain's dynamic organization in terms of "causal connexions between physiological impulses," and it will show that this structure "determines the peculiar functional significance of the individual impulses, or groups of impulses, which we know as their sensory qualities."[15] Later in the book he describes his effort specifically as one of developing the Gestalt notion of organizational field:

As was then pointed out, the present approach may be regarded as an attempt to raise, with regard to all kinds of sensory experiences, the question which the gestalt school raised in connexion with the perception of configurations. And it seems to us that in some respects at least, our theory may be regarded as a consistent development of the approach of the gestalt school.[16]

These are rather rarified sentiments, but it must also be conceded that Hayek's book, for all its many theoretical insights into the workings of the brain, passed almost unnoticed at the time and even today is little discussed. But this does not detract from its essential importance, as the more recent modelers of the phenomena of perception, memory, and consciousness are beginning to document.

Hebb's Neuropsychological Theory

This lack of recognition, at least in retrospect, is not the case with the nearly contemporary study of the brain's neurological structure by the psychologist Donald O. Hebb, who, in 1949, published his epoch-making study, *The Organization of Behavior*.[17] It appeared just as Hayek's manuscript was nearing completion, and the latter even thought of withholding his study from publication because of the "physiological detail" of Hebb's book.[18] In the end, however, Hayek's decision has proved justified in that the two theoretical models were indeed complementary. Hebb's book provided the physiological explanation for Hayek's theory of sensory classification.

The Canadian Hebb was trained in physiological psychology under Karl Lashley, the noted biologist who had devoted his lengthy career to searching for the neurological principles of learning and memory. Hebb thus brought an anatomical propensity to his work, although he subtitled his book "A Neuropsychological Theory" and described his principle of learning as principally a psychological one. He wrote it in answer to two neurological models of his day. One was connectivism, whereby the brain was seen as a kind of "telephone exchange" connecting the sensory and motor systems. The other was the Gestalt model of field theory, in which the brain was viewed as a homogeneous system entertaining diverse and interchangeable fields of activities. Hebb, in his thinking, takes the middle ground. He allows aspects of the connectivist model but not in a linear fashion, while he at the same time radically alters some of the premises of field theory. He points out, for instance, that the new technology of electroencephalograms (EEGs) had demonstrated that the brain is continuously active, even spontaneously so, in all its parts, and that there are local patterns among these neuronal firings or maps. This activity was nothing less than human thought implicated with the neural processes, operating through the vehicles of attention, expectation, and the like.

His criticisms of Gestalt psychology are also instructive, especially as Hebb was not unsympathetic to their important insights. First, with regard to the most general premise of field theory – the absence of localization in neurological events – he argues that "we do not know that the pattern is everything, locus nothing."[19] The place or location of the neural activity is significant, he argues, in that cells responding to specific events are excited in specific sectors within the brain. Gestalt psychology was correct in their emphasis on pattern, but they were wrong in insisting that it could take place anywhere in the brain. Hebb also brings something new to field theory in that if some objects are perceived as distinct wholes, he reasons, it is because these wholes depend on a series of neural excitations, some of which have to be learned. In his reasoning, some rudimentary perceptual aptitudes, such as the recognition of vertical and horizontal lines, may exist at birth, but ordinary visual perception (especially with higher mammals) has a relatively long learning curve and Gestalt theorists give too little regard to those associations connected with past experiences. Therefore, he argues, drawing in the associative areas of the brain into this neural activity "may make it possible to adopt a halfway position in which one can take advantage of some of the obvious values both of configurationist and of connectionist theories."[20] Neural associations, he goes so far as to say, are even an essential part of every perceptual event.

With this matter decided, Hebb is free to propose his neural theory of learning, based on the "bald assumption" that "repeated stimulation of specific receptors will lead slowly to the formation of an 'assembly' of association-area cells."[21] Thus learning, in all cases, is a result of synaptic growth connecting the brain's neurons, a point he makes with the often-repeated principle or law that is the basis of modern neuroscience:

> *When an axon of cell A is near enough to excite a cell B and repeatedly or persistently takes part in firing it, some growth process of metabolic change*

takes place in one or both cells such that A's efficiency, as one of the cells firing B, is increased.[22]

Hebb's principle – sometimes expressed with the formula "neurons that fire together wire together" – carries with it an abundance of implications. When one neuron causes another to fire, the bond between them is strengthened, increasing the likelihood that they will fire again in response to similar stimuli; through repeated firings, they form well established patterns or maps that, in his view, eventually draw in or entail associative circuits or memories. Hebb attributes this synaptic growth to an increase in the "synaptic knobs" themselves, or what one might today describe as growth conditioned by the repeated chemical release of neurotransmitters. The end result of growth or bonding between the brain's neurons, however, is the same. The fact that the connecting neurons can be altered by experience is also referred to as the brain's "plasticity" or openness to synaptic changes. In a converse way, if previous neural circuits are not reinforced with repeated firings, the growth eventually deteriorates and the connection disassembles.

There is a second part to Hebb's neurological theory, which he terms "phase sequence." Here, with more complex perceptual events, different perceptual units (sensory, motor, and thought) are integrated into sequences of patterns or circuits firing, leading to the phenomenon of consciousness:

> Consciousness then is to be identified theoretically with a certain degree of complexity of phase sequence in which both central and sensory facilitations merge, the central acting to reinforce now one class of sensory stimulations, now another.[23]

For Hebb, human consciousness also arises out of the high ratio (compared to other mammals) of non-sensory cortical areas to sensory cortical areas, which in turn have very distinct effects on learning. The human being, for instance, is extremely inefficient in his perceptual and conceptual mastery of the world in early years, yet he becomes extraordinarily efficient at maturity because of the abundance of associative areas that have been implicated into maps. Hebb goes on in his book to apply these principles to such other issues as attention, motivation, pain, hunger, and emotions, but all of this work – the bulk of his book – remains far less important than his underlying intention: "Ultimately, our aim must be to find out how the same fundamental neural principles determine all behavior."[24] Whereas some today would not agree with his verb "determine," everyone recognizes the essential correctness of his insight into how brain cells or neurons establish their firing patterns.

Neutra's Biorealism in Architecture

At first glance, Richard Neutra's *Survival through Design* (1954) can be paired with the studies of Hayek or Hebb only by virtue of its date of publication. But when we look at the juxtaposition of texts more closely, we find that the connection is actually a deeper one. Not only does Neutra share with Hayek a nearly identical Viennese background and interdisciplinary curiosity but he also holds with Hebb the conviction that the neurological activity of the brain cannot be divorced from the physical environment in which it takes place. The architect who ignores this fact, Neutra argues in very alarming terms, places the future of the human race in peril.

"Nature has too long been outraged by design of nose rings, corsets, and foul-aired subways."[25] With these indignant words Neutra opens his book, a collection of 47 essays on how architecture must transform itself from being a entrepreneurial enterprise in service to commercial interests to a profession that takes cognizance of our essential "neurological entity."[26] The issue is in fact twofold. On the one hand, the architect should attend to repairing the deleterious effect or "baneful influence of such man-made surroundings"; on the other hand, one must strive to become "a gardener of nervous growth," that is, the architect must realize that one's potential for doing good or harm to the human species is "staggering."[27]

Neutra completed his book in the late 1940s, and thus he was unfamiliar with Hebb's study. The majority of his many referenced sources in physiology and psychology, such as George Coghill's *Anatomy and Problem of Behavior* and Naum Ischlondsky's *The Conditioned Reflex, Neuropsyche and Cortex*, date from the 1920s and 1930s, yet his results are eerily modern, a fact that underscores the rich scientific literature of these earlier times. And then there is the matter of his Viennese education and background.[28] In his early years he reveled in the *fin-de-siècle* climate of the arts and cultivated his interest in Freudian psychology (he was a childhood friend of Freud's son Ernst and often vacationed with the family). In 1912, after starting his architectural studies at the Technische Hochschule in Vienna, he became a regular at the informal lectures of Adolf Loos. There he met Rudolph Schindler (five years his senior) and the two made a pact to travel to the United States to work for Frank Lloyd Wright. Schindler departed in 1913, but Neutra was retained by the completion of his studies. World War I intervened and Neutra was sent to the Balkan front, where he contracted tuberculosis and malaria. After the war, and yet another year in a sanitarium in Switzerland, the architect – lacking an American work visa because of the slow resumption of formal diplomatic relations – moved to Berlin to work for Erich Mendelsohn. It was not until 1923 that he left for Chicago, and it was only after meeting Wright at Louis Sullivan's funeral in the following year that he at last received his desired invitation to Taliesin. When Wright's practice collapsed shortly thereafter, Neutra made his way to Los Angeles where he joined Schindler.

He was thus a mature architect when he settled in southern California and it was here that he turned his attention to physiology. In 1922 Schindler had received the commission to design the weekend house of Dr Philip Lovell in Newport Beach, a physician well known in the Los Angeles area for such natural health treatments as regular exercise, massages, vegetarianism, and hydrotherapy. In 1926, in collaboration with Lovell, Schindler composed a number of essays for the *Los Angeles Times* on the physiological requirements of the healthy house: discussing issues such as ventilation, plumbing, heating, lighting, furniture, exercise areas, and landscape. When, in 1927, Lovell decided to build a new home in the Hollywood Hills – the so-called Health House – he turned not to Schindler but to Neutra, who responded by designing the most biologically refined residence of the 1920s, one that was conceived entirely around physiological, psychological, and environmental concerns. The commission established Neutra as an international modernist, but more importantly it began a successful practice that would land him on the cover of *Time Magazine* in 1949. Human psychology and physiology remained principal interests for the architect, as during the 1930s and 1940s he experimented with a number of low-cost prototypes for housing and schools that focused on the health and comfort of occupants.

It is within that context that *Survival through Design* has to be considered. If one of the intentions of the book is to downplay the role of the architect as a commercially minded practitioner, it also challenges any approach to design based on simple aesthetics. Commenting on the uniquely human endowment of a large cerebral cortex, Neutra notes that it is "in this more complex world, as we see it in the light of current organic research, that the coming designer must operate, not in the *pure* aesthetics of a bygone brand of speculation."[29] This new era of the scientific understanding of the brain means, for instance, that the level and duration of the neural excitation caused by architecture must be fitted to the environment and the effects of a well-crafted sensory field. If our minds are continually assailed with chaos or with an "amorous intake of senses," the mind responds by seeking a sense of order to maintain a biological balance. "Plato," he goes on to argue, "ascribes a solemn mystical significance to abstract ideas, to simple numerical relations and geometrical patterns. Mental economy evidently favors what can be easily conceived, visualized, memorized, and communicated."[30] For this reason, "we must strive cautiously to appraise the physiological function of consuming, absorbing, assimilating *forms*, be they simple, organized entities, habituated complexities, magic remnants, or novel and puzzling technogen necessities – requirements of the industrialized age in which we find ourselves."[31]

But none of this implies that architecture should be simple in its compositions. Architecture is first of all a multisensory art, and therefore one in which emotions are always in play. Emotions (regulated, says Neutra, by blood circulation, glandular secretion, respiration, the peristalsis of the bowels, and metabolism) not only color every experience, but "our neuromental performance is acted out on a multiple level stage, like a medieval mystery play. Emotion is near to all the levels and never exits."[32] With the notion of multisensory design, Neutra stresses again and again that architecture has to be conceived in more than just visual terms, and must take into account not only the other senses but also the effects of spores due to dampness, humidity, air currents, heat loss, tactile stimulation, the gravity or resilience of the floor, and other muscular-skeletal responses. Even such a formerly abstract issue as architectural space has a very existential coloration of "vector properties" that we impose on it as we move forward in time. The sound of a room is also vitally important to this experience: "Whether we are conscious of it or not, the constructed environment either appeals to us or harms us also as a complex auditory phenomenon and is often effective even in its tiniest reverberations."[33]

All of this leads Neutra to propose a twofold strategy to design. On the one hand he encourages the architect to become familiar with the most recent research on color, illumination, comfort and fatigue, involuntary reflexes, habituation, and nervous shock. On the other hand he proposes that architects undertake new research in the areas of "sensory significance" (shapes, colors, texture, consistencies), materials (as sensory stimuli), and arrangements and compositions (optical, acoustical, chemical, mechanical, thermal responses). Underlying these strategies on the negative side is the fear – citing the genetic work of Tracy M. Sonneborn – that willful and arbitrary design, in a genetic sense, "may bring about mutations more fateful than nature's."[34] On a more positive side, he stresses the fact that the entire nervous system is but one neurological organ and that architects, through a physiological and psychological understanding of its necessary stimulation and balance, have the capacity to affect the deepest reaches of our existence:

> A house, then, can be designed to satisfy "by the month," with the regularity of a provider. Here it satisfies through habituation. Or it may do so in a very different way, "by the moment," the fraction of a second, with the thrill of a lover. The experience of a lifetime is often summed up in a few memories, and these are more likely to be of the latter type, clinging to a thrilling occurrence, rather than of a former, concerned with humdrum steadiness. Here is the value of a wide sliding door opening pleasantly onto a garden.[35]

Neutra's book is a vast repository filled with trenchant observations, as he was the first architect in recent times to consider design from a strict neurological perspective. He ponders, for instance, the architectural transformation that Japanese houses will undergo when the people adopt tight-fitting leather shoes and Western clothes.[36] He comments on the neurological relaxation that accompanies the "Eureka!" moment, when the brain creatively breaks through a mental impasse.[37] He dwells on the enormous sensitivity of our tactile sensations as well as the nuances of our spatial perception. In one extraordinary chapter on the city he harshly rebukes the scale of postwar planning induced by the automobile, in a way that still retains high cogency:

> What can be called a *neighborhood* has an optimal size that will not change greatly so long as phases of infantile development, human stature and gait do not change. Man is still the measure of things, as was proclaimed thousands of years ago. Modern means of traffic may extend settlements and shrink the planet; but we repeat that within a neighborhood, humanly conceived, they should not be allowed to cause significant dimensional changes. And there are also reasons for this other than pedestrian musculature. There are significant limitations to human brains and nervous systems.[38]

All in all, Neutra's book remains a milestone in looking at architecture from the vantage point of human ecology – which, in fact, was proffered around the same time by one sociologist as the study of the human community in relation to its built environment.[39] And even if today his book still might be a little too "cerebral" for mass consumption, it deserves to be rediscovered and become standard fare within our architectural schools, for many of which theory is still only remotely connected with the vital issues of design. It certainly provides one possible way out of the impasse at which the profession currently finds itself.

9

The Phenomenal Brain

Merleau-Ponty, Rasmussen, and Pallasmaa

Flesh of the world – flesh of the body – being. (Maurice Merleau-Ponty)[1]

The French philosopher Maurice Merleau-Ponty is best known for his book *Phenomenology of Perception* (1945), so much so that few reviewers of his ideas consider his first book of three years earlier, *The Structure of Behavior*. Perhaps one reason for this oversight is that his earlier study reads as much a psychology textbook as it does a philosophical study. It nevertheless serves as an essential introduction to his thought, if only because it reveals quite explicitly the psychological and physiological grounding to his later phenomenology.

The Structure of Behavior is, above all, a critique of behavioral psychology and other forms of what he terms physiological atomism, and in this regard he follows the critical lines of both Gestalt theory and Kurt Goldstein's more holistic physiology – namely, that it is impossible to reduce the perceptual whole to a sum of individual parts, and perception is fundamentally an event of the entire organism. Merleau-Ponty is also intrigued with the Gestalt notion of isomorphism or the tying of consciousness to specific neurological events, and philosophically his intention is to do away with the Cartesian dualism of mind and body. His most telling criticism of contemporary models of psychology is the argument that the lived world or constructed milieu that we inhabit is a very different one from that which might be dissected experimentally in a psychology lab. He therefore desires to approach the notion of a *Gestalt*, or structural whole, within an experiential framework, one that in its perceptual quest for meaning integrates consciousness, but not as its most essential element. It is the structure of the perception itself that now becomes "indispensible to the definition of man."[2]

Our psychological world, Merleau-Ponty argues, in fact unfolds in three dialectical "orders." The perceptual wholes of which the Gestalt theorists spoke constitute an initial grounding or dialectic with the physical world that we inhabit, but this world is at the same time transformed into a higher vitalistic order by the intentionality that we bring to our acts. Walking, for instance, is more than a series of muscular contractions; it is an activity animated by the fact that we generally walk toward a goal. Similarly, the phenomenal body "is not a mosaic of just any visual and tactual sensations" but one ordered with gestures and attitudes already imbued with meaning.[3] These meanings thus constitute the vital structure of our existence. Finally, on a cultural level, or what Merleau-Ponty terms the "human order," we are continually creating new milieus with our books, music, architecture, and language. Each of these three orders forms a structural synthesis with the lower ones. If such a synthesis is inherently ambiguous, it is because all three orders always remain embodied within the primacy of "perceptual consciousness."

It is the primacy of the perceptual order that also emerges as the leitmotif of *Phenomenology of Perception*, where the Hegelian dialectic of his earlier book is now recast into explicit phenomenological terms. If there is one all-powerful principle to this impressive study, it is that there is for everyone "an autochthonous significance of the world," one that is always and everywhere conditioned by our essential incarnate existence and therefore accessible only through our embodied dealings with the world.[4] We are our bodies and even the rationalizing mind cannot operate outside of this condition. A thing in the world is no longer "given" in perception, as classical psychology would have us believe, "it is internally taken up by us, reconstituted and experienced by us in so far as it is bound up with the world, the basic structures of which we carry with us, and of which it is merely one of many possible concrete forms."[5] Thus the perception is always a process of creative receptivity, a composing rather than a copying of the external world, but more importantly, "a formation already bound up with a larger whole, already endowed with meaning."[6]

Ultimately, this too is a Gestalt premise, and Merleau-Ponty does not shy away from crediting this school (from which he again draws an abundance of experimental evidence) for bringing "home to us the tensions which run like lines of force across the visual field and the system: our body-world, and which breathe into it a secret and magic life by exerting here and there forces of distortion, contraction, and expansion."[7] The one problem with many Gestalt psychologists, Merleau-Ponty argues, is that they misunderstood the radical implications of their findings and cast the issues within the conventional terms of naive realism – when in fact the Gestalt, or the significant form, is much more "the very appearance of the world."[8] We therefore experience the world as forms on many levels: forms of spatiality, sexuality, temporality, motility, and the like. In this reading – the body, for instance, cannot be objectified; it does not exist *in* space and time, "it *inhabits* space and time," that is, the body is the very precondition for the appearance of space or time.[9] Similarly, it is not the objective body that we move during the act of perception; rather, our phenomenal body "surges toward objects to be grasped and perceives them."[10] Once again, the perceptual world is a vast potential field of human activity, one that exists always in relation to one's body awareness, and my body is the "frontier which ordinary spatial relations do not cross."[11] If I make a complicated gesture in the air with my hand, I always know where my hand is. Its location and nearness are a given.

The same is true for consciousness, which – in a strict phenomenological sense – is always a consciousness of something, an intentional act of perception. It too is now fully integrated into our corporeal condition with its "intentional arc" that both situates us with respect to our past and future and at the same time "brings about the unity of the senses, of intelligence, of sensibility and motility."[12] Because consciousness operates only through the body and its senses, the union of the mind and body is implied throughout every moment of our existence. Such a formulation also expands Merleau-Ponty's notion of perception, or rather, he conflates it with phenomenal consciousness and the senses. At one point, for example, he defines vision as a "*thought subordinated to a certain field*, and this is what is called a *sense*."[13] The field of vision, as we might suspect, is one that is always pregnant with meaning. A familiar object that we fail to recognize in an inverted position does not lose its essential configuration but rather its significance. In a similar way, ocular convergence and apparent size are not the causes of our readings of visual depth, "they are present in the experience of depth."[14] In this way Merleau-Ponty observes that the "body is the fabric into which all objects are woven, and it is, at least in relation to the perceived world, the general instrument of my 'comprehension'."[15] Summarizing this point another way, he concludes the book by quoting a passage from the French aviator and writer Antoine de Saint-Exupéry: "Man is but a network of relationships, and these alone matter to him."[16]

What has changed here with regard to his earlier psychology is not only the tone of his critique of psychological realism but also its epistemological footing. Merleau-Ponty's thought, almost from the very beginning, has been characterized as a "philosophy of the ambiguous," both for the ambiguity that is inherent in the perceptual process and for the indeterminate nature of consciousness itself.[17] There is, however, a third layer of ambiguity that shadows *The Phenomenology of Perception*, which resides in the fact that the idea of the *cognito* still hovers somewhere in the background. Even though he had steadfastly tried to do away with the conventional mind/body duality through his phenomenological reduction or bracketing of the world, the duality nevertheless remains. This was, at least, how he criticized his earlier work in *The Visible and the Invisible*, an incomplete manuscript that was found after his death in 1961.

The Visible and the Invisible

The 150 pages of the manuscript, which begins as a critique of Sartre's phenomenology, are not only unfinished but excessively opaque in their literary style, save perhaps for one chapter, "The Intertwining – The Chiasm." The author's notes appended to the text also shed light on some key points. The noted chapter opens with a seemingly straightforward question regarding our sense of touch: "How does it happen that I give to my hands, in particular, that degree, that rate, and that direction of movement that are capable of making me feel the textures of the sleek and the rough?"[18] His answer is that we can do so because we are not foreign to the world that we inhabit. In a way recalling Wölfflin, we are capable of reaching out and feeling the world through our hands because our hands know what it feels like to be touched. The "body sensed and the body sentient" are two moments of one and the same body; they are reciprocal activities and the intertwining of each other's presence. They are, to use his preferred ontological term, "flesh." With this vivid corporeal term (here used as a metaphor for our profoundly embodied existence), Merleau-Ponty strives to dissolve the traditional mind/body duality as well as the seeming cleavage between the subjective and objective worlds:

> We have to reject the age-old assumptions that put the body in the world and the seer in the body, or, conversely, the world and the body in the seer as in a box. Where are we to put the limit between the body and the world, since the world is flesh? Where in the body are we to put the seer, since evidently there is in the body only "shadows stuffed with organs," that is, more of the visible? The world seen is not "in" my body, and my body is not "in" the visible world ultimately: as flesh applied to a flesh, the world neither surrounds it nor is surrounded by it.[19]

If this passage suggests an underlying pantheism, such as we saw earlier in the theory of Robert Vischer, Merleau-Ponty specifically evades it through the notion of a chiasm. The last is a physiological term indicating an intersection or crossing over of anatomical strands – the most notable of which is the optic chiasm, where the optic nerves from each eye bifurcate and send information to both hemispheres of the brain. This ontological bifurcation of the body seeing and the body seen, for Merleau-Ponty, provides a kind of space or what he terms a "dehiscence," from which we gain an identity without allowing any semblance of a dualism back into philosophy, "so that we must say that the things passed into us as well as we into the things."[20]

Nevertheless, Merleau-Ponty does indeed draw upon the ideas of Vischer, as this last comment intimates. In his notes under the heading cited at the start of this chapter ("Flesh of the world – Flesh of the body – Being"), the philosopher specifically recalls Vischer's concept of *Einfühlung* (empathy). Our ontological relationship with the world is such that "we are already *in* the being thus described, and we *are of it*, that between it and us there is *Einfühlung*," and what this means is that "my body is made of the same flesh as the world (it is a perceived), and moreover that this flesh of my body is shared by the world, the world *reflects* it," and it encroaches upon the world.[21] It also means that my body is both the starting point and the measuring rod of "all of the dimensions of the world."[22]

Flesh, for Merleau-Ponty, thus acquires almost a symbolic meaning that engulfs what was previously called mind. On the one hand it defines our essential embodied or incarnate condition as corporeal and sentient beings; on the other hand it retains that Gestalt structure of significance that was evident in his earlier phenomenology. Our brain interprets the world not as a spatial/temporal sequence of forms, but as expressive sounds, movements, and gestures. When we inhabit the world we at the same time borrow its inner framework of ideas. What is different now is that this ideality (and this is Merleau-Ponty's most important contribution to philosophy) cannot ever again be considered as separate from flesh:

> There is a strict ideality in experiences that are of the flesh: the movements of a sonata, the fragments of the luminous field, adhere to one another with cohesion without concept ... Is my body a thing or an idea? It is neither, being the measurant of the things. We will therefore have to recognize an ideality that is not alien to the flesh, that gives it its axes, its depth, its dimensions.[23]

Rasmussen on the Experience of Architecture

Almost simultaneous with the efforts of Merleau-Ponty to compose his last philosophical study, there appeared a small book by the Danish architect and town planner Steen Eiler Rasmussen, entitled *Experiencing Architecture* (1959). The book shares none of the philosophical rigor of the Frenchman's book, and it is little concerned with the mechanisms of the human brain. But in its own way it draws upon themes very similar to those of Merleau-Ponty and other theorists with whom we have been concerned. Written within the heyday of the "International Style," when architecture was largely measured by the photogenic qualities of its sleek, black-and-white detailing, Rasmussen's book considers architecture as a variegated experience particular to the senses, that is, architecture not as phosphoric sheen but as flesh.

In the author's expressed intention to forego normative standards, the book is a masterpiece of understatement, with the scarcely articulated theme that "in our highly civilized society the houses which ordinary people are doomed to live in and gaze upon are on the whole without quality."[24] Although no sources are cited and no bibliography is given, the book clearly has an intellectual pedigree – both psychological and biological. In his chapter on "Solids and Cavities in Architecture," for instance, the idea of *Einfühlung* is clearly evoked around the very active and creative process of perceptual "re-creation, which is often carried out by our identifying ourselves with the object by imagining ourselves in its stead."[25] If primitive peoples expressed such empathetic feelings by investing inanimate objects with spiritual life, the modern individual now reads "an impression of straining muscles" in the *entasis* of a column, "a surprising thing to find in a rigid and unresponsive pillar of stone."[26] Such a feeling cannot be read from a photograph (or in our case on a computer screen), but must be experienced on the spot, for which reason Rasmussen prefers the word "cavity" to the more abstract notion of architectural "space."[27] Only the former term with its sense of mass or flesh expresses a genuinely physiognomic experience of spatial perception in the manner of Wölfflin. In such a way, Gothic architecture becomes the architecture of construction, while the Renaissance, with its domed spaces, becomes the architecture conceived as cavities.

Rasmussen notes that he is little concerned with the atomic elements of architectural design, because, in a Gestalt manner, *"the object of all good architecture is to create integrated wholes."*[28] Nevertheless, the book abounds with observations of details from a highly tactile perspective – from early comments on the curvature of the English riding boot, to the basket weaves of Cherokee tribesmen or the clinker paving patterns found in Dutch streets and sidewalks. Chapters also consider such topics as rhythm, texture, and color, but his intention is obviously to move beyond a purely visual reading of the architectural experience. Thus he has a chapter on "Hearing Architecture" that discusses the merits of varying the levels of reverberation throughout a building. Similarly, one of the longest and most informative of his chapters concerns "Daylight in Architecture," which, he insists, "is of decisive importance in experiencing architecture."[29]

Rasmussen's objective is obviously to engage architecture first and foremost as a multisensory experience, which he finds most satisfying in his favorite city of Rome. He had not fully appreciated the church of Santa Maria Maggiore, he admits, until one day he came upon a group of schoolboys playing a game of bouncing a ball off the exterior wall of its apse: "As I sat in the shade watching them, I sensed the whole three-dimensional composition as never before."[30] The "tensely coiled volutes" and the other "unbelievable number of Baroque details" of Michelangelo's design for the Porta Pia, which Arnheim would also find so satisfying, portray for Rasmussen a highly empathetic "clash in mighty conflict," both restless and dramatic in its accretion of forms.[31]

Figure 9.1   Pietro da Cortona, Santa Maria della Pace, Rome (1656–67).
Photograph by the author

Meanwhile, the "boldly curved portico" of Pietro da Cortona's Santa
Maria della Pace, when set within its urban court, is nothing less than
a respiratory, thermal, and theatrical revelation: "It is a breath-taking
experience to come from the dark, narrow passage out to the sunlit
courtyard and then turn and see the church entrance like a little round
temple surrounding a cool, shadow-filled cavity. And as you gaze upwards
the extraordinary arrangement of the reduplication columns is even more
dramatic."[32] There is clearly a phenomenological perspective driving
Rasmussen's conception of architecture, although the word itself was
still a few years away from being evoked within architectural circles.

Frampton and Pallasmaa

In fact, the Norwegian theorist Christian Norberg-Schulz, in his
Existence, Space & Architecture of 1971, was one of the first architects
to make this evocation. In his first book, *Intentions in Architecture*,

published eight years earlier he had attempted – by his own later admission without success – to stitch together aspects of Gestalt psychology, Jean Piaget, structuralism, information theory, and semiotics into a "satisfactory *theory of architecture*."[33] With his book of 1971, however, he turned to the phenomenology of Martin Heidegger and Merleau-Ponty, and delineated no fewer than six types of space (pragmatic, perceptual, cognitive, abstract, existential, and architectural). His central concern was how architectural space "concretizes" existential space, through such symbolic means as place/node, path/axis, domain/district. Norberg-Schulz followed this effort with two other phenomenological studies during this decade, *Meaning in Western Architecture* (1975) and *Genius Loci: Towards a Phenomenology of Architecture* (1979). Both again focused on the viewing of architecture in sensory and emotive terms, and the latter even proposed to explore the "*psychic* implications" of this field.[34]

Norberg-Schulz was not alone in this regard. In 1972 the Polish-born Joseph Rykwert published *On Adam's House in Paradise*.[35] While not overtly phenomenological in structure, the book nevertheless approached architecture in a hermeneutic way. Since the early 1960s Rykwert had been highly critical of rationalist strategies of design and had stressed the need to take into account the importance of meaning, emotions, and the ritualistic values of *poiēsis* – all of which would culminate in his impressive study, *The Dancing Column* (1996).[36] Rykwert was based at the University of Essex in the 1970s and worked alongside the Czech-born architect and theorist Dalibor Vesely. The latter had studied with Hans-Georg Gadamer and thus brought a strict phenomenological perspective to his own architectural analyses, the fruits of which have become manifest in his recent study, *Architecture in the Age of Divided Representation* (2004).[37]

Also becoming influenced by phenomenology in the early 1970s was the British theorist and critic Kenneth Frampton, whose editorial of 1974 for the American journal *Oppositions*, "On Reading Heidegger," lent important credibility to phenomenology on yet another continent.[38] Frampton had studied at London's Architectural Association in the 1950s and had been part of the beat generation of British architects who had been inspired by the modernist polemics of Reyner Banham. Relocating to Princeton University in 1965, he admits he became radicalized politically, first with the critical theories of Theodor

Adorno and Herbert Marcuse, and to a lesser extent with the political arguments of Hannah Arendt. Thus his editorial of 1974 signals a new direction in his thinking, as he seizes upon Heidegger's notion of "place" (*Raum*) as a way to counter what he terms the "Charybdis of elitism" (formalist or highly conceptual approaches to design) and the "Scylla of populism" (the commercialization of practice). Frampton insists that the phenomenological notion of "place" not only endows the practice of building with a more genuine topological and tectonic footing for design but it also acknowledges a "public sphere" that good architecture must also accommodate. Hence the formula "*place, production, and nature*" becomes a new "homeostatic plateau" for design.[39]

Such a perspective was once again articulated almost a decade later in his well-known essay "Towards a Critical Regionalism: Six Points for an Architecture of Resistance." Here Frampton proffers the *arrière-garde* position of "critical regionalism" as an act of "resistance" against the technological forces of universal civilization.[40] What is particularly interesting is the means by which this resistance takes place. First and foremost is the notion of "place-form," which in the Arendtian connotation of "the space of human appearance" both lends to the polis a certain conservative or blocking authority and suggests such timeless and resistant urban forms as the perimeter block, galleria, atrium, forecourt, and labyrinth.[41] Critical regionalism also favors design strategies taking into account the variables of local topography, context, climate, the use of natural light, and tectonic form. If the first four concerns are largely circumscribed by the concept of regionalism itself, the new emphasis on tectonics, or the constructional aspects of building, serves as both "a potential means for distilling play between material, craftwork and gravity" and as "the presentation of a structural poetic rather than the re-presentation of a facade."[42] Even more surprising is the last section of his essay, "The Visual versus the Tactile," as he now overtly draws in Rasmussen's earlier themes:

> It is symptomatic of the priority given to sight that we find it necessary to remind ourselves that the tactile is an important dimension in the perception of built form. One has in mind a whole range of complementary sensory perceptions which are registered by the labile body: the intensity of light, darkness, heat and cold; the feeling of humidity; the aroma of material; the almost palpable presence of masonry as the body

senses its own confinement; the momentum of an induced gait and the relative inertia of the body as it traverses the floor; the echoing resonance of our own footfall.[43]

Frampton, of course, explores the poetics of tectonics in much more detail in his later book *Studies in Tectonic Culture* (1994).[44] By this date, however, the idea of a phenomenological reading of architecture was being explored in a more encompassing way by his close friend Juhani Pallasmaa. In fact, the Finnish architect allows us to complete the circle that began with Merleau-Ponty and Rasmussen, as both are now incorporated into a theory considering architecture first and foremost as an experience of the perceptual senses.

Pallasmaa came to this position from a varied background.[45] In his early professional years he was drawn to prefabrication and to the technological theories of Buckminster Fuller and John McHale, yet by the mid- or late 1970s, his faith in rationalism had dwindled as he became attracted to the phenomenological writings of Norberg-Schulz, Heidegger, and especially Gaston Bachelard and Merleau-Ponty. All of this was headlong into the rush of the postmodern and poststructural movements that tended to overshadow such viewpoints.

We can follow his intellectual trajectory over the years through his lectures and essays, all of which grow increasingly rich in terms of the ideas he brings to them. In one essay of 1983, "Architecture and the Obsession of Our Times," Pallasmaa invokes Bachelard's *Poetics of Space* to bemoan the loss of architecture's "plasticity and sensuousness," as well as its antipathy toward "illusion, ornament, and framing."[46] In his essay of 1985, "The Geometry of Feeling," Pallasmaa's phenomenology becomes fully explicit. It opens with the question "Why do so few modern buildings appeal to our emotions, when an anonymous house in an old town, or an unpretentious farm building, will give us a sense of familiarity and pleasure?"[47] Part of the answer must lie in the intensifying rationalism of the last few centuries, but part also has to do with the excessive formalism of the last few decades. By contrast, "an authentic work of art always pushes our consciousness off of its commonplace track and focuses it onto reality's deeper structure."[48] The role of phenomenology, he argues, is to probe this deeper structure and with it to articulate the "language of metaphors that can be identified with our existence."[49] Phenomenology further underscores the fact that architecture is first and foremost a multisensory experience, one that in the best of situations "sensitizes our whole physical and mental receptivity."[50] Both of these issues – his aversion to highly rationalized formalism and his view of architecture as a metaphoric and multisensory experience – compose the basic core of Pallasmaa's beliefs.

With the 1990s came another evolution in his thinking, brought on by the resurgent environmental movement. In his essay of 1993, "From Metaphorical to Ecological Functionalism," Pallasmaa not only pillories the last vestiges of poststructural nihilism but also laments the loss of architecture's once-proud social mission. In a manner recalling Neutra, he calls for architecture to return to its "biologically-driven Functionalist ideals," an ethical stance that espouses "an aesthetics of noble poverty, as well as the notion of responsibility in all its philosophical complexity."[51] In a follow-up essay of 1994, "Six Themes for the Next Millennium," he lists his six points for architecture's re-enchantment: slowness, plasticity, sensuousness, authenticity, idealization, and silence. If several of these points are self-explicable, slowness (in the face of the digitalization of the design process and excessive attention to novelty) pleads for a deliberate taking account of the "archaic, bio-cultural dimensions of the human psyche," whereas silence, as with all great art, allows human individuals to listen to their own being.[52]

In 1994 Pallasmaa joined with Pérez-Gómez and Steven Holl in editing a special issue of the Japanese journal *a+u*, which carried the title *Questions of Perception: Phenomenology of Architecture.* Pallasmaa's essay, "An Architecture of the Seven Senses," now draws the writings of Merleau-Ponty explicitly into the mix, as the Finnish theorist registers his deep concern with our "retinal" or ocular bias of architecture, resulting in an overemphasis on the "intellectual and conceptual dimensions of architecture."[53]

As with Rasmussen, Pallasmaa discusses the sensory realms of acoustic intimacy, silence, scents, and taste, but the new aspect of his argument is the high value he attaches to haptic sense, which unfolds in the three realms of "Shape of Touch," "Images of Muscle and Bone," and "Bodily Identification." The first is not only the skin's capacity to read the texture, weight, density, and temperature of the physical world but also how this sense – presaging what the new scanning technologies were likewise discovering – engages in "an unconscious bodily mimesis" with visual perceptions. "Our gaze strokes distant surfaces, contours and edges, and the unconscious tactile sensation determines the agreeableness or unpleasantness of the experience," he says, thus good architecture should offer "shapes and surfaces molded for the pleasurable touch of the eye."[54] Moreover, he observes, emotional states also alter these perceptions, as when under an emotional condition "sense stimuli seem to shift from the more refined senses towards the more archaic, from vision down to touch and smell."[55] Images of muscle and bone further emphasizes this liaison of our bodies with the world, because "we behold, touch, listen and measure the world with our entire bodily existence and the experiential world is organized and articulated around the center of the body."[56] The same is the case with bodily identification, for every architect and spectator "internalizes a building in his body," when "movement, balance, distance and scale are felt unconsciously through the body as tension in the muscular system and in the positions of the skeleton and inner organs." Therefore, he concludes,

> understanding architecture implies the unconscious measuring of an object or a building with one's body, and projecting one's bodily scheme on the space in question. We feel pleasure and protection when the body discovers its resonance in space.[57]

"Pallasmaa further explored these themes in his book The Eyes of the Skin: Architecture and the Senses (1996). What he now brings to the table, above all, is the realization that his earlier observations, "based on personal experiences, views and speculations," were beginning to find some scientific support.[58]"

Part II

Neuroscience and Architecture

10

Anatomy

Architecture of the Brain

For better or for worse, the future of the earth and all its forms of life are presently ruled by a single species, whose cranial mass of gray, white, and other matter is deemed by many to be the most incredible phenomenon of evolution. Although this assembly of highly specialized components, in its chromosomal structure, does not differ in many ways from that of other primates or mammals, the human brain does in one particular sense. Over the course of its 1.5 million-year evolution (since the advent of *Homo erectus*), it has cultivated the awareness of our brief existence, the ability to think and speak within a logical framework, and the gift to view ourselves within the context of a past, present, and future. With modest success, the human brain has explored the principles of the physical universe. For its own biological reasons, it has constructed an elaborate play of cultural forms that we call music, art, and architecture. And particularly in the last quarter-century or so, it has, with its new technologies, trained its lens of curiosity on itself and today is reaping wondrous breakthroughs and insights. For we are now coming to understand that at least some of the philosophical and psychological questions that humans have posed over the last 10,000 years or so have a very cogent, and perhaps a very different neurological answer than we might have presumed only a few years ago. The Nobel laureate Francis Crick has christened this new endeavor as nothing less than "the scientific search for the soul."[1]

But what exactly is the brain, this bundle of neurons that is biologically conditioned to explore, interpret, and classify events? One might start by noting that it is a living, throbbing entity consisting of 100 billion neurons or nerve cells, weighing about three pounds, and capable of generating about 14 watts of electrical power. During its pre-human evolution the rate of change was much slower than it has been during its human history, and like all nervous systems it arose to mediate the survival of a species within a specific environment. Moreover, only those species exhibiting motility developed a brain. It is thus a goal-oriented organism focusing its activities around the basic needs of finding food, drink, sex, and generally more favorable environments.

The human brain has another curious feature. It arrives at birth without having formed many of its higher functions, and thus over the first years of a baby's life the brain undergoes singular growth and development. Some nerve cells die, even before birth, while others flourish shortly thereafter by developing elaborate electro-chemical pathways that effectively bind specific areas of the brain to one another. Perhaps the brain's most salient characteristic is that it continues to grow in its neural complexity even after it passes through specific stages of early development in which it is most accessible to linguistic, musical, and mathematical learning. The controlling factors for this growth are the particular environmental circumstances into which we are thrown, the food substances with which we feed the brain, and most importantly, the level of neural stimulation by which we either enhance or neglect its propensity for growth.

Neurons

The building blocks of the human brain are the 100 billion neurons or brain cells, which are sandwiched among an even larger number of glial cells and an extensive system of supporting blood vessels. Without putting the matter in mechanistic terms, each neuron, with its enormous computational powers, is in some respects a small battery with a full complement of DNA, and it consists of a cell body, axon, and dendrites. It operates by generating an action potential or tiny electrical charge through the passage of ions (positively and negatively charged atoms, such as potassium and sodium) along its main stem or axon. There are perhaps as many as 1,000 different types of neurons in the brain, but they fall into the two general groups excitatory and inhibitory. In a very loose analogy, most cells can be likened to a tree. The cell nucleus is located toward the middle of the tree, in the knobby area where the furcating branches begin. The limbs with their branches

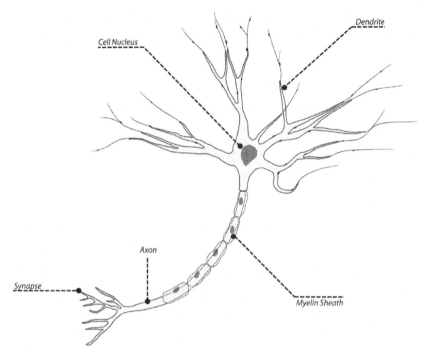

Figure 10.1   Neuron or brain cell. Illustration by Amjad Alkoud

and twigs are the dendrites, which receive messages from other neurons. The trunk of the tree is the axon, which passes the message from the cell body to other neurons through its roots (as many as 10,000), which are capable of connecting with an equal number of other dendrites. Axons, or tree trunks, can be anywhere from less than a millimeter to several feet in length; the longer ones are wrapped in a white myelin sheath, which enables the signal to travel faster. These myelinated axons, which connect neurons to each other and form about 40 percent of the brain mass, are the "white matter" of the brain.

The point of connection between the axon of one neuron and the dendrite of another is the synapse or synaptic cleft (it is a tiny gap). When the ionized charge or action potential moves down the axon to the synaptic cleft it causes a spill of chemical neurotransmitters to the adjoining dendrite. Neurotransmitters, like the cells themselves, can be of several types, in fact as many as 50 have been identified. Because the number of synapses is estimated to be as many as 200 trillion, the human brain, for all intents and purposes, possesses an infinite number of neural connections. If these numbers are astounding, no less so is the overall neural efficiency of the structure itself. One scientist, György Buzsáki, likens the brain, especially its scalability, to a tensegrity structure of R. Buckminster Fuller, in which neurons, over the long course of genetic engineering, have mapped out their shortest possible paths and thereby minimized the volume of axons required.[2] Bernard J. Baars reports that neurons are so interconnected that a message can pass from any one cell in the brain to another in seven steps or fewer.[3] Norman Bryson has described this neural activity as "the orchestration of myriad plays of lightning across the ramifying branches of the brain."[4]

The first major breakthrough in our understanding of the brain in recent years was Donald O. Hebb's principle that when two neurons fire together the synapse is altered through growth and they will tend to wire together. This biological principle is the reason for the brain's great efficiency, because the organ from the beginning of its development tends to link neural groups into loops or maps that oscillate in synchronous rhythms (which principle has long underlain the practice of meditation), allowing actions to be coordinated and thereby enhancing the output among different populations of neurons. The complexity of these neural rhythms has only been recently intimated, yet precisely how and why they work in this manner remains a mystery. The three principal rhythms – alpha, beta, and gamma – operate in the approximate frequencies 8–12 Hz, 13–30 Hz, and greater than 30 Hz, respectively, and certain oscillations are believed to be essential for such events as cognition and consciousness.[5] Another interesting feature of these rhythms is that their default condition, similar to our nervous system as a whole, is one of pulsating firings (not silence), which means that the brain does not simply process outside stimulation; rather, it continually generates its own patterns of information. As Buzsáki describes it: " 'Representation' of external reality is therefore a continual adjustment of the brain's self-generated patterns by outside influences, a process called 'experience' by psychologists."[6]

This fact becomes doubly important in that neurons and their circuits are highly specialized in the stimulation to which they respond. Not only are neural circuits continually processing the inputs of touch, color, form, motion, smell, and sound in different areas of the brain, but some neurons respond only to individual colors, while others

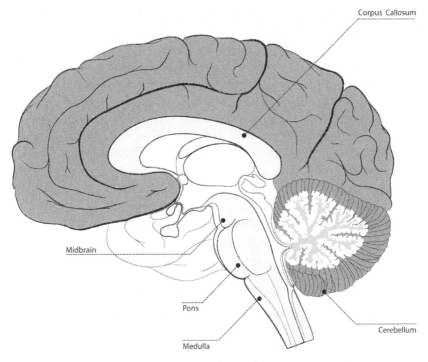

Corpus Callosum

Midbrain

Pons

Medulla

Cerebellum

Figure 10.2 Brainstem. Illustration by Amjad Alkoud

only to vertical or horizontal lines. Hence, the mental world that we inhabit is minutely parceled by the brain before it is subsequently integrated into our seemingly simple sensory perceptions – all within a few hundred milliseconds. Perhaps this creative ordering of events, as Kant and Hume vaguely suggested, is the ontological essence of the brain's underlying microbiology. "Comforting or disturbing," notes Rodolfo R. Llinás, "the fact is that we are basically dreaming machines that construct virtual models of the real world."[7]

Brainstem and Limbic System

The brain is more than a simple organ. In fact it consists of many distinct parts that have been overlaid on each other over its long evolutionary history. The oldest part in evolutionary terms is the brainstem, which resides at the top of the spinal cord. It consists of three parts: the medulla, pons, and midbrain. Science has known for many years that it is involved with a variety of metabolic functions, such as the regulation of the cardiac and respiratory systems, the central nervous system, sleep, pain, temperature, and the musculoskeletal frame, but what has recently become apparent is the enormous microbiological complexity of these areas. In the brainstem there are more than 40 heterogeneous nuclei or cell groups, each with different cell structures that store and release different neurotransmitters.[8] One part of the midbrain is critical to consciousness, while another area of the midbrain's gray matter (known as PAG or periaqueductal gray) is much involved with the production of emotions. It controls the movements of the face, tongue, expressions, as well as the conversion of chemical signals carried by the bloodstream into neural signals.[9]

Behind the brainstem, at the base of the brain, lies the cerebellum, which at one time in our mammalian history was the main brain. Today it regulates some of our fine motor skills (such as riding a bicycle or playing a piano), and it seems to have acquired more recently the cognitive function of assisting some types of memory. Imaging techniques have demonstrated that it is also involved with some aspects of our auditory, visual, tactile, and emotional processing, which is not surprising in that it is one of the oldest parts of the brain.

The brain becomes especially interesting as we pass above the brainstem into the area known as the limbic region: two assemblies of modules (one in each hemisphere) that Rita Carter refers to as the "powerhouse of the brain."[10] They lie at the very core of the brain and they form two identical groups of mini-organs wrapped in the surrounding white and gray matter of each hemisphere. And if the term "limbic system" (relating to emotion) is losing credibility with a number of scientists, it is because we are once again beginning to understand the great complexity and vital importance of these two regions. Some of their components, such as the hypothalamus, amygdala, basal ganglia, and pituitary gland, are indeed largely regulatory in nature and participate in such activities as movement, eating, drinking, sexuality, and emotions. The "motor tapes" of the basal ganglia, five large interconnected nuclei between the thalamus and cortex, are crucial for such complex tasks as playing a violin, as Rodolfo Llinás reports. Two other nodules in each hemisphere are of interest to architects – the hippocampus and the thalamus.

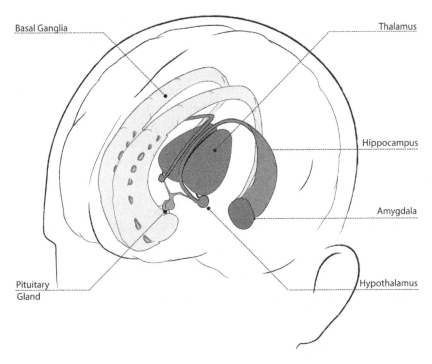

Basal Ganglia

Thalamus

Hippocampus

Amygdala

Pituitary Gland

Hypothalamus

Figure 10.3   Limbic system. Illustration by Amjad Alkoud

The hippocampus is shaped a little like a seahorse, from which it derives its name, and it lies along the folded edge of the temporal lobe of the cortex. It is an area of intense study today because it is the seat of Alzheimer's disease and thus it is critical to the retrieval of both short- and long-term memories. The two hippocampi, together with the surrounding cortical tissue, also have another interesting function, which is spatial orientation and navigation. Through a series of discoveries (the last being made as recently as 2005), we know that spatial understanding is mediated through groups of specialized cells in the hippocampus and the surrounding region, and it has been demonstrated that London taxi drivers, for instance, have an enlarged hippocampus. Given the spatial abstractions involved with design, we might expect this also to be the case with regard to architects. The two hippocampi, in turn, wrap around two egg-shaped appendages, the two thalami. Each thalamus is subdivided into about two dozen regions, and each seems to be concerned with a particular area of the cortex. For this reason it is sometimes called the gateway to the cortex, and in many respects can be considered its dynamic hub as it has been implicated in nearly all activities of the brain, including attention and consciousness. And although neuroscientists shy away from referring to it as a control center, the thalamus both scans and helps coordinate the various activities of the brain. Even the neural stimulation recorded on the retinas of the two eyes pass through the thalami before being processed by the visual cortex at the rear of the brain.

Cerebral Cortex

When most people think of the brain, however, they visualize the outer mantle of the upper brain called the cerebral cortex. It is only one-eighth of an inch thick and consists of six layers of neurons (from 30 billion to 50 billion cells), so densely packed that in a laboratory vial it takes on a gray coloration. Beneath the mantle is a fibrous tract of axons, connecting the many parts of the brain to one another. The gray mantle is rather neatly divided into sections. There are right and left hemispheres, and each hemisphere is further divided into frontal, parietal (middle rear), temporal (side), and occipital (rear) lobes. The various fissures and folds of the cortex have come about because it has grown so large in recent evolutionary history that it has to be scrunched and folded to fit into the cranium. If it were laid flat, it would be about the size of a large handkerchief.

Each of the two hemispheres is to some extent a brain in itself, each with its own limbic assortment of appendages. They are connected to one another along the center by a large bridge of axons known the corpus callosum, which has 600 million fibers sending messages back and forth anywhere from 40 to 1,000 times per second. The two hemispheres are to some extent specialized or differentiated in their functions, but not as simply as often described. Language and analytical skills are to a large extent, although not exclusively, concentrated in the left hemisphere, whereas the processing of feelings, certain spatial skills, and the ability to grasp wholes tend to take place in the right. Many skills, such as the processing of sound, are carried out in both hemispheres, but music slightly more so on the right.

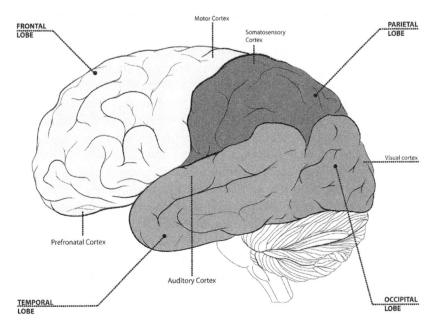

Figure 10.4 Lobes of the brain. Illustration by Amjad Alkoud

The various lobes of the brain also tend to be functionally specialized. Nearly all of the occipital lobe at the back of the brain is given over to visual processing, and is often called the visual cortex. Areas of the parietal lobe work closely with the occipital lobe in sensory processing, and the parietal lobe, near the top of the head, also contains the somatosensory cortex, which registers both our tactile senses and monitors the movements of muscles and bones. The somatosensory cortex is also famously partitioned according to the different parts of the body, sized by their neural sensitivity. The largest areas, by far, are given to our hands, lips, and genitalia. The temporal lobes are multifunctional and engage in such activities as language recognition, spatial visualization, and the processing of sound (auditory cortex).

The frontal lobe, the last part of the brain to develop both in evolution and in a child's brain, is where the planning and reasoning processes are located. It not only makes up close to a third of total cortical area, but it is also the region most tightly packed with neurons. Along its rear, adjacent to the somatosensory cortex in the parietal lobe, is the motor cortex, which regulates our conscious movements. As we move forward toward the prefrontal cortex, however, sensory processing gives way to such functions as volition, attention, emotional reflection, speech, and thought. None of these sites of specialized activity within the cortices are strictly fixed in size, compartmentalization, or neural complexity. The auditory cortex of a musician, for instance, is larger in size and more complex in structure than someone without musical training. We have learned this only recently because of the technical refinement of the various imaging or scanning technologies, such as functional magnetic resonance imaging (fMRI), positron emission tomography (PET), electroencephalograms (EEG), and magnetoencephalography (MEG). Their accessibility and use have proliferated in particular since the mid-1990s, and it seems that scientists – almost on a daily basis – are making major breakthroughs in understanding the neurological complexities of a brain. In addition, the final sequencing of the 30,000 genes of the human genome, which was completed only in 2006, will undoubtedly add further details to this knowledge on a microbiological level. We are in fact sitting on the cusp of momentous discoveries that will revolutionize how we think about ourselves.

Embodiment and Plasticity

There are two further recent insights into the brain that are relevant to our theme. The first is the relative autonomy of the brain, by which we mean that the brain is a self-contained organism capable of spontaneous activity on its own, or independent of environmental influences. Dreams are perhaps the most obvious manifestation of this power, but the implications of this activity are seen as even more profound today. The old model of the brain as a computer or processing center, passively taking its stimuli from the senses, is fundamentally flawed and has been discarded. The brain has a long evolutionary history and over the course of its development it has acquired certain unique skills, not the least of which is its biological self-organization. The brain does not merely sense the world; it actively confronts it with its own representational models and it continually tests and retests its hypotheses. The brain is also highly motivated and selective in its perceptual engagement, and it pares away what it is not seeking or does not need. Because all of this happens on a molecular level, many scientists will now argue that it is obsolete to speak of a human "mind" as something cognitively distinct from the brain. That old Cartesian duality of a *res cognitas* (immaterial thinking consciousness) and *res extensa* (brute matter) is collapsing.

Along with this understanding comes the realization of the brain's embodiment. If you remove a brain from a cadaver and look at it from below, you see immediately that the eyes are simple neural extensions of the rear portion of the brain. What this suggests is that vision is not a "sense" separate and distinct from the brain, as we say in our everyday language, but biologically an appendage of the brain conveniently located at two portals in the skull. The same is true if you attach all of the neural circuits that extend down through the arms and legs. Quite simply, the brain is an embodied organ, and in this regard even that old distinction between the mind and body is breaking down. The neurons in the big toe are as much a part of the brain as those neurons in the fontal lobe that allow us to think about the big toe. The brain is the body in all of its workings, and vice versa.

The second issue of importance that has come into view in the last few years is the extent of the brain's plasticity, which is a biological term for the brain's ability to alter its synaptic networks. At birth, the human brain weighs between 12–14 ounces and its weight increases fourfold as it reaches maturity. This discrepancy might not seem unusual in light of what other parts of the human anatomy undergo during growth, but the brain differs from other organs in one important respect. It is essentially born with nearly the full complement of roughly 100 billion brain cells, yet with relatively little connectivity among them (around 50 percent or so). A genetic code, of course, guides the basic homeostatic mechanisms and provides a general plan for future development, but these regulatory systems and intellectual endowments by no means direct all aspects of the brain's subsequent development. We simply lack the genes to specify the synaptic complexity of the brain's higher functions.

The implications of this plasticity are myriad. Because so many of our neural networks are determined by our experiences or contact with the world, the brain is extraordinarily variable from person to person, even between identical twins. We are, in good part, the specific neural circuits or maps that we build over the course of a lifetime. Much of this synaptic growth takes place in the earlier stages of life, to be sure. A child, for instance, is born with the visual cortex in place, and its parietal cortex becomes active shortly after birth. Yet the frontal lobe, whose development allows cognition and a sense of self, does not come on line until about six months of age. How and when we develop areas of the brain is therefore crucial for the brain's structure. We have long known, for instance, that a child is more open to learning a second language or training in music at specific points in childhood, and that delay makes these tasks more difficult and sometimes impossible. We now know the reason why this is true. It is because particular synaptic structures are ready to be formed during certain stages of neural growth. These structures will deteriorate or be taken over by other functions if they are not developed. For instance, the neural connections needed for reading and writing (which are quite recent evolutionary skills and not encoded in the human genome) have to be learned or formed in childhood, or else the brain will be permanently altered with regard to these capacities.[11] This is not to say that someone older cannot learn to read and write – only that it will be more difficult and the outcome will generally be less efficient.

Musical training provides a graphic demonstration of this principle of plasticity. An experiment recently conducted by a group of German scientists, led by Thomas Ebert, scanned the areas of the brain controlling the fingers of both hands from groups of musicians and non-musicians. The brains of musicians, specifically violinists and cellists, displayed a marked disparity. The area of the motor cortex controlling the right hand, which simply moves the bow, was no different in size from that of non-musicians. Yet the area of the cortex controlling the four fingers of the left hand, which are essential to modulate the sound of the instrument, was as much as five times larger than this area in non-musicians. These disparities were most pronounced with those musicians who had been trained at an early age.[12] We might some day be able to deduce the similar outcome for the brain of the architect, even if this development comes at a later time.

Another aspect of plasticity that we are only beginning to understand is that the brain remains pliable in its neural wiring throughout most of our lives. Existing synaptic circuits, as we noted, strengthen or weaken, depending on their use. New connections, when prompted, are created, while existing connections infrequently utilized will wither and dissolve. This fact may never allow us to become concert violinists if we lack the early training, but it does underscore the fact that the more we (and our larger culture) stimulate the brain, the more we enrich our cortical maps with knowledge, memories, and creative associations, the more the brain will continue to grow in its neural complexity. Susan Greenfield terms this process the "personalization" of the brain, and she relegates the "mind" to that "seething morass of cell circuitry that has been configured by personal experiences."[13] What this suggests is that aspects of creativity might indeed be learned; the contrary is also true, as the colloquialism "vegetate" aptly suggests.

Such an understanding of the brain speaks volumes to architects, whose education generally takes place in the late teens and early twenties, that is, when the brain is undergoing the last significant phase of major growth and development. It may also explain why architects are often said not to attain the full height of their creative powers until the age of 40 or even later. If one reason for this might be the acquisition of such a large body of technical skills and professional knowledge, still another might be the great sophistication of cortical mapping necessary to excel in this highly competitive field.

This "sculpting" of the brain, as Warren Neidich calls it, also carries with it a reverse implication.[14] If so many of the brain's synaptic connections are shaped by the particular culture into which we are born and how we ultimately choose to "play" the brain through our interests, then we can deduce that there is such a thing as an architect's brain. Moreover, given the massive cultural changes over the short course of our literate body of architectural theory, it is not far-fetched to suggest that the basic structure of the architect's brain has indeed changed over time, altering itself with changing cultural and environmental conditions. Palladio's brain in its neural circuitry, for instance, was arguably different from that of Pierre de Meuron. Such a statement, of course, has to be considered within such recent cognitive models as that of Merlin Donald, for instance, which, in a larger evolutionary context, view the modern human brain and its unique representational powers as "a mosaic structure of cognitive vestiges from earlier stages of human emergence."[15] We thus bring along many visceral and cultural attributes from our ancestral past, but all the while continually adapting and modifying them – today, seemingly, at a much accelerated pace.

Such a legacy, and its potential loss, allows us to pose a few basic questions. What implications does this new understanding of the brain hold for present and future design? And how is the nature of design affected by the areas of the brain that our twenty-first-century culture conditions us to exploit? Neurologists, even with all of the wealth of results now being published, are certainly not ready to answer these questions in any detail, but here and there we can find some intriguing hints along the way.

11

Ambiguity

Architecture of Vision

I am convinced that there can be no satisfactory theory of aesthetics that is not neurobiologically based. (Semir Zeki)[1]

Perhaps no area of neurological investigation in recent years has made more progress than that directed to how we see the world. The older model of vision that had been around for centuries was largely a passive one. In this explanation, an image of the world is mechanically impressed on the retinas of our two eyes from where it is then transmitted through the optic nerves to the area at the back of the brain known as the visual cortex. There this image is processed by the "higher" surrounding areas of the brain known as the association cortex. This theory, through its many permutations, always preserved the neat Cartesian boundary between the camera-like, sensory process of viewing the world and the mental process of understanding it. The new and far more neurologically active model bypasses and antiquates such distinctions, and its details and nuances have several important things to say to architects.

What then is the process of viewing an object? It turns out to be far more complex than we previously imagined.[2] Light reflected from the object passes through the lens and stimulates the retinal nerves of the eye – actually a part of the brain. Nerve cells (cones and rods) are unevenly distributed along the surface of the retina and thus selectively favor or distort the information, with the greatest concentration of nerves surrounding the very small area of the fovea, which is the focal point of our field of vision. The three types of cones used for daytime vision are sensitive to specific ranges of wavelengths. In addition, the right side of the

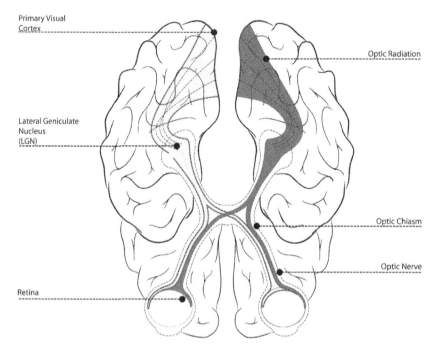

Primary Visual
Cortex

Optic Radiation

Lateral Geniculate
Nucleus
(LGN)

Optic Chiasm

Optic Nerve

Retina

Figure 11.1   Optic nerve. Illustration by Amjad Alkoud

retina of both eyes scans the left half of the field of vision, while the left side does the reverse. The axons of the nerve cells – about 100 million rods, five million cones – form the optic nerve, which then transmits the information to the optic chiasm in the center of the brain, at which point about half the information from each eye passes over into the opposite hemisphere. This partial crossover allows a reconstruction of the full image in both halves of the visual cortex at the rear of the brain.

Yet along the optic tract, beyond the optic chiasm, there is another important stop for the visual information: a part of the thalamus (of which there are two) called the lateral geniculate nucleus or LGN. The two thalami in each hemisphere, which are connected to many parts of the brain, are in fact a second important processing station, as the axons of the optic nerve breaks up into branches. The LGN consists of six layers of two types of nerve cells that sort bits of optic stimulation. One group of "M cells" specializes in processing fast-moving, coarse-grained stimuli, while the other group of "P cells" focuses on slower-moving,

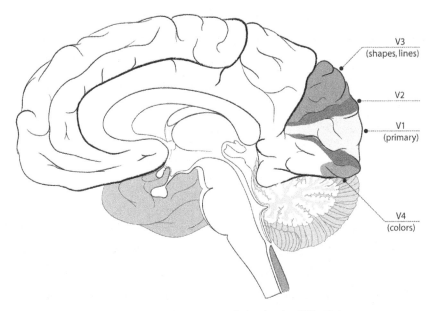

Figure 11.2 Visual processing areas of the brain (V1–V4). Illustration by Amjad Alkoud

finer-grained stimuli, as well as sorting the different wavelengths of light. It is also likely, given the number of feedback circuits from the visual cortex, that the LGN also enhances and suppresses the character of the retinal input. Therefore, not only is the eye itself selective in the assimilation and processing of data that it takes in from the world, but so is the LGN, which, incidentally, also sends some of its circuits to other areas of the brain. The brain, both the retina and LGN, is thus already breaking down or abstracting the visual stimulation before it actually arrives at the visual cortex, the main processing area in the occipital lobe of the brain.

It is in the visual cortex that the processing of visual data intensifies, and the axons of the LGN arrive first at the area known as V1. As the work of David H. Hubel and Torsten N. Wiesel first suggested in the late 1950s, the features of the visual image, in both hemispheres of the brain, are organized in a highly selective way into columns of nerve cells that further segregate the details of object recognition into such categories as lines, shapes, color, and motion.[3] Therefore, V1 not only receives the data but arranges the impulses by type and then transmits this complex of information to the adjoining area called V2, which, now joining pathways from both sides of the brain, continues to process such things as contrasts, edges, depth, and shape.

But all of the work described thus far constitutes only the earlier stages of a visual perception. For the bits of information that are assembled and sorted in V1 and V2 are then sent out into other adjoining and geographically distinct areas of the brain where further selective processing takes place. The neurons of the area V3, for instance, are sensitive especially to shapes and the orientation of lines in motion (with some neurons responding only to lines of a single orientation), while those in the area V4 are particularly sensitive to color (some neurons responding only to a single color), curving lines, and some angled lines. The area V5 (which is not shown in Figure 11.2 because it is on the outside of the occipital lobe) processes stimuli relating to motion, and there is even a large area of the brain involved only with facial recognition, no doubt a vital attribute for early human survival.[4] The principle by which the different elements of an object are ultimately "perceived" in different parts of the brain is known as "functional specialization."[5] In effect, the brain first analyzes and parcels the different elements of each image, then somehow consolidates the distinct attributes in different areas of the brain according to its own system of rules – as the Gestalt psychologists at least partially surmised.

And the parcelization or functional processing does not stop here, for most of the images that we perceive also call memories and other associations into play. Therefore, from the areas V1–V5, the perceptual image passes out into other areas in the brain: the temporal lobes (for form, color, recognition of objects), parietal lobes (for space, motion, depth), and frontal cortices, the thalami, and a dozen or more other areas. This level of complexity found in our visual perceptions is also true for the other senses as well, as each sense has its particular region of the cortex in proportion to its importance as a sensory organ. The area processing touch, for instance, is very well defined, and the part of the cortex that receives signals from the fingers has a much larger processing area than that of the other parts of the body.

The details of this model are replete with a number of implications. Although we perceive the world as a unitary event, our overall visual consciousness, as Semir Zeki suggests, is actually formed from a series of spatially and temporally distinct "microconsciousnesses," in that there is a temporal lag in the processing of these events – because these different nodes complete their processing at different times. Locations, for instance, are perceived before color, which in turn is perceived before form, motion (as much as 80 milliseconds before), and orientation.[6] What this means is that we are never really in a "present," at least with regard to our perceptual understanding of the world.

Second, this incredible system of processing has no single cortical zone to which all other areas report, although, as we noted, these outlying areas are reconnected back to each other and to V1 through reentrant neural circuits. In fact this description of the visual perception as a linear process is somewhat misleading. Not only does the thalamus send signals of what the LGN has recorded to other parts of the brain than V1, but it is now known that each perception is constructed through the "parallel processing" of assemblies of neurons in distinct cortical areas, that is, along highly selective neural pathways that relay information in a fraction of a second. Such a process has led one neurologist to describe the perception that we compose in our brains, perfectly synchronized as it were, as "written in the 'wiring' between the nerve cells."[7] Thus, the philosophical question of what distinguishes perception from understanding – that long-standing epistemological issue – loses much of its relevance. It does so because perception and the thought involved with the perception are in fact one and the same neurological process.

If this seems like a complicated neurological undertaking, we can also add to the complexity by noting that we do not see the world in terms of single fixed images, but as a continuum of movement and sensory change. This in itself raises yet another series of questions as to just what constitutes "consciousness" in a healthy brain, for by what means does the brain go about registering or synchronizing these many different "microconsciousnesses" of color, motion, and form, and thereby construct the mental world that we inhabit? If we limit ourselves simply to vision for the moment, what issues does this discrete visual processing raise for the architect?

Zeki's Neuroaesthetics

Semir Zeki, who has been pursuing the problem of vision since the late 1960s, posed a few of these questions in the late 1990s when he ventured to where few scientists before him had dared to go. He focused the new scanning technologies on vision, specifically with regard to the arts, and in the process opened up a new realm for artistic and scientific investigation, which he christened neuroaesthetics. The premises that he outlined for this field are quite simple. The visual apparatus of the brain has the Darwinian task of acquiring knowledge about the world in order to insure its survival. It does this by selecting the essential properties of objects it encounters, first by discounting all information that lacks relevance, and second by comparing the selected information with past experiences. To make this difficult task manageable, it has to generalize the visual event, or, as Zeki says, "the brain is only interested in obtaining knowledge about those permanent, essential, or characteristic properties of objects and surfaces that allow it to categorize them."[8]

On this basis Zeki defines the purpose of art, another evolutionary byproduct of this selection process, "as a search for the constant, lasting, essential, and enduring features of objects, surfaces, faces, situations, and so on."[9] From this perspective, the visual arts are therefore "an extension of the major function of the visual brain" and the specific role of the artist in this regard is to exploit "the characteristics of the parallel-processing perceptual systems of the brain."[10]

Let us, for example, take the issues of color perception and color constancy. The conventional explanation that has come down to us over centuries is that an object appears to have a specific color because it reflects light from a particular electromagnetic wavelength. An object appears blue because we see more light reflected from this range of the spectrum. One problem with this explanation, which has also been known for centuries, is that a blue object appears blue in lighting conditions of vastly different luminance. If the retina of the eye is simply recording wavelengths of light, the color of objects would continually change depending on specific conditions. But blue appears as blue in the brightest morning light and in the dimmest evening light. The earlier explanation for this phenomenon was that the "higher" areas of the brain somehow imposed their understanding on perceptual process.

In the middle decades of the twentieth century, Edwin Land, the inventor of the Polaroid, began to formulate another explanation.[11] Through a series of ingenious experiments, he concluded that the perception of color was in fact a far more complicated process involving the brain, but in a different way than previously thought. He demonstrated that in focusing on an object we assess the wavelength of light in a particular patch of the visual field with respect to its surroundings, not only for one but for all the different wavelengths in the surrounding field. With the discovery of the area V4 in the visual cortex, we now know precisely what area of the brain does this elaborate computational processing. Therefore color, far from being something out there in the world (photons have no color), is rather a creation of our biological or neurological apparatus. Zeki in fact has defined color in a very compelling way as "an interpretation, a *visual language*, that the brain gives to the constant property of reflectance."[12]

The realization that nerve cells within the visual cortex were highly selective as to the stimuli to which they respond was still another landmark in understanding the sophisticated nature of visual perception. Single cells or columns of cells in the visual cortex, as we noted, might respond only to lines, but some even more selectively to just horizontal lines, others to vertical or diagonal lines. Similarly, some respond only to one color or to one color placed against a specific background. If we extend this principle to the realm of art, we begin to see visual perception from a different perspective. The horizontal line of a gable on a Greek temple, for example, might be processed in one part of the visual cortex, while the diagonal sides of the gable are read in another part, the vertical columns in a third part. In no one part of the brain are the results of these different processing stations joined again.

Therefore, the issue of whether a work is purely abstract or representational becomes an important one. An abstract composition consisting of a few colors or forms may be processed only in the areas V3 or V4, whereas a representational scene, as brain scans reveal, engages these areas as well as other parts of the cortex, no doubt soliciting memories or knowledge of previous experiences. And since the different arts, such as architecture, also possess different means, knowledge of these means and the areas in which they are processed might say something about design.

Such a question led Zeki to consider the work of such artists as Piet Mondrian and Kazimir Malevich – artists that he considers to be "neurologists" for their intuitive exploitation of how the brain works.[13] In the case of Mondrian in the late 1910s and the 1920s, Zeki interprets his self-limited use of horizontal and vertical lines and a few colors as an attempt "to put on canvas the constant elements of all forms," and therefore an as effort "to reduce the complexity of all forms into their essentials or, to put it in neurological terms, to try and find out what the essence of form as represented in the brain may be."[14] At the same time, this pursuit raises for Zeki the issue of whether or not there are indeed "universal aspects of forms" that have a particular resonance within the brain, or if there are primary neurological forms (such as squares, circles, or particular rectangles) from which all other forms may be constructed.[15] Zeki in fact argues that in the early abstract experiments of such artists as Mondrian and Malevich the painters intuitively tailored their artistic intentions to the single-cell neurology of the visual brain.[16] In other words, these artists, in seeking what they themselves described as the essence of form and color, were in their own way functioning as neurologists, probing how the brain puts together a perception.

It is within this context that Zeki returns to Robert Vischer's idea of *Einfühlung* or "empathy" as an explanation for this phenomenon. He defines it in an updated fashion as "a link between the 'pre-existent' forms within the individual and the forms in the outside world which are reflected back."[17] The "pre-existent" forms are none other than the formal predilections of the working brain, as they have evolved along with its biological features. This is an intriguing suggestion and one that is rife with implications, which Zeki seems to suggest is on at least three levels. First, there is the fact that we approach every act of perception with a stored visual record of forms and colors, which we have acquired over the course of a lifetime. These patterns, as it were, interface with new perceptions and of course affect the way we view new images. Zeki even likens these visual records to Platonic Ideas, in much the same way that Gestalt psychologists spoke of "good forms" or perceptual proclivities.[18]

A second implication of the "pre-existing forms," one very much related to architecture, concerns those highly selective cells that are active only with certain colors, lines, or forms. Mondrian, of course, broke with Theo van Doesburg over the issue of the diagonal, perhaps because he realized that the particular effect he was seeking could only be produced by restricting himself to horizontals and verticals.[19] But architects have often done the same. Early Renaissance architects, as we see in the mezzanine and temple story of Alberti's new facade for the church of Santa Maria Novella, broke with the diagonal forms and triangulated geometries of the Gothic style by stressing the simple forms of squares, rectangles, and circles. In a similar way, do the curved

Figure 11.3 Leon Battista Alberti, Santa Maria Novella, Florence (1448–70).
Photograph by the author

and buckled forms of a Frank Gehry concert hall speak to a particular single-cell language?

Still a third area that is at least suggested by Zeki's "pre-existing forms" is the whole realm of proportions and geometries. The idea that there are privileged or harmonic ratios, as we have seen, was certainly not foreign to the thought of Alberti or Palladio, or in fact to most architects up to the middle of the eighteenth century. Zeki, in a similar way, credits Cezanne with his great revolution in painting because he simplified nature by returning it to certain prototypical forms, such as cones, spheres, and cubes, and because he placed great values on the qualities of his lines, squared angles, and edges – forms that are fundamental to the visual discrimination of the brain.[20] None of this, as Zeki himself has noted, is to suggest that art can be or should be reduced to these particular neurological sympathies. Nevertheless, as we might suspect, on this point his theories have met with resistance from at least a few art historians.[21] Our interest, however, is not with the aesthetic issues that he raises but rather with their implications for design.

Abstraction and Ambiguity

We can explore this theme further by turning to his concept of ambiguity, which Zeki regards as fundamental to great art. It is a term also defined somewhat differently from elsewhere. On a neurological level, the theme arises out of the single-cell process and functional specialization by which the brain organizes its perceptions, and the fact that perceptions are formed through a series of "microconsciousnesses" within the brain, scattered in location and formed over time.[22] The various processing sites are in fact the perceptual sites, as imaging scans demonstrate, and thus the image of one event exists not in one site but is fragmented in several locations. To carry out this distributed parallel-processing task, the brain will thus tend to abstract or draw out the essentials of each visual event by searching for constants. The brain is in essence genetically programmed not to get bogged down with particulars because they would only complicate the process, and because the mature brain in fact has an experiential bank to draw upon. Thus a level of ambiguity is a characteristic of every perception, as the brain essentially makes a "best guess" or fills in the details of what may be missing. Zeki thus argues that ambiguity is inherent in the perceptual and interpretative process:

> My aim here is to show that there are different levels of ambiguity dictated by neurological necessity and built into the physiology of the brain. These different levels may involve a single cortical area or set of areas; they may involve different cortical areas, with different perceptual specialization; or they may involve, in addition, higher cognitive factors such as learning, judgment, memory, and experience. Whether the result of activity in a single area or in different areas, these different levels are

tied together by a metaphoric thread whose purpose is the acquisition of knowledge about the world and of making sense of the many signals that the brain receives.[23]

But art, too, deals with metaphoric threads or essential meanings, and thus in a similar way it too often exploits this condition of ambiguity. In fact, ambiguity for Zeki is a primary characteristic of all great art, in that art presents the brain with particulars from which the brain extracts more general representations. The key to this transposition for Zeki is in how he defines ambiguity, which he does not in the conventional sense of "uncertainty," but rather as "*certainty – the certainty of many, equally plausible interpretations, each one of which is sovereign when it occupies the conscious stage.*"[24] Ambiguity, in this neurological definition, is thus the obverse of constancy; it is a neurological play as it were that, like a Shakespearean passage, engages and challenges the brain to allow multiple meanings. In another place, he defines ambiguity as "the ability to represent simultaneously, on the same canvas, not one but several truths, each one of which has equal validity with the others."[25] A prime example of ambiguity, for Zeki, is the work of Jan Vermeer, particularly the facial expressions of his characters, which often defy any single reading of their emotions.[26]

What Zeki seems to be touching upon here is the fact that the brain, in its everyday activities, canvases the world, rapidly constructs and organizes its images, and with its highly organized propensity for structural patterns, expends little or no cognitive energy on easily categorized or familiar events. Such viewing, as we often complain, is tedious. Yet art, in exploiting the brain's biological quest for knowledge about the world, offers something different. It invokes something less familiar, something that forces the brain to pause, engage multiple areas, and reflect upon the new phenomenon it encounters. To follow the logic of his argument – the brain enjoys the teasing of an enigma, although more so in its capacity for "multiple experiences" rather than for the nature of ambiguity itself.

Such a thesis, one might argue, offers nothing new, in the sense that novelty, as Richard Payne Knight earlier suggested ("the attainment of new ideas; the formation of new trains of thought"), has long been regarded as a psychological need.[27] What we now know, however, is that this psychological need is in fact grounded in the brain's biological necessity to enrich or enhance its neural efficiency – new trains of thought are in fact the formation of new synaptic growth. It also offers us a novel grounding for perceptual understanding, which invites new possibilities and elevates the discussion about design above the level of a simple aesthetic discourse.

Ambiguity in Architecture

It can also be argued that the notion of ambiguity (in Zeki's specific sense of a neurological event open to multiple interpretations) has long been an important part of architectural design. Surprisingly, however, the notion has received very little discussion in architectural circles, although this seems to be largely a problem of terminology, as a brief review of our earlier authors will show. Alberti's notion of architecture as a "form of body" consisting of many (corporeally defined) architectural parts is a metaphor pregnant with ambiguous interpretations, and in fact the whole Renaissance notion of embodiment is itself a highly ambiguous one. Similarly, the fascination of Perrault, Burke, and Le Roy with the colonnade was an appreciation of the perceptual richness or visual ambiguity produced by a continually changing sensory experience. Again, Price's definition of the picturesque, particularly the fact that he distinguished it from the clarity and regularity of beauty, is grounded in an appreciation of the ambiguous. Semper's "masking of reality" and "haze of carnival candles" likewise epitomize the concept of ambiguity, while the concept is certainly implied and discussed in various writings of Pallasmaa.[28]

One author to give the notion extensive discussion was Rudolf Arnheim, as we saw in his book *The Dynamics of Architectural Form*. His defense of the "mannerist complexity" of Michelangelo's Porta Pia is a paean to the notion of ambiguity, as was his broader defense of the baroque against the charge that it was but a fragmented "multiplicity of partial images."[29] Arnheim also championed an "orderly ambiguity" against his reading of Robert Venturi, because it allowed an "enriching complexity" rather than disorder and confusion.[30] In another part of the book, Arnheim discusses the ambiguous experience of walking down the nave of the church and coming to the transept, housing the sacred place of the altar. Here the path of the nave transforms itself into a "place" but not one free of tension with respect to the centering of the altar: "This ambiguity in the basic arrangement, the presence of two competing centers, enables the layout of the Latin Cross to function as a highly dynamic image of the meeting of man and God." Even the cupola above this area functions in an ambiguous way, both as "an image of the sky" and as "a canopy for man."[31]

Of course the strongest supporter of ambiguity in recent years has been Robert Venturi, who nevertheless devotes only three pages to discussing the meaning of the term in *Complexity and Contradiction in Architecture* (1966). Yet his definition approaches that of Zeki, as he defines it as "a paradox inherent in perception and the very process of meaning in art."[32] He also argues, in several instances, that an "architecture which includes varying levels of meaning breeds ambiguity and tension."[33] Several of his chapters, particularly "The Phenomenon of 'Both-And' in Architecture" and "The Double-Functioning Element," abound with examples of visual ambiguity, but in the end the idea is somewhat eclipsed by his preference for the terms "complexity" and "contradiction." His use of all three terms is also focused almost entirely on the purely visual considerations of the building as an object or formal composition. Other possible types of ambiguity that one might experience in a building or cityscape are only occasionally discussed.

Yet what Arnheim's comments on the church transept make clear is that ambiguity in architecture can exist in ways other than on a purely visual level. And we can find it in many places. Let us take the example of the "Prairie Style" of Frank Lloyd Wright, whose work is rarely cited as particularly ambiguous. The Prairie houses of Wright were largely designed in the first decade of the twentieth century and thus their reductive forms and design intentions precede by a few years the abstract formal simplicity of Mondrian and Malevich. Like the work of Mondrian, they are often characterized by their lines, and in particular by the horizontal line, which Wright once referred to as the "line of domesticity."[34] For Wright, as for Mondrian, it also assumes metaphysical importance. In Wright's main essay on this period, "In the Cause of Architecture" (1908), he conflates the horizontal line with the theme of simplicity – that is, simplicity of ground plane and the horizontal "wall surfaces," simplicity of "axial law and order," simplicity of the unpretentious "simple line" and "clean through living form."[35] This linear and planar simplicity is raised in opposition to the present "skylines of our domestic architecture," that is, to those "fantastic

Figure 11.4 Frank Lloyd Wright, Robie House (1908–10).
Photograph by the author

Figure 11.5 Frank Lloyd Wright, Robie House (1908–10) (detail).
Photograph by the author

abortions, tortured by features that disrupted and distorted roof surfaces" from which chimneys and other accoutrements, "like lean fingers" threaten or disrupt the serenity of the sky.[36] Thus Wright's artistic innovation, in a way similar to Mondrian, lies precisely in his reduction of the confusing palette of forms largely to horizontal lines and unbroken wall planes, occasionally punctuated with a low-slung or embracing gable.

But this intention on his part does not mean that Wright's cleansing of the design palette lacks ambiguity, in the sense of which Zeki speaks. Wright, in one of his later books, acknowledged that in "breaking" the box he was forced to come up with a new and ambiguous conception of the wall, one that exalted in disrupting the relationship of inside to outside:

> My sense of "wall" was no longer the side of a box. It was enclosure of space affording protection against storm or heat only when needed. But it was also to bring the outside world into the house and let the inside of the house go outside. In this sense I was working away at the wall as a wall and bringing it towards the function of a screen, a means of opening up space which, as control of building-materials improved, would finally permit the free use of the whole space without affecting the soundness of the structure.[37]

Neil Levine has characterized the ambiguity of Wright's work in more expansive ways. He describes Wright's stylistic development – between the design of the Willits House (1902) and Robbie House (1908) – as a period "of high tension between the poles of abstraction and representation."[38] If "fragmentation and decomposition," "interpenetration of volumes," the "half-inside, half-outside interstitial spaces" of the Willits House define the start of a march toward abstraction, the Robbie House, for Levine, culminates this process in an even more forceful way.[39] Here, he argues, "within the traditional framework of the house-type, Wright dissected and pulled apart the planes, fracturing the image and opening it up to a freedom of space and ambiguity of relationships that was quintessentially modern."[40] Levine even describes this breakthrough as something "akin to the invention of Cubism in painting by Picasso and Braque," in other words, to one of those rare artistic moments when architecture, now reduced to its most primal formative elements, re-invents itself anew.[41]

Figure 11.6   Andrea Palladio, Church of Il Redentore, Venice (1577–92).
Photograph by Marco Frascari

Wright's ambiguity of inside and outside exploits the notion of
ambiguity both perceptually and conceptually, but even a simple form
of visual ambiguity, as Venturi has suggested, can have dramatic or
intriguing neurological effects. Perhaps one of the more lauded examples of ambiguity in architectural history is Palladio's facade design for
the Venetian church of Il Redentore. This long-admired masterpiece is
a votive church, the design for which was approved by the Venetian
Senate late in 1576. It was commissioned as a plea for the city's deliver-
ance from a plague that had claimed one-third of its population, or
more than 50,000 people. Its location on the isle of La Giudecca was
the third site considered after two earlier ones had been rejected, and
Palladio and his Venetian supporter Marc'Antonio Barbaro, the former
Consul to Constantinople and the brother of Palladio's major patron,
preferred a centralized design.[42] The Senate, after much deliberation,
ultimately rejected the centralized proposal in favor of a church with a

Figure 11.7 Andrea Palladio, San Giorgio Maggiore (c.1565–80).
Plate from Ottavio Bertotti Scamozzi, *Le Fabbriche e i Desegni di Andrea Palladio*, vol.
3 (Vicenza, Francesco Modena, 1731)

traditional nave and side chapels. Nevertheless, the church has long been recognized as one of Venice's greatest artistic treasures, a jewel within a city renowned for its abundance of art and architecture. And for four centuries now, Redentore has attracted architects from around the world – because of its intricate and somewhat challenging facade as well as for its grand interior spaces.

Architectural historians have been nearly unanimous in their praise of this work. The first major historian of the Renaissance, Jacob Burkhardt, extolled its waterfront elevation in 1862, especially for culminating in the "single-order facade" of the high Renaissance. And even though he was less than enamored with its architectural verity (he regarded the Renaissance church facade, in general, as a "splendid mask"), he readily admitted that Palladio had "performed wonders" with it.[43] Almost a century later, the historian Rudolph Wittkower devoted a dozen pages of *Architectural Principles in the Age of Humanism* to analyzing the main facade. He too describes it as the "climax" to a long line of tentative Renaissance church designs, beginning with Alberti's facade for Santa Maria Novella in Florence in the second half of the fifteenth century.[44] Alberti had dealt with the different heights of the nave and side aisles, as we have seen, by introducing a mezzanine and upper temple front – mediating the different heights with a large scroll. A little more than a century later, Palladio had seemingly solved the problem in a far more elegant way with his design for San Giorgio Maggiore. In this Venetian showpiece, he simply overlaid a major (two-story) temple pediment over the minor (one-story) pediment defined by the side aisles, resulting in a playful overlapping of the two forms.

Yet at Redentore, designed a little over a decade later, Palladio intensified the drama by incorporating or suggesting no fewer than four temple pediments. Wittkower was appreciative of this solution, even while conceding that the "peculiar repetitions" of the four, superimposed, gable motifs scattered throughout different planes of the facade might actually overstep the bounds of correct classicism. He therefore characterized the design as a Mannerist work inspired by a multiplicity of sources, including classical antiquity.[45]

Wittkower offered what became the standard view of this church throughout the second half of the twentieth century. James Ackerman, for instance, saw the church as combining elements of a Roman temple and bath, a Byzantine dome, Gothic buttresses, as well as the humanist system of proportions. He also interpreted Redentore's grand podium, its lavish and separate choir, its limited ornament, and the "chaste whiteness" of its facade as an effort to conform to Counter-Reformation guidelines.[46] Deborah Howard stressed its Ottoman influence and ties to Barbaro's consulship in Constantinople between 1568 and 1573.[47] Leonardo Benevolo was simply a great admirer of Redentore's "compact and articulate" composition, and he praised its multiple gable motifs for functioning "as a perspective section of the three-dimensional organism which extends behind it," and for establishing "the geometrical ratios between all the measurements."[48] He also defended the grandeur of the overall design as entirely suited to the large "sheet of water" on which it is situated.[49]

Nevertheless, not all twentieth-century historians were so sanguine about Redentore's ambiguous facade composition. In one of the more detailed analyses of its compositional massing of pediments, Staale Sinding-Larsen pointed out several infelicities of its detailing and overall organization, and in fact argued that it was incorrect to view it, as Wittkower did, as "two interpenetrating temple fronts."[50] Rather, he saw the facade as a compromise derived from an earlier design, one that resulted in "a confused statement of what might actually lie behind it, a confusion which becomes compounded if we consider the unusual manner in which Palladio treated the attic and antae."[51] Finally, in reviewing his findings regarding the city's purchase of the site, he reached the rather startling conclusion that the design of the facade had largely come about for no other reason than last-minute political deliberations. In Palladio's original, centralized design for the church, Sinding-Larsen surmises, the architect had imposed the central temple motif directly onto a narthex fronting the central space, and when the Venetian Senate ultimately decided to go with a basilican plan, Palladio, out of the sheer exigency of time, was forced to push his temple front forward and add the nave and side aisles. These additions, in turn, required that he attach the double-pedimental lateral wings to integrate and conceal both the roof of the side aisles and the structurally necessary buttresses above that propped up the nave wall.

But Sinding-Larsen's insightful analysis, as I think most architects would agree, does not detract from or diminish the great visual power of the composition, because its formal ambiguity is precisely what allows us to appreciate better Palladio's ability to attend to the original temple front, the addition of the side chapels of the nave, and the piers that rise above the lower roofs of these chapels. In short, he had to weave his design out of a series of competing demands, even though – except for one day a year – it is only from Bertotti Scamozzi's elevation of this church that we can appreciate the full ingenuity of his design, which in fact contains the suggestion of a fifth pediment with the hip of the attic. The one-day exception arises because of the large lagoon on which it is situated. For it is only on the feast day of the church's dedication that a ceremonial bridge of boats is erected across the lagoon, allowing participants the single full, frontal view of the design

Figure 11.8   Andrea Palladio, Church of Il Redentore.
Plate from Ottavio Bertotti Scamozzi, *Le Fabbriche e i Desegni di Andrea Palladio*, vol. 3 (Vicenza, Francesco Modena, 1731)

from a reasonable distance. It is therefore only on this day that Redentore fully displays exactly the strong ambiguity of which Zeki spoke, that is, the ability of the artist "to represent simultaneously, on the same canvas, not one but several truths, each of which has equal validity with the others."[52]

12

Metaphor

Architecture of Embodiment

Just as we think architecture with our bodies, we think our bodies through architecture. (Marco Frascari)[1]

Palladio's Redentore provides an intriguing visual example, but architecture is at heart a more deeply embodied phenomenon than the merely visual; it deals with many more sensory and subliminal dimensions (spatial, material, and emotional) and therefore engages many other areas of the brain. Neuroscience is reminding us of the enormous complexities of what were once viewed as simple sensory reflexes to stimuli, and these new neurological models, along with the implications they entail, are today being greeted with excitement across the various sciences and arts. Limiting herself simply to works drawn from the visual arts, and then to those "spatialized/sensorial 'chunks' of thought," the art historian Barbara Maria Stafford has recently emphasized not only the brain's "primitive perceptual order" but also the "visceral dimension of an organism's awareness."[2] Such a biological view, as we have seen, would not have been opposed by Heinrich Wölfflin, who charged architecture with the specific task of tapping into those *"great vital feelings,* the moods that presuppose a constant and stable body condition."[3] And Wölfflin was not alone in articulating this theme even in his day. His professorial arch-rival August Schmarsow – who opposed Wölfflin's corporeal formalism with the non-material thesis that architecture was simply the "*creatress of space*" – nevertheless found architecture's perceptual genesis in "the residues of sensory experience to which the muscular sensations of our body, the sensitivity of our skin, and the structure of our body all contribute."[4] Maurice Merleau-Ponty, with all of his insight, did not express it better.

The neurologist V. S. Ramachandran likens the significance of these current breakthroughs to the intellectual markers of Copernicus, Darwin, and Freud, and insists that this work will not only revolutionize the sciences but also have a decisive impact on the parallel culture of the arts, philosophy, and humanities – presumably architecture as well. Taking the matter to another level, he points out that with 100 billion neurons in the brain, each with the potential to form 10,000 synapses, "the number of possible permutations and combinations of brain activity, in other words the number of possible brain states, exceeds the number of elementary particles in the known universe."[5] When looked at in this way, the human being, or rather the human brain, no longer seems so small.

And such a model does not take into account the choreographing of those microconsciousnesses of which Zeki spoke, the synchronization of anatomically distributed neural networks pulsating in dynamic and coordinated rhythms. The "tantalizing conjecture" to be inferred from this, in the words of György Buzsáki, is that informative models of "perception, memory, and even consciousness" can be derived from understanding these rhythms.[6] If televisions, computers, cell phones, bridges, and tall buildings oscillate to their particular rhythms, he asks, why should anyone doubt that the brain does the same? [7] Thus what Jean-Pierre Changeux cast in hypothetical terms in the 1980s as "neuronal man" no longer seems so metaphysically unspeakable out-side of biological circles – although for Changeux at least, such a state-ment is by no means synonymous with a mechanistic or causal view of biological life.[8] What then are the architectural implications?

Memory

Perhaps a good place to begin these deliberations is with the issue of memory. What exactly is that picture that we have in our minds, say of Chartres Cathedral or the Athenian Parthenon? What constitutes the memory bank of our autobiographical experiences and where is it located within the brain? Some fascinating answers are coming forth, although we should not forget that it was only a half-century ago that scientists were still on the trail of that elusive "engram," or memory cell, that would neatly store those pictures. By the second half of the twentieth century, the idea of a single cell or a single area of the brain housing memory rapidly began to lose favor. It would be highly inefficient for the human brain, as several authors have pointed out, to store or commit to memory all of the images that we receive on a daily basis over a course of a lifetime. In addition to the logistical problems in housing these fleeting images (the vast majority of which we perceive unconsciously), the brain would have the impossibly difficult task of retrieving such images in any expeditious manner among the billions of brain cells. Finally, there is the insurmountable problem that there is no known biological mechanism for coding or symbolizing pictorial representations, and what is more, there exists no homunculus or tiny person inside our brains to read the results.

Through a series of experiments started in the 1970s, a number of neurologists, among them the Nobel laureate Eric R. Kandel, began to explore a different approach, which was to relate memories not to neurons but to neural circuits.[9] The key to this approach, made possible by the theories of Donald Hebb, was the understanding that all forms of learning (invariably a process of memory) result in synaptic changes. Kandel probed the nature of these changes and discovered, for instance, that short-term memory, sometimes called working memory, strengthened synapses through a release of glutamate, while the different phenomenon of long-term memory not only strengthened synapses with proteins but also created new synapses to enhance the neuronal bond. Hence memories, as this new working model suggested, were to be found at no specialized site within the brain, but rather were scattered throughout the brain within its neural circuits, that is, within the synaptic connections that were initially involved with processing the event. But if this is the case, how is it that our lives consist of a stream of perceptual and recalled pictures? How do synaptic exchanges, circuitry, and brain rhythms give us pictures?

Let's assume that you just returned from a trip to Greece where you visited the Parthenon in Athens. The perceptions that you would have formed of this experience are myriad. You would have seen the pattern of horizontal, vertical, and gabled lines of the fractured ruin, the size and scale of the huge marble blocks, the marble's texture and golden crust, its reflective brilliance under the Mediterranean sunlight, the discolorations, and ornamental reliefs. You would have viewed the blue

Figure 12.1   Parthenon, Athens (447–432 BC). View of the east facade. Photograph by the author

sky against which the monument is silhouetted, the faded vegetation and houses on distant hills of the smoggy city, experienced the midday heat under which the visual examination took place and, perhaps, a mild throbbing in your calves due to the climb up the Acropolis. All of these stimuli, as we have seen, would be processed in different areas of the brain: the Athenian heat in one area, the color of the marble in another, the brightness of the sunlight in still another, the forms of the columns and entablature in other areas.

Figure 12.2   Temple of Hephaestus, Athens (449–415 BC).
Photograph by the author

Now suppose that before you had viewed the Parthenon you had visited the classical Temple of Hephaestus adjacent to the old Athenian agora. Here you would have had a similar perceptual event of a fifth-century Doric temple, and its memory would have brought something to the new experience. For instance, the smaller scale of the Hephaestus might have given you a better appreciation of the scale of the Parthenon, and the relatively intact condition of the Hephaestus might have allowed you better to imagine the former glory of the Parthenon – that is, before its lateral columns were exploded by a canon ball in the seventeenth century. Hence your perception of the Parthenon would have been altered by this earlier experience. But with the insertion of this memory of the Hephaestus into your perceptual process, what indeed has happened in a neurological sense?

The answer, which has already been suggested, is surprisingly very little. If memories are nonrepresentational, then they do not reside in the molecular structure of our brain's neurons but rather in the brain's specific firing patterns – that is, in the circuits that are likewise dispersed over various parts of the brain and lie dormant until reignited. Indeed, one of the more dramatic results of the new scanning technologies is the realization that perceptual images are often processed in the same areas of the brain as are imagined images. If you sit back in your living room a few months later and recall the image of the Parthenon, you pretty much activate the same neural circuitry that you excited when first viewing the monument.

The neuroscientist Joaquín M. Fuster concludes from this discovery two important results with regard to memory: first, that all memory is in essence "associative," or an act of classification (in the sense that Hayek previously noted), and second, that in viewing a new event in light of a previously recorded perception, the "processing and representation are practically inseparable at all levels, from the lowest to the highest. The cortical cell groups and networks that represent previously stored information are the same ones that will process and incorporate new information as it comes through the senses."[10] He thus places all our knowledge of the world – objects, facts, concepts, and events – under the rubric of "perceptual memory."[11] Gerald M. Edelman offers a slight variation to this theme by noting the highly variable nature of neural circuitry (defined as "degeneracy" or the ability of different neural structures to function similarly or yield the same output), and thus admits only the necessary "similarity" of circuits that are re-engaged. Memory for him is recategorical (constructive) rather than replicative.[12] Both men, however, emphasize the dynamic process of continuous interaction between new experiences and existing memory circuits.

But during a perceptual event, what allows these and only these specific circuits to re-fire? The answer, as has only recently become clear, seems to lie with another part of the brain that is of particular importance to architects – the hippocampus. As we will later see, this tube-shaped, curved structure in the limbic region of the brain is one of the principal sites of our spatial navigation and imagination, but it (and the surrounding entorhinal cortex) also seems to direct storage retrieval by reactivating circuits. As Joseph LeDoux describes it, "memory is initially stored via synaptic changes that take place in the hippocampus. When some aspect of the stimulus recurs, the hippocampus participates in the reinstatement of the pattern of cortical activation that occurred during the original experience. Each reinstatement changes cortical synapses a little."[13] Buzsáki, who has also focused his research specifically on this region, points to the unique nature of the hippocampal-entorhinal system with its "large connection space that is ideally built for the construction of episodes and event sequences from arbitrary relations by providing a spatiotemporal context for the information to be deposited."[14] His experiments have also shown that it is a particular set of hippocampal oscillations or rhythms that activates this system and binds it with the activities of the cerebral cortex. Thus, the fact that both spatial navigation and memory are located in this region is not an evolutionary accident.

What is interesting in all of these explanations is that even though they have fundamentally altered our view of how the brain works, they have at the same time confirmed what indeed has long been obvious. Because of the plasticity of the brain's synaptic structures, we can assume that neural patterns associated with memory can be strong or weak, complex or simple, depending on the level of experience, or in consideration of such variables as the passage of time. For instance, if the Parthenon were a one-time encounter that you visited many years ago with no subsequent perceptual or mental reinforcement, your capacity to evoke a neural pattern of its image might be quite faint or even non-existent. Then again, the neural patterns induced by the Parthenon constituted a complex sensory experience of different factors, all of which were processed in different parts of the brain. Even long after the synaptic connections related to the visual image may have come unraveled a trip through the Panama Canal could spark another pattern recalling the Athenian summer heat. You may also, some day, come upon a block of Pentelic marble in a museum and find the color or texture curiously familiar although you do not remember where or when you may have seen it. What this new understanding of memory also underscores is that memory is not a fixed portfolio of previously recorded events but is rather (following the fragmentary nature of how our perceptions are constructed) a series of perceptual or generalized categories that we re-simulate. Lines, forms, colors, and bodily feelings – these are its categorical patterns that the brain may or may not stitch together in later reconstructing the image of the Parthenon from different corners of the brain. They, together with the perceptual input from the other senses and from fantasies, emotions, and dreams, are the elements that we fashion into memories.

Consciousness

Alongside memory is the riddle of human consciousness, which in many ways is the big prize on the not-too-distant horizon. Consciousness entails the process by which we come to be aware of ourselves, the world, and the constancy of this relationship over time. And although most animals have this awareness and emotional engagement at varying levels, our ability to plan our immediate circumstances and place them within a past and future is uniquely a human ability. Even the higher primates, which have brain sizes and DNA complexes not so different from those of humans, are worlds apart in most cognitive pursuits. In an evolutionary sense, higher-level consciousness is a rather recent development within human history.

Dozens of books and articles on the theme of consciousness have appeared since the late 1990s from a variety of linguistic, cognitive, psychological, and philosophical points of view, but from a neurological perspective the various models, in the last few years, seem to be converging. Francis Crick, the British biochemist who collaborated with James D. Watson in the 1950s in discovering the molecular structure of DNA, turned to this matter in the mid-1980s by teaming up with Christof Koch. Their first joint paper was published in 1990, and their results (both preliminary and more recent) have been published in two books: Crick's *The Astonishing Hypothesis: The Scientific Search for the Soul* (1993), and Koch's *The Quest for Consciousness: A Neurobiological Approach* (2004).[15] The "astonishing hypothesis" of which Crick speaks, quite simply, is "that *all* aspects of the brain's behavior are due to the activities of neurons."[16] In this overtly mechanistic scenario, there is no separate "I" or "self" apart from these neural activities.

Crick and Koch's theory is essentially a local one, in the sense that they are restricting themselves to visual awareness or visual consciousness (a part of a larger system of cerebral consciousnesses), and their objective is to identify the "*neural correlates of consciousness*," or "the minimal set of neural events and mechanisms jointly sufficient for a specific conscious precept."[17] Their underlying contention is that consciousness is a discrete event that involves the activity of many essential cortical nodes, as well as the parallel firing of special sets of neurons in synchronization, which they initially believed to be in the range of 40 Hz. In their model, the perceptual processing of stimuli taking place within the visual cortex also passes into the lateral and parietal lobes for additional processing for such features as form, color, objectification, space, depth, and motion. This information is here filtered, as it were, as only a fraction of the sensory data passes forward once again and converges in an area or areas of the prefrontal cortex. Consciousness, in their view, is thus a biological version of an "executive summary." Its purpose is "to produce the best current interpretation of the visual scene, in the light of past experience either of ourselves or of our ancestors (embodied in our genes), and to make it available for a sufficient time, to the parts of the brain that contemplate, plan and execute voluntary motor outputs (of one sort or another)."[18]

The key to this model, in which "front of the cortex" is essentially "looking at the back," is the involvement of the thalamus and one or more neurotransmitters from the brainstem that facilitate the multiple series of thalamocortical loops or cycles of information being passed between the thalamus and cortex.[19] Another feature of their model is that the work of the visual cortex, the related motor activities, and even our thoughts are not immediately accessible to consciousness; only "their sensory reflection and re-representation in inner speech and imagery" are directly knowable when consciousness flares up.[20] For them, consciousness is likely an all-or-none event, in that it comes into being abruptly when a certain neural threshold of activity is met and it does not evolve continuously with perception. It is also not identical with attention, and Crick and Koch even go so far as to characterize perceptual awareness as "a series of static snapshots, with motion 'painted' on them," akin to a cinematic event.[21]

The model of consciousness of Gerald Edelman also dates from the mid-1980s. It is not dissimilar in many respects from that of Crick and Koch, but it varies in the fundamental sense that it, following the earlier neurological theories of Kurt Goldstein, stresses the global or holistic integration of these local areas for the appearance of consciousness. Edelman won his Nobel Prize in 1972 for work on the human immune system, but since the late 1970s he has been preoccupied with unraveling the mysteries of the brain from a strict Darwinian perspective. His pivotal work in this regard, *Neural Darwinism* (1987), was the first of a trilogy of theoretical studies that set out in a comprehensive way his "theory of neuronal group selection" (TNGS).[22] He followed this work with a string of books in the 1990s and 2000s that have both popularized his theories and considered their many implications.[23]

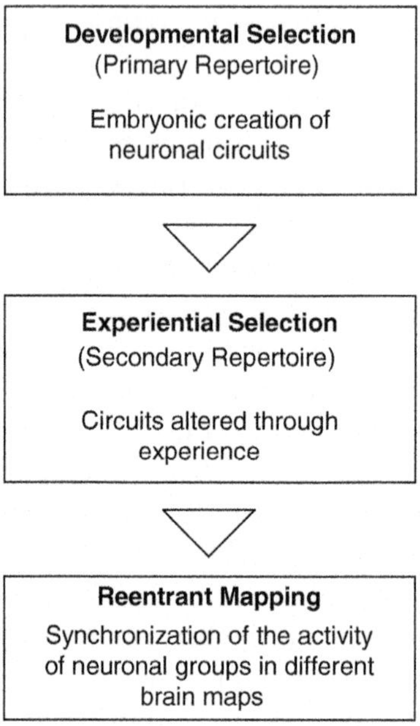

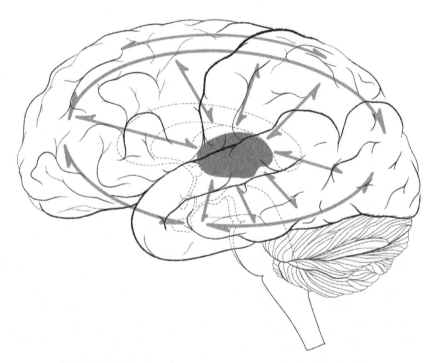

Developmental Selection
(Primary Repertoire)

Embryonic creation of
neuronal circuits

Experiential Selection
(Secondary Repertoire)

Circuits altered through
experience

Reentrant Mapping
Synchronization of the activity
of neuronal groups in different
brain maps

Figure 12.3 Gerald Edelman's "Theory of Neuronal Group Selection"

Figure 12.4 Thalamocortical Loop (after Gerald Edelman).
Illustration by Amjad Alkoud

Two aspects of Edelman's model are especially important to note. First he makes the distinction between primary consciousness (an attribute we share with other animals) and higher-order consciousness, which entails perceptual categorization, a semantic capacity (conceptualization), memory (sense of self), and adaptive value systems that are particularly open to change. Second, as this terminology suggests, his model is thoroughly biological, although not in the mechanistic sense of Crick and Koch. The brain, for Edelman, is a highly dynamic system that arrives at birth not extensively programmed, and it continues to emerge over time through its selectional interaction with the world. Therefore, it demands a high degree of variability in a biological sense.

With these premises in place, his model unfolds in three stages.[24] At the start of life, largely in the womb, humans undergo a phase of "developmental selection" by which a primary repertoire of neural circuits is formed. Here the human genome constitutes itself as a basic set of circuits, although one with few specific instructions. After birth, through "experiential selection," a secondary repertoire begins to be formed. Here one's personal and environmental experiences initiate the process of adapting and modifying the existing synaptic structures, a process known as plasticity. In this stage, neurons that act together tend to form groups or maps in response to similar stimuli. One can look at this process as evolution acting not over eons but rather over the course of a lifetime, as each individual has very different experiences and therefore builds very different neural maps.

All animals share this process of perceptual categorization, but there is a third stage of biological development that largely distinguishes the human species, which Edelman terms "reentrant mapping." At some point within our evolutionary history, he argues, the spatially discrete functional groups, such as those dealing with sensory perception, emotions, and language, began to synchronize or link up, as it were, with local and distant circuits in an elaborate process of parallel processing. Edelman identifies several topographical systems or loops linking the many parts of the brain, but the most important for the appearance of consciousness is the loop connecting the thalamus with the cortex, whereby the two thalami in each hemisphere bind the cortex and its sensory-motor areas with the hippocampus, basal ganglia, brainstem, cerebellum, and other systems.

Consciousness in this scenario is quite simply a "remembered present," or an awareness of being conscious. Here the brain reciprocally synchronizes its activities and incorporates within them the additional phenomenon of circuits following the brain's own neural activities. One might formulate this in another way by saying consciousness resides in various parts of the brain speaking to one another through reentrant or reversible maps. It is no small matter, neurological speaking, but an intense synaptic event involving millions of looped circuits firing simultaneously, or at least within an extremely short period of time. Biological value systems (constraining elements in a Darwinian selectional system) help to regulate this activity.

Consciousness, as with the model of Crick and Koch, is quite fleeting for Edelman and exists on various levels. We lose "ourselves" in sleep and countless daily tasks that require little conscious awareness. Hence consciousness, or, more specifically, higher-level consciousness, must involve "strong and rapid reentrant interactions," as well as the condition of "constantly changing and sufficiently differentiated" neuronal groups.[25] Higher-level consciousness also demands increased neurological curiosity and an active engagement with the world. Once again, consciousness is a complex system of parallel processing that is neither controlled by nor located in any one area of the brain, but one that resides in the neural and humeral circuits scattered throughout the brain. It possesses sensory, emotional, rational, and biochemical coordination (transmitted via neurons and by chemicals in the bloodstream), and in this sense consciousness is perpetually recreating itself with each new thought or willful focus. In fact, for Edelman, it is difficult to look at consciousness as something centered in the brain at all, because the brain is of course *embodied* in a much larger, neurally interconnected, anatomical system. And if we wanted to cast this highly evolved complex of biological forces in Emersonian terms, the body at the same time is *embedded* in a larger ecology from which it extracts most of its essential stimulation. Only the human brain, it seems, stands apart by virtue of its capacity – through feelings, reason, memory, and language – to recreate a "small world" of its own.

In still a third model of consciousness, which has been put forth by Semir Zeki and Andreas Bartels, we find a slight variation on these two models.[26] Drawing upon their work in functional specialization as well as their demonstration that the individual processing sites for vision (V3, V4, V5, etc.) are indeed the perceptual sites, the two scientists suggest that consciousness consists of a series of temporally and spatially distinct hierarchies. At one level are the perceptual microconsciousnesses scattered among the temporal and spatial nodes where, for example, color, form, and motion are processed. A series of macroconsciousnesses appears when individual attributes are bound together or integrated over time into a perception (temporally discrete because one color binds with another, for instance, before it binds with motion). The phenomenon of a unified consciousness forms only at the end of this hierarchic process, that is, when the individual – note the lag time – becomes aware he is experiencing a perception.

Most of these associative, classificatory, or recategorical models for consciousness and memory support another pivotal insight of recent neurological research, which is that the brain in its nonlinear operations does not run by the force of human logic, as the overwrought computer analogy wrongly suggests. The ability to reason, or think logically, is a very late evolutionary phenomena, while the brain, like all biological organisms, has honed its neurological operations over a much longer time, specifically in the refinement with which it generates and categorizes its fields of neural patterns. These new models also have their ramifications for the designer or architect.

Creativity

In a laboratory at Northwestern University in 2006, a team of neuroscientists from three universities, led by John Kounios and Mark Jung-Beeman, conducted two experiments in which they attempted to peer into that "Eureka!" or "Aha" moment when a solution to a difficult problem seemingly descends from thin air – that is, the moment of a creative breakthrough. Wiring their subjects first to electroencephalograms (EEGs), and then running them under functional Magnetic Resonance Imaging scanners (fMRIs), the experimenters gave their subjects a series of word problems that demanded a series of semantic associations; then they followed the trail of neural activity with scans. One of the first areas of the brain to become involved was the anterior cingulate cortex (ACC), which is deemed to be one of the executive centers of the brain that focuses attention by suppressing irrelevant thoughts or secondary perceptual activity. Another area to become active was the language-processing area of the left temporal lobe (Wernicke's area, see Figure 13.2), which begins the process of actually wrestling with the semantic problem. Sometimes it solves it without fanfare, but other times it struggles and reaches an impasse. The "Eureka!" moment arrives when that impasse is suddenly broken, and the area that undergoes "a sudden burst of gamma-band oscillatory activity" is not in this region but on the other side of the brain, in the right anterior superior temporal gyrus, just above the right ear.[27] The fact that a word problem is solved not in the language area of the left hemisphere but rather in the right hemisphere is significant in itself, but so too is the researchers' conjecture that the ACC, aware of the failure of the language area to solve the problem, turns the matter over to the right hemisphere of the brain, where a "coarser semantic coding" (the ability of the brain to generate larger associative patterns or recognize "new connections across existing knowledge") allows a more creative solution.[28]

What was unusual about these particular experiments was not so much that neuroscientists have become concerned with some of the more abstruse areas of the human brain (these particular scientists have worked in the field for years), but the fact that we are beginning to gain demonstrable knowledge of what actually takes place in the human head – issues about which people have pondered and theorized for millennia. Thanks to the marvels of technology, we now have high-resolution, almost real-time, 3-D images of exactly what goes on, and obviously we are learning much. If one peruses Kenneth M. Heilman's *Creativity and the Brain* (2005), for instance, one can find a half-century of rich speculation about the causes of creativity, which range (on a physiological front) from hemispheric asymmetry, handedness, and the number of axons connecting the two hemispheres, to (on the psychological side) depression and novelty seeking. In the 1960s it was generally assumed that the IQ was directly correlated with creativity, although this hypothesis soon began to crumble. In fact, in one study done with architects in the 1970s, it was found that there was a minimum IQ of around 120 necessary for creativity (which nearly all architects met), but beyond this threshold there was no correlation between increased IQ and creativity.[29] Something more was obviously needed.

Edelman's theory of neuronal group selection suggests something more. If half of our neural circuits are formed after birth, then its stands to reason that the more we build these circuits – the more we experience people, the world, and its architecture, the more we contemplate, discuss, read, practice, and enmesh ourselves in the nuances of our fields of activity – the richer and more efficient our mental processing and associative networks will become. Juhana Pallasmaa expressed this idea well when he pointed out that design is not a unique exercise in problem-solving, but "creative work of all kinds, I believe, is a matter of working on one's own self-understanding and life experience as much as on the concrete object of work."[30]

This may also explain in part the widespread belief that it takes architects an unusually long time, generally into their forties, to begin to approach the height of their creative powers – Thomas Edison's 99 percent perspiration. And in this sense it may be true, as Steven Pinker has suggested, that geniuses are wonks – that is, they have paid their dues by mastering the nuances of their fields and thereby laying the neurological ground for novel patterns of associations.[31] But it is also true that the patterns in themselves will not suffice, that it is also important to "think outside of the box," so to speak, and explore new realms. Gregory Berns, in a recent book on creativity and neuroscience, makes this point by noting that for one to think creatively, one "must develop new neural pathways and break out of the cycle of experience-dependent categorization."[32] Heilman, in drawing upon his EEG studies, has also supported such a thesis:

> A greater measure of creativity might be achieved by using networks representing knowledge in one domain to help organize a quite different domain that might nevertheless share some attributes, a sort of creativity by metaphor. Many different network architectures probably exist within the association cortices of the brain. This raises the possibility that this creativity by metaphor might involve the recruitment of networks of substantially different architecture in order to escape the constraints of existing (learned) internal models represented in the networks usually used for thinking in a particular domain.[33]

Heilman goes on to characterize creative individuals as having a "flatter associative hierarchy," by which he means that during the creative process they recruit input from more spatially distributed areas of the brain, as his EEG studies document. The contention of Heilman's "creativity by metaphor" is strengthened by the "Eureka!" experiment noted above, as the anterior superior temporal gyrus in the right hemisphere has also been implicated in the detection of literary themes and the interpretation of metaphors.[34] It seems to be able to draw in more distant and creative connections.

The connection of creativity with metaphor that continually seems to crop up in scientific literature is given both a curious and fascinating twist at the hands of the highly respected neurologist Ramachandran. One of the neurological issues that he has explored in his brain studies is the phenomenon of synesthesia, whereby some people, when hearing a particular musical tone or viewing a number on a page, experience the sensation of color, or some other sensory crossover. Our everyday language, he notes, is also riddled with synesthetic metaphors, such as the connection of "sharp" with a particular cheese or "dry" with a particular wine. Neurologists generally attribute this cross-modal phenomenon to the fact that we are born with an excess of connections in the brain and that in these few individuals endowed with such sensory richness their " 'pruning' gene is defective, which has resulted in cross-activation between areas of the brain."[35]

But Ramachandran also reports two other odd things about this phenomenon. One is that there seems to be a conceptual hierarchy among synesthetics – for example, one might associate the shape of a numeral (its form) with a color, while another might associate a day of the week with a color (thereby implying the abstract idea of ordinality). The second is the fact that synesthesia "is seven times more common among artists, poets, novelists" than among the non-artistic population. And what "artists, poets and novelists all have in common," he goes on to argue in an intriguing way, "is their skill at forming metaphors, linking seemingly unrelated concepts in their brain, as when Macbeth said 'Out, out brief candle,' talking about life."[36]

Ramachandran therefore speculates that creativity is an outgrowth of "hyperconnectivity," which allows a person to be more prone to metaphor and therefore relate seemingly unrelated things. It is not something restricted (as is lower-level sensory synesthesia) to just one or two sensory areas of the brain accidentally being wired together but rather to a more thorough-going facility: "So it's possible that other high-level concepts are also represented in brain maps and that artistic people, with their excess connections, can make these associations much more fluidly and effortlessly than less gifted people."[37] Ramachandran also goes on to locate the source of this particular gift – the angular gyrus at the TPO junction (the junction of the temporal, parietal, and occipital lobes). The neuroscientist even conjectures, on the basis of some early testing, that this region specializes in specific types of metaphors in each hemisphere, that is, the left angular gyrus deals with cross-modal metaphors ("loud shirt"), while the right angular gyrus deals with spatial metaphors.[38]

Marco Frascari, a student and former associate of Carlo Scarpa, is convinced that this Venetian architect worked entirely through a synesthetic process that entailed, on the same pages of sketches, different colors and styles of drawing with different media. It was through these "bundles of intertwined sensory perceptions," Frascari argues, that Scarpa was able to modulate his multisensory ideas – say, red of a waxy pencil from the red of a brick from an identical red of India ink: "Architectural drawings then became metaphors, not in the literal meaning, but factually they are a *metaphorein*, a carry over, a moving of sensory information from one modality to another modality, from one emotion to another emotion."[39] This "joining of the information received by one sense to a perception in another sense," Frascari also argues, "is the essence of the architectural thinking."[40]

Embodied Metaphors

We can pursue these dual themes of creativity – coarse semantic coding and the hyperconnectivity of sensory, emotional, and conceptual areas of the brain – by considering the nature of metaphor. Rudolf Arnheim has already provided us with an important clue in this regard by suggesting that the most effective architectural metaphors were in fact "sensory symbols," and that the most powerful ones were those embodied or grounded in "the most elementary perceptual sensations," such as morning light streaming through a window. The reason for this, as we cited earlier, being that "they refer to the basic human experiences on which all others depend."[41]

The psychologist Steven Pinker has an ingenious explanation for why "people form concepts that find the clumps in the correlational texture of the world," and why these tend to fall into generic conceptual categories such as space and force.[42] He points out that the human brain evolved not in order to master the nuances of science or chess, but because our immediate ancestors thought a lot about "rocks, sticks, and burrows" and it was only through the mastery of these "force simulators" that we were able to command our immediate environments and outwit predators. Therefore, the neural circuits that were conditioned for perceptual matters were only later appropriated for other activities:

> The circuits could serve as a scaffolding whose slots were filled with symbols for more abstract concerns like states, possessions, ideas, and desires. The circuits would retain their computational abilities, continuing to reckon about entities being in one state at a time, shifting from state to state, and overcoming entities with opposite valence. When the new, abstract domain has a logical structure that mirrors objects in motion ... the old circuits can do useful inferential work. They divulge their ancestry as space- and force-simulators by the metaphors they invite, a kind of vestigial cognitive organ.[43]

Pinker's thesis is supported by George Lakoff and Mark Johnson's now classic study of a quarter of a century ago, *Metaphors We Live By*. The original intention behind this book, which first appeared in 1980, had been "to awaken readers throughout the world to the often beautiful, sometimes disturbing, but always profound, realities of everyday metaphorical thought."[44] Their presumed modesty, however, was soon outpaced by the implications of their findings, as the authors came to realize that nearly all of our everyday language and its concepts are metaphorical, even though we are generally unaware of it. They neatly organized our metaphors into categories, such as "Time is Money" metaphors and "Theories (and Arguments) are Buildings" metaphors. In the first instance we say such things as

> That flat tire *cost* me an hour
> You need to *budget* your time
> He's living on *borrowed* time
> *Thank you for* your time.[45]

Among the many architectural metaphors, we say

> Is that the *foundation* for your theory?
> We need to *buttress* the theory with *solid* arguments
> They *exploded* his latest theory.[46]

The essential point that the authors are making is that metaphors are not just flourishes of language; they are the essential rudiments out of which we conceptualize or think about the world. They are the brain's way of carrying abstractions back to an experiential or perceptual footing (to use both a motion and architectural metaphor). Of course, when Shakespeare suggested that life was little more than "sound and fury signifying nothing" (a composite metaphor employing aural, emotional, and semantic images), he was reclining on a figurative cloud of his unique creation.

In 1987 Mark Johnson advanced this premise with his book *The Body in the Mind*, in which he argued that not only is the mind and imagination conditioned by the very patterns of our bodily experience, but also that "metaphor is perhaps the central means by which we project structure across categories to establish new connections and organizations of meaning and to extend and develop image schemata."[47] This theme was subsequently developed by Lakoff and Johnson in their ambitious study of 1999, *Philosophy in the Flesh*, which brought their earlier ideas in line with contemporary neurological research. This happy conjunction of linguistics and philosophy with neuroscience proved enlightening in several respects. First, there was their realization that if our conceptualization is largely metaphoric in nature, it is carried out for the most part unconsciously (95 percent or so).[48] Second, it is likely, they hypothesize, that metaphoric categories are likely hard-wired into our neural maps, sometimes at a very early age. Citing the work of Christopher Johnson, Lakoff and Johnson use the example of the "Affection is Warmth" metaphor, such as we use when saying "she is a warm person" or "she's as cold as ice." They argue that these metaphors arise from the experience of a child being held affectionately by a parent and thus experiencing warmth.

> There is neuronal activation occurring simultaneously in two separate parts of the brain: those devoted to emotions and those devoted to temperature. As the saying goes in neuroscience "Neurons that fire together wire together." Appropriate neural connections between the brain regions are recruited. These connections physically constitute the Affection Is Warmth metaphor.[49]

As suggestive as this statement is in itself, Lackoff and Johnson take the matter one step further. They surmise that much of our thinking takes place through what they term an "embodied concept," that is, "a neural structure that is actually part of, or makes use of, the sensorimotor system of our brains. Much of the conceptual inference is, therefore, sensorimotor inference."[50] They see the implications of this thesis as pivotal for Western philosophy: "We will suggest, first, that human concepts are not just reflections of an external reality, but that they are crucially shaped by our bodies and brains, especially by our sensorimotor system."[51]

Lackoff and Johnson were not alone in the 1990s in reorienting their respective fields (linguistics and philosophy) in light of the advances of neuroscience. During this same decade the psychiatrist Arnold H. Modell took note of Edelman's selectionist theory, and in his later study, *Imagination and the Meaningful Brain* (2003), he also drew upon the work of Lackoff and Johnson.[52] The complementary nature of the two theories, in fact, led Modell to fashion his later book on the very premise that "If we combine Edelman's selectionist principle with Lakoff and Johnson's unconscious metaphoric process, metaphor becomes the selective interpreter of corporeal experience."[53] What he means by this is that the metaphoric process is embedded in our conceptualization process because it in fact springs from the core of our corporeal existence. To cite his own words: "I suggest that sensations arising from the interior of our body are subject to the same metaphoric transformations as are sensations arising from the external world."[54] A sense of balance, for instance, is a sensation arising from within our body, and because of this it is also a structural metaphor that we project into the world, whether it be the Eiffel Tower or an abstract painting. Modell, in also citing Zeki's discussions of color constancy, goes on to suggest that corporeal metaphors – perhaps for reasons of bodily continuity – provide a necessary "illusion of constancy" of self within a world of continuous change.[55] In a curious way, such a contention is reminiscent of Robert Vischer's concept of *Einfühlung* (empathy).

All of this returns us to the model of consciousness of Edelman, who also connects the issue of creativity with the idea of metaphor.[56] His theory of neural Darwinism, as we noted, rests on the assumption that selectional systems must rely on a biological generation of diversity, and that the neural repertoires that result must have a very large number of variants. Yet the number of possible connections between the cortex and thalamus is, to use his term, "hyperastronomical." Then how does the brain in fact function or even file its classifications with infinite possibilities for connections? His answer, which resemble Zeki's deliberations regarding the visual cortex, is that the brain does so by foregoing a great deal of specificity in its neural events in order to increase its conceptual range – once again, by pattern recognition. And at least one of the neurological ways to achieve this efficiency is through the use of metaphor and its broader categories. As he points out, we have heard people describe artistic activity as child-like, but even after a child grows up and acquires the abstract powers of mathematical logic, metaphor "continues to be a major source of imagination and creativity in adult life."[57] He continues,

> The metaphorical capacity of linking disparate entities derives from the associative properties of a reentrant degenerative system. Metaphors have remarkably rich allusive power but, unlike certain other tropes such as simile, can neither be proved or disproved. They are, nonetheless, a powerful starting point for thoughts that must be refined by other means such as logic. Their properties are certainly consistent with the operation of a pattern-forming selectional brain.[58]

Metaphor, if we can summarize this section, seems to underlie the creative patterns that the brain constructs. It is therefore understandable that metaphoric associations have always been a fundamental part of the arts, not the least of which is that very plastic and sensuous art of architecture.

Architecture and Metaphor

Up until this point we have been discussing the term metaphor in two senses. On the one hand, metaphor seems to be inherent to that neurological process by which we classify and conceptualize the very thinking processes of the brain, a neurological shortcut or rule of pattern-making by which 100 billion neurons are brought into some kind of working order. Metaphors, in this sense of the word, are embodied in that they are grounded in, if not synonymous with, our neurological activities. On the other hand, metaphor is a very specific creative tool for the arts, a powerful juxtaposition or "transfer" of ideas, as its Greek etymology indicates. But what indeed do these two senses of metaphor have in common, and especially with respect to architecture? The answer that seems to be coming from neuroscience is actually quite surprising.

As we have already seen in our earlier chapters, metaphors have been a part and parcel of architectural conceptualization, probably since the first womb-like huts were conceived with vaginal-shaped entrances.[59] When Alberti said that a building is a "form of body," he was not using the body as a simile for architecture but rather discoursing on an immediate metaphoric fact of life, one with important implications with regard to such things as proportions. Similarly, when Vitruvius recounted the three architectural orders as representing the forms of human bodies – the Corinthian child born of Ionic female and Doric male – he was stating what to him must have seemed to be an obvious architectural fact, but one also reflecting a higher "order of the cosmos."[60] Indra Kagis McEwen has called attention to the fact that when Vitruvius advertised in one Preface that he was setting out "to write about the whole body of architecture," he was also the first Latin author to associate the term "body" (Latin *corpus*) with a literary work.[61]

It seems evident that architecture in all of its pre-classical and classical manifestations was based on such metaphoric thinking. John Onians, for instance, has interpreted the colonnades of the Periclean period as metaphors for the "strength, erectness, and disciplined regularity" of a phalanx of warriors, whom they valued as defenders of the homeland.[62] Joseph Rykwert, in *The Dancing Column*, interprets the meaning of architecture in both classical antiquity and Renaissance times principally as the explication of metaphor:

> But the metaphor with which I have been concerned is more extended – a double one – in that it involves three terms: a body is like a building, and the building in turn is like the world. The metaphor returns in a more global similitude: the whole world is itself understood as a kind of body.[63]

Building as a metaphor for the human body continues throughout the Renaissance and into much of the baroque period of course, but in the late-seventeenth century, beginning with the rationalist spirit of Claude Perrault, the situation begins to change. Perrault's attitude – especially his startling rejection of the "Ancients" or the sway of any inherited authority – was a signal of the coming Enlightenment or, more fittingly, the Age of Reason. And notwithstanding the allegorical exuberance of architects engaged in *architecture parlante* in the last years of the eighteenth century, it was the anti-metaphorical functionalism of

Jean-Nicolas-Louis Durand that took command, at least in post-revolutionary France. Durand's first theoretical act, not insignificantly, was to jettison both Vitruvian mythology and the "rustic hut" of Marc-Antoine Laugier.[64]

Of course this is the principal theme of Alberto Pérez-Gómez's well known book, *Architecture and the Crisis of Modern Science* (1983). His contention is that Western architectural thought underwent a radical transformation around 1800, one in which the rational sciences assumed the upper hand within architectural deliberations, much to the demise of the mytho-poetic content of the classical tradition. Architecture in the industrial age, in effect, was forced to choose between art and science, and with the gradual ascendance of the latter's positivistic outlook, the profession began a well-ordered march in which the "poetical content of reality" became increasingly "hidden beneath a thick layer of formal explanations."[65] This architectural crisis, for Pérez-Gómez, culminated in the structuralist and poststructural theories the 1960s and 1970s, in which design methodologies, urban typologies, and linguistic formalism – all entirely rational in their high conceptualizations – summarily carried the day.

Written more than 25 years ago, Pérez-Gómez's book offers many valuable insights, even if he at times overlooks the complexity of the intervening conflicts. He downplays, for instance, the heated debates of the nineteenth century over the issue of just how to mediate the new "Newtonian worldview" with the old art – as Semper's metaphoric thesis of the "dressing" (curtain wall) and "masking of reality" makes transparent.[66] The tone of Pérez-Gómez's polemic again suggests an anti-technological bias, which seems unfair because the rapid increase in the use of iron and glass as building materials was not the cause of the loss of metaphor but rather the result of the same industrial and rationalist spirit. Even Otto Wagner's attempt at the start of the twentieth century to square technology with Semper's symbolic "dressing" can be interpreted today as a last-ditch attempt to salvage some vestige of classical metaphor for architecture.[67] The wreath-bearing angels placed atop the Vienna Postal Savings Bank (the wreath was Semper's metaphor for the inception of art) attests to this architect's artistic/rationalist conflict – in the era of Freud, of course.

Nonetheless, Pérez-Gómez's thesis remains insightful, especially in light of the context in which it was written. It appeared during the first beery rush of postmodernism's popularity and as the movement's obsession with semiotic issues was fully manifest. Yet, arguably, the movement in the late 1970s was conceived as a response to the semantic muteness or metaphorical silence of twentieth-century modernism. At least, this was the view of the movement's most influential champion, Charles Jencks. His wildly popular book, *The Language of Post-Modern Architecture* (1977), indeed exalted metaphor as its leading theme. The plague-bearing, child-eating dragon that needs to be slain, in Jencks's account, is none other than modernism's dreary "factory metaphor" or "machine metaphor," as found in abundance in the steely vocabulary of Mies van der Rohe and other International-Style architects.[68] The lance of St. George that will slay the dragon, for Jencks, is nothing less than compound metaphor or multivalent architecture, which the author sees, *in nuce*, in the TWA terminal in New York, the Sydney Opera, and Cesar Pelli's "Blue Whale" in Los Angeles.

What Jencks actually succeeded in showing, which is germane to the timing of Pérez-Gómez's book, is that architectural metaphors can appear on sundry levels, not all of them especially profound. In the realm of literature, for instance, the phenomenologist Paul Ricoeur has defined the range of metaphor – "the power to 'redescribe' reality" – as everything from the individual word to the hermeneutic "strategy of discourse."[69] Architecturally, this might translate into everything from a beam of sunlight on the wall to the spiritual transcendence of a Gothic cathedral. Yet Jencks does not venture here, and he employs building-as-objects for nearly all of his examples of architectural metaphor. To view the forms of the TWA terminal as a metaphor for flight, for instance, defines it on a level that Arnheim, in his own way, was simultaneously condemning as "shallow" and "superficial."[70] By contrast, to raise (as Jencks did in the last pages of his book) the corporeal and political allegory of Antonio Gaudi's Casa Battlo in Barcelona, with its variegated "sleeping monster sprawled out" on the roof, is to elevate the idea of metaphor to the embodied level of a classical Greek drama.[71] With it, Jencks had in fact touched on something of great significance.

Perhaps it is better to begin a consideration of architectural metaphor by first excluding what Arnheim – following Alfred Lorenzer – once called "intentional and consciously applied symbolism."[72] It is not that architects, like other artists, cannot or should not engage in semantic references or operate on highly abstract planes of thought, but we should also recognize that few users of buildings perceive the

Figure 12.5 Antonio Gaudi, The roof of the Casa Battlo, Barcelona (1904–6). Photograph by Romina Canna

world in this way. In fact, what the bulk of the brain scans are indicating at present is that the vast preponderance of our conceptualization – recalling the insights of Merleau-Ponty – is perceptually and emotionally driven from below. Our basic engagement with the world, the world of architecture, is forged from our more basic corporeal responses, which always precede and are often subliminal to our propensity for rationalizations.

An interesting experiment might shed some light on this point. In 2004, in search of "the neural correlates of beauty," Semir Zeki and

Hideaki Kawabata conducted an experiment on 10 subjects.[73] Each subject examined 300 paintings and, after classifying them as "ugly," "neutral," and "beautiful," they were shown the same images when inside an fMRI scanner. The results were both expected and surprising. The works judged beautiful, as expected, produced the highest activity in the orbito-frontal cortex, an area that is intimately linked with the emotional limbic centers of the brain and known to be associated with such emotional states as romantic love. The works judged ugly, quite unexpectedly, activated the motor cortex, as if the subjects wanted to take evasive action. The architectural translation is clear. Good buildings fill us emotionally with a sense of happiness and gratification, while bad buildings cause us to take flight. Such a result assumes another dimension of meaning when considered alongside another fMRI experiment carried out in 2008, in which it was determined that decisions made in the prefrontal and parietal cortices can take place up to 10 seconds before they enter our conscious awareness.[74] In other words, our judgments about buildings and other things may take place long before we stand back and ponder their "higher" meaning.

Therefore, we have to look elsewhere for the power of metaphor, which is not in the conceptual propensities of our linguistic affectations. Peter Zumthor opened his book *Thinking Architecture* with a useful observation, "When I think about architecture, images come into my mind."[75] It sounds quite simple, but it says what every architect or designer recognizes in their professional experience, and it reinforces what so many writers cited in this chapter have suggested about metaphor – which is that the brain rarely thinks in terms of abstract concepts or words, especially when it is thinking creatively. For all of the neurological complexity of the brain, the metaphoric activity of the architect is primarily a process of image-making: a re-simulation of familiar or associative neural patterns drawn from experience and on occasions bringing something quite new to the result. Images, moreover, are always perceptually driven, which to say that they are inherently material and textural in nature, rather than abstract or semantic. To say that architecture is a language, as so many of the early postmodernists were prone to do, is almost counter-intuitive, because the concept of language, even when metaphorically inclined, in no way explains, as Juhani Pallasmaa has noted, the emotional force of a poem, or indeed how to string words together to compose one.[76] Steven Holl has made a similar argument in remarking that architectural thinking, "more fully than other art forms, engages the immediacy of our sensory perceptions."[77] Holl, in his essay, then goes on to pay homage to the archetypal architectural experiences of color, light and shadow, space, time, water, sound, hapticity, proportion, and scale. Neurologically, it seems people do respond specifically to these phenomena. Even the silent chords of the piano placed in Louis Kahn's Exeter Library induce the auditory experience of sound careening off the hard teak and concrete.

In another early challenge to postmodernism's semiotic drift, Vittorio Gregotti, in a series of editorials that appeared in *Casabella* in the early 1980s, offered a critique of architecture's accepted linguistic analogy. He was concerned with the question of "what constitutes the nature of architectural quality" and how this quality might be conveyed to others outside the field – to which he responded with the notion of "mimesis."[78] He invoked the term not in the sense of imitation (as it is unfortunately usually translated today), but as he found it in Erich Auerbach's book of this title, which discussed it as a powerful exercise of the imagination in its literary reconfiguration of the world.[79] A few months later Gregotti connected the concept of mimesis with the issue of architectural detailing and the possibility that architecture could also be read as a mimetic or representational text.[80] He did so by raising Alberti's corporeal notion of ornament as an "expressive form," rather than as something simply ornate.

Since Gregotti's comments, the notion of mimesis has enjoyed currency in a few architectural circles. Frascari soon thereafter embraced the theme and called attention to the definition of mimesis by the eighteenth-century Venetian Antonio Schinella Conti, for whom it was also an exercise in detailing. Schinella defined mimesis as "nothing else than to make a representation in such a fashion that it will make sensory and mental impressions analogous to those which are in the things themselves."[81] If this "anatomical understanding" hints at affinities with some of the present neurological contentions, Frascari's summary point makes the metaphoric connection even more explicit:

> Buildings are texts which can be read in their architectural possibilities bringing to light the imaginary nature of human thoughts. This process is based on the construing of details: an anatomical procedure singling out the meaning of the bodies of buildings through a reasoning based on the understanding of the parts of construction. Such reasoning is

instantaneous; when a mind perceives an architectural text, it discerns the parts, and interprets them. Expressive details are thus endowed by the mind. This is a hermeneutical process which liberates the symbolic images embodied in the materials of architecture.[82]

A few years later Pérez-Gómez pointed out the relationship of the original concept of mimesis with the act of catharsis in the Greek drama. He suggested that mimesis for the pre-Socratic Greeks signified "not imitation but rather the expression of feelings and the manifestation of experiences through movement, musical harmonies and the rhythms of speech."[83] From such a perspective, Pérez-Gómez called for architecture to be "articulated as a narrative 'metaphoric' projection grounded on recollection."[84]

Joseph Rykwert, whose book *The Dancing Column* might be seen as a 400-page exegesis on the concepts of mimesis and *poiēsis* (both implicating the technique by which things are made), not only stressed the Greek heritage of the two terms but he also called for a contemporary interpretation of mimesis grounded specifically in "technical skill and invention," as well as in a "prerational empathy" that allows "an interdependence of imitator and imitated in dialogue and play, not in hegemony and domination."[85] Metaphor for him was one of the principal means to achieve this experiential depth.

Finally, Dalibor Vesely has also argued on behalf of the mimetic nature of architecture and indeed in its original sense as "a particular form of *poiēsis*."[86] The inhibiting factor in this regard, suggests Vesely, is the modern instrumental perspective, whose "main characteristic is the confusion of the distinction between sense and intellect and a naive belief in the ability of sight to see intelligible reality directly, without any mediation with sensible reality."[87] For him, some ways to draw the senses back into an embodied architecture are metaphor, analogy, and proportion.

My reason for calling attention to mimesis is that the concept, in its original sense as a stylistic reconfiguration of the world, is in many ways a perfect metaphor for architectural creativity – that is, if we view the brain (as neuroscience is now disclosing) as a rhythmic and holistic process of neural activity not only imbued with sensory and emotional coloration but also structured by metaphoric pattern-making. In his fascinating study *Origins of the Modern Mind*, Merlin Donald has hailed mimesis as the first essential step in human evolution: the bridge between the episodic life of our primate ancestors and the ritualized and symbolic culture of modern humanity. Nevertheless, Donald still locates mimetic impulse "at the very center of the arts," specifically because of its supramodal capacity to engage all of the emotions and senses.[88] What all of this suggests is that it is not by logic or abstract reasoning that the brain and its internal rhythms generally engage the world. This is especially true for the architectural experience, which is much more primal in its principal effects.

13

Hapticity

Architecture of the Senses

The architecture of the eye detaches and controls, whereas haptic architecture engages and unites. (Juhani Pallasmaa)[1]

Our perception is visceral. Reason plays a secondary role. (Peter Zumthor[2])

If we trace the course of architectural theory over the past 500 years, from the days of Alberti forward, we see a more or less consistent process of increasing abstraction and rationalization. But today neuroscientists are reminding us that the one-eighth of an inch mantle of "gray matter" that abuts the inner circumference of the skull is but a small part of a much larger neurological and visceral biological operation that is driven internally and externally from below – that is, by sensory-emotive activity as well as by its own spontaneous rules of engagement. This old, but at the same time new, realization holds a very important lesson for designers. Architects may like to rationalize the variables of design, but people *largely perceive buildings emotionally through the senses.* Moreover, in doing so they employ those 'higher' cognitive powers to only varying extents.

"Hapticity" is a term that has been traditionally ascribed to the sense of touch, but this definition has been expanding in recent years. Jean Piaget referred to haptic perception as the process whereby a child, in an early stage of spatial development, translates "tactile-kinesthetic impressions" into a "spatial image of a visual kind."[3] His contemporary James J. Gibson emphasized that hapticity is a system that yields "information about solid objects in three dimensions."[4] Juhani Pallasmaa and others have proffered the term as a way both to counter the ocular bias of our architectural culture and as a holistic means of enhancing "materiality, nearness, and intimacy."[5] I would like to use the term as a synonym for the emotive and multisensory experience of architecture, which includes the visual dimension. Neuroscience is now showing that such a vantage point has a solid biological basis.

Neurobiologists, of course, approach the matter from a different direction. Semir Zeki, to the best of my knowledge, has not used the term "hapticity," but he refers to "abstraction," alongside constancy, as one of the two "supreme" laws of vision. He defines visual abstraction as the process by which "the particular [of the perceived object] is subordinated to the general, so that what is represented [in the visual brain] is applicable to many particulars."[6] This perceptual shortcut of abstracting forms from the real world, he goes on to argue, at the same time carries with it a steep price. If we are principally sensory animals, abstraction in this reductive form can never suffice. Thus art (and presumably architecture), he reasons, is the way that we "download" our conceptualizations back into particulars, or invest our creative world with materiality.[7]

Many architects, it seems, have come to a similar conclusion. When Peter Zumthor speaks of architecture as preeminently a visceral experience, he is referring to architecture as a haptic process that "sets out from and returns to real things." In the case of his widely praised baths at Vals, he notes that his design was preceded by a meditation on three sensory elements: "mountain, rock, water."[8] Steven Holl, who has considered the matter from a phenomenological perspective, has also spoken of finding some kind of "pre-theoretical" ground for architecture, one that "bridges the yawning gap between the intellect and senses of sight, sound, and touch, between the highest aspirations of thought and the body's visceral and emotional desires."[9] None of this is meant to deny the importance of rationally grounded explanations or other aesthetic pursuits, but simply to underscore the sensuous reality of that biological organism that lives and breathes beneath this culturally conditioned layer of linguistic clothing.

The Emotional Brain

A good place to begin this consideration of the senses is with the phenomenon of emotion, which was already a component of the earliest reptilian brain. The psychologist Joseph LeDoux defines emotion as "the process by which the brain determines or computes the value of a stimulus."[10] The word "value" in this definition is laden with evolutionary overtones. It suggests a genetic conditioning device by which the brain rapidly evaluates a threat (a dangerous animal) or a reward (the possibility of a meal) and responds accordingly. Emotions, therefore, are genetically-coded, chemical, and neurological activities directed to maintaining our homeostasis, and in certain cases are essential for our survival. Laughter, for instance, releases morphine-like chemicals into our bloodstream called endorphins, which flood targeted areas of our cortex and induce neurological activity leading to a highly pleasurable state that in its own way engages the present.[11]

The neurologist Antonio Damasio underscores the fact that emotions cause changes in our body's homeostatic conditions as well as in the supporting brain structures involving thought. In effect they are "multidimensional maps" reflecting "the organism's internal state."[12] He also distinguishes emotions from feelings. If emotions are the initial expressions of affective states that are visible for others to observe, feelings are quite simply the brain's interpretative (that is, cerebral) response to an aroused corporeal condition. More explicitly, a feeling is "*the idea of the body being in a certain way,*" that is, an actual perception taking place in the "*brain's body maps.*"[13]

Damasio and his colleagues were also among the first to track the neurological activities of emotion and feelings through positron emission tomography or PET scans. Emotions precede feelings, and they are triggered in such sites as the brainstem nuclei (part of the reptilian brain), the amygdala, hypothalamus, basal forebrain, and prefrontal cortex. No one site triggers an emotion in itself, and different emotions arise from the coordinated activities of several regions in a generation of neural patterns. Feelings engage these same areas, but also the somatosensory cortex, cingulate cortex, and insula.[14]

The somatosensory cortex, which is the home of our corporeal awareness and is therefore intimately connected with feelings, will be discussed below, but the insula is also an interesting area in that it is a fold of the temporal lobe deep within each hemisphere and adjacent to the limbic system. It not only concerns itself with feelings but also monitors sensory experience. In fact, one of Damasio's findings is that the peripheral nerves for touch terminate not in the

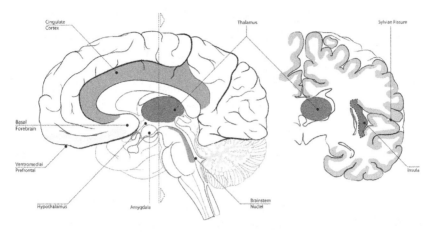

Figure 13.1 Longitudinal section through the brain showing areas activated by emotions and feelings, with a transverse section through the brain showing the location of the insula. Illustration by Amjad Alkoud

somatosensory cortex (in which tactility is processed) but rather in the insula – again underscoring the close relationship between feelings and the senses.[15]

Susan Greenfield views emotions as a kind of primeval id, that is, as an atavistic conflict in which emotions surge upward from the brainstem only to be dampened in the limbic areas and the cortex.[16] Neurologists more often than not stress the more positive aspects of emotions by emphasizing their biological role in organizing the brain's activity and maintaining the body's homeostatic equilibrium. Different emotions also have different neurological maps. Happy people, as Diane Ackerman expresses it, display more "mind glow" in the left prefrontal cortex and little activity in the amygdala, whereas sad people activate the amygdala along with the right prefrontal cortex.[17] Feelings of joy are also known to stimulate some higher cortical processes (while de-activating others), whereas feelings of sadness have been shown to depress the operations of the larger biological field and they therefore have a pejorative effect on our overall health.

The importance of our emotional well-being cannot be overestimated by architects, if only for the reason that designers are principally engaged in constructing the habitats in which we live. Little research has thus far been done on how the variables of the built environment affect our emotional life, but it might very well be demonstrated in the near future, as John Eberhard has recently suggested, that a well-designed building or city may lead our biological organism toward a greater sense of functional harmony, whereas we have long known that an uninspiring building or a blighted urban area contributes to a condition of functional disequilibrium.[18] Damasio also raises the possibility that our understanding of feelings "can inspire the creation of conditions in the physical and cultural environments that promote the reduction of pain and the enhancement of well-being for society."[19] Such a possibility has scarcely been uttered in architectural circles over the last 40 years.

Still another scientist who has long been involved with the investigation of emotions is Jaak Panksepp, and he stresses another very important aspect of their influence: their relationship to our behavior. He defines emotions in a traditional sense as "psychoneural processes that are especially influential in controlling the vigor and patterning of actions in the dynamic flow of intense behavioral interchanges between animals, as well as with certain objects during circumstances that are especially important for survival."[20] But Panksepp's focus has been on what he terms the "primary-process emotional feelings," rather than with sensory-based affects. He argues that affective sensations, which we share with most other animals, profoundly color our emotional consciousness. He further identifies seven endophenotypes, or core emotional instincts, that are found in all mammals: seeking, lust, care, panic, rage, fear, and play.[21] Two of these – seeking and play – are vital to the various fields of artistic creation and appreciation.

Seeking (and its emergent emotions of curiosity, anticipation, and interest) has certainly long been viewed as a cornerstone of human nature. Edmund Burke termed curiosity and its pursuit of novelty "the simplest emotion which we discover in the human mind," and insisted that "some degree of novelty must be one of the materials in every instrument which works upon the mind," otherwise life would habituate itself into a state of "loathing and weariness."[22] Uvedale Price, as we have seen, found his curiosity nourished by the "partial and uncertain concealment" of nature, while Richard Payne Knight believed that novelty was the centerpiece of all aesthetic enjoyment, in that it allowed "the attainment of new Ideas; the formation of new trains of thought."[23] More recently, the neuroscientist Kenneth Heilman has termed novelty a "major criteria of creativity," and related it in the visual arts to the manipulation and transformation of images.[24]

For Panksepp, seeking has a vital biological footing. To begin with, it is "characterized by a persistent positively-valenced exploratory inquisitiveness, with energetic forward locomotion – approach and engagement with the world – consisting of probing into the nooks and crannies of interesting objects and events."[25] It does so not on whim or blind impulse, but in order to increase "the future efficiency of behaviors through the emergence of cognitive maps, expectancies, and habit structure."[26] As a result it, along with the chemicals it sets in motion, evoke "feelings of environmentally engaged aliveness," specifically within the limbic and brainstem areas of our brains.[27] Seeking again drives all learning, and it is therefore one of the principal ways in which the brain enhances its neural efficiency. Artistic innovation may transpose itself into a polite or recreational pastime in a museum setting, but from a biological perspective it seems to be as primal a human instinct as anger or fear.

Play also has long been viewed as one of the driving instincts behind art, and in a biological sense the ludic instinct offers several positive benefits. In the young it helps to foster the brain circuits necessary for social companionship and it thereby provides a structured system for friendly competition. It often entails physical exercise and therefore assists in muscular and visceral development as well. With adults, play is associated with the emotion of happiness and with the release of those satisfying endorphins, but perhaps the most important biological benefit of play is that it promotes "neuronal growth and emotional homeostasis."[28]

Over the past decade this theme of artistic play has been especially pursued in neurological studies focusing on music, which Arthur Schopenhauer equated with humanity's innermost being and emotional wellspring. Historically, the origin of music has been traced to such things as the mimicry of sounds and rhythms of nature, tribal hunting, warfare, harvesting, and the ritualizing social bonds of chanting and dance. Neuroscientists are beginning to explore music's eurhythmic relationship with the health and development of the brain. Douglas F. Watt's affective model of consciousness, for instance, stresses the "seamless integration of homeostasis, emotion, and cognition," while suggesting that musical play, in particular, epitomizes "how higher cognitive processes recruit primary emotions" in order to enhance and intensify the complexity of emotional life."[29] He therefore sees music as the process whereby the brain turns inward and feeds off its own evolutionary and emotional complexity. Panksepp and Günther Bernatzky, once again, emphasize that musical play is indeed the "language of emotions" and is therefore a fundamental part of our biological fitness: "Our overriding assumption is that ultimately our love of music reflects the ancestral ability of our mammalian brain to transmit and receive basic emotional sounds that can arouse affective feelings which are implicit indicators of evolutionary fitness."[30]

The many cognitive and scanning experiments of Robert Zatorre and his associates in Montreal, along with the work of Gottfried Schlaug at Harvard University, have recently shed much light on the importance of musical play. In one notable experiment Zatorre's team used positron emission tomography (PET) scans to observe the brains of individuals experiencing "shivers down the spine" from music. They too found a complex web of brain activities that activated the brainstem, amygdala, left ventral striatum, right orbito-frontal cortex, and ventral medial prefrontal cortex. The complexity of the cerebral areas involved underscore the fact that musical play is no simple emotional exercise driven by a few casual instincts but one that "links music with biologically relevant, survival-related stimuli via their common recruitment of brain circuitry involved in pleasure and reward."[31] It also "supports the general idea that the ability to perceive and process music is not some recent add-on to our cognition, but that it has been around long enough to be expressed from the earliest stages of our neural development."[32]

Schlaug's imaging scans have demonstrated that musical play not only increases the number of neural circuits in the auditory, motor, and visual spatial areas of the cortex, but it also results in an enlarged corpus collosum connecting the two hemispheres – emphasizing the earlier point of hyperconnectivity.[33] We also now know that the musical arts, as with other perceptions, engage or assist other areas of the brain relating to attention, focus, anticipation, memory, motor programming, and sensory integration.[34] Other studies have shown that listening to music aids the cognitive recovery of people who have suffered a stroke, and that it lessens depression and increases the diameter of blood vessels to the point where the body manufactures less LDL or bad cholesterol.[35] Zatorre has documented the contribution of the cerebellum as a mutual timing device for both visual and auditory rhythms.[36] A pianist, for instance, may activate areas of the frontal, somatosensory, and motor cortices, the thalamus, basal ganglia, and cerebellum.

Zatorre's last finding – the transference of musical rhythm to the visual world of form – lends some credence to Gottfried Semper's characterization of architecture, alongside dance and music, as a "cosmic" art, that is, one in which early humans took especial "delight in nature's creative law as it gleams through the real world in the rhythmical sequence of space and time movements, in wreaths, a string of pearls, scrolls, round dances, the rhythmic tones attending them, the beat of the oar, etc."[37] Wolfgang Köhler, more than a half century later, described musical articulations (*crescendo, diminuendo, accelerando, ritardando*) in similar terms as intrinsic forms of "inner life," whose metrics once again traverse all artistic boundaries.[38] Merlin Donald, as we have seen, views rhythm as a primordial mimetic skill, one that is related to all forms of human learning and expression.[39]

Still one other issue related to emotion was the announcement made in the 1980s by a team of Italian scientists that there are groups of neurons in both the frontal and parietal cortex that have the capability of mirroring the actions and emotional behavior of others.[40] Although still disputed in neurological circles, these "mirror neurons," have spawned an inter-disciplinary realm of research consolidating itself under Robert Vischer's old term of "empathy," and they are being studied for such things as language development, learning, and autism. V. S. Ramachandran, even more boldly, speculates that their appearance – the human capacity to imitate the complex skills of other humans – may have led to the "explosive evolution" of culture roughly 50,000 years ago.[41] They become architecturally relevant if we accept Wölfflin's thesis that emotional effects of architecture are, in large part, physiognomic.[42]

Spatiality

Another series of interesting neurological discoveries over the last few decades has been that we navigate spatial fields with at least three highly specialized groups of neurons coordinating our actions in space. John O'Keefe's and Lynn Nadel's research on rats in the early 1970s laid the basis for this insight with the discovery of "place cells" in the hippocampus.[43] Spatial perception regarding such features as depth and motion takes place in the occipital, parietal, and temporal lobes of the cortex, but as this information is passed into the hippocampus the latter seems to create spatial maps or "place fields" detailing the experience. These fields are non-anthropocentric, that is, they seem to be related only to the spatial geometry of the environment. As we move through an area, groups of place cells (of which there are millions) fire at very specific points within the field and at no other points. If the environment is altered, spatial fields are remapped, which leads to the explanation that they depend at least in part on landmarks. The firing of place cells tell us we are "here" within a map and they fire even though we might not be paying attention to our environment.

Place cells, as we learned in the 1980s, are assisted by "head-direction cells" in an adjacent parahippocampal area, which activate when the head and its cone of vision are pointing in a specific direction, regardless of its location.[44] They effectively serve as a compass for the activation of the adjacent place cells. And, in 2005, a group of Norwegian scientists found another group of spatially active cells in the entorhinal cortex, which they called "grid cells." It seems that the brain, when entering any environment, is hardwired to lay down (unconsciously) a directionally oriented, topographic map or triangular grid within a spatial field, and specific neurons fire when we cross each of the vertices. The functional similarity of this grid with the place cells raises the possibility that some of the sensory information about space in the hippocampus, which is specific to a context, is actually computed "upstream" in the entorhinal cortex "by algorithms that integrate self-motion information into a metric and directionally oriented representation that is valid in all contexts."[45] As with place cells, the map created by the grid cells is anchored to external landmarks but can also persist without them, which suggests "that grid cells may be part of a generalized, path-integration-based map of the spatial environment."[46]

Obviously the ability not to get "lost" in a hunter-gatherer world was an important key to our evolutionary success, but what does such an elaborate, built-in navigational system (incidentally affirming Kant's "pure form" of space) really mean for architecture? The answer is as yet not entirely clear, although it certainly suggests the importance of considering the spatial aspects of our built environment. One study carried out by a team of Dutch scientists in 2004, in which 20 subjects navigated their way through a virtual museum, found that during route-learning the parahippocampal area of the brain responds to the relevance of landmarks, and it does so on a highly selective basis, that is, "the brain automatically distinguishes between objects at navigationally relevant and irrelevant locations," and independently of the participant's attention to them.[47]

This same area of the brain has also been demonstrated to be involved in object–place associations and recording scene details and layouts.[48]

In another study, in which experienced taxi drivers were tested with MRIs while navigating virtual streets of London, Hugo Spiers and Eleanor Maguire found that this activity in the parahippocampal area was conjoined by activity in the prefrontal cortex and the parietal cortex. At the outset of the journey, the parahippocampal area is most active in planning the route, but it becomes less so as the drivers approach their goals and as activity in the prefrontal cortex picks up. These scientists suggest that the prefrontal cortex, which in general processes future goals, integrates "information from long-term memory about the Euclidean distances between locations in a familiar environment," while the parietal cortex appears "to aid navigation by coding information about the egocentric direction to the goal."[49] In an interesting aside, the parahippocampal areas of the taxi drivers were larger than those of the general population, similar to the way that musicians have altered the structure of their brains. What does this say about a designer's parahippocampal area?

Given the amount of the research that is now being focused on this region of the brain (the hippocampus is one seat of Alzheimer's disease), we can expect a relatively comprehensive model of human spatial navigation in the not too distant future. And with the knowledge of how we structure or perceive space, how we measure it and most easily move our way through it without loss of direction, we should be able to pose some very specific questions or experiments of use to the architect. To some extent, this research has already begun. A few studies have looked at how we form images of buildings and navigate our way through virtual cities on foot.[50] One interdisciplinary group of architects and scientists at San Diego State University has attempted to apply such findings to the design of a nursing home and hospital environments, as well as to relate it to the topological theories of Kevin Lynch.[51] Such research will no doubt continue in the future.

Architecture of the Senses

We have already seen the very elaborate neural processing that takes place in dozens of distinct areas of the brain with the perception of a simple visual image. The same is true for the other so-called senses.

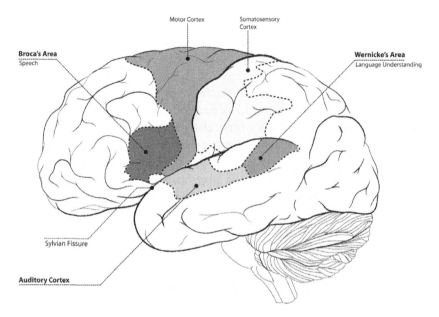

Figure 13.2   Areas of the brain involved with hearing, speech (Broca's area), language comprehension (Wernicke's area), and sensorimotor activities. Illustration by Amjad Alkoud

The perception of sound, for instance, is in many ways similar to that of vision. Vibrations in the air make contact with the functionally asymmetrical ear – first through the tympanic membrane or eardrum and then through the mechanisms of the middle ear, which in turn transmit the sensations into the cochlea. It is here that the first stage of sound processing begins, as sounds move across the basilar membrane and resonate with some of the 16,000 sensory receptors or hair cells in each cochlea. These nerves transmit the information to the auditory nerve that, after an elaborate number of intermediate stations that include the thalamus, sends the signals into the primary auditory cortex. This is located along the temporal lobes (a few centimeters above the ears) and is folded into the Sylvian fissure, separating the temporal from the parietal and frontal lobes.

Yet once again, as with vision, the auditory cortex only begins a larger interpretative or perceptual process. In its quest for perceptual constancy, the cortex must break down the encoded elements of sound, segregate it from its background, analyze it for several factors, and send out signals to sub-regions of the auditory cortex in which neurons are particularly sensitive to specific qualities of sound, such as intensity or frequency. At the same time, it sends signals back to the cochlea to attend to certain sounds or to remain dormant for others. For obvious evolutionary reasons, the auditory cortex is particularly keen on locating the "what" and "where" of a sound, which of course it coordinates with the other senses. In the human brain, it is also extremely receptive to the nuances of both speech and music. Musical perception takes place in the auditory cortices of both hemispheres, and is aided by a connection between the auditory cortex and motor cortex that is unique to humans. Language perception and comprehension is carried out in the upper part of the temporal lobe of the left hemisphere, known as Wernicke's area. It is linked to the area of the left frontal lobe known as Broca's area, which controls speech. The latter, in turn, is wired to the motor cortex, which initiates the physical movements of speech. Scanning images demonstrate that conversation engages all of these areas in one continuous loop.

Still another feature of auditory perception, as with visual perception, is that imagined sounds engage the same neural circuitry as perceived sound. Talking to oneself silently, for instance, will activate the same neural loop as a conversation with another person, with the exception that the motor cortex and primary auditory cortex are left out of the loop. Similarly, an imagined musical tune of a sonata will activate the same secondary areas of the auditory cortex as the heard musical passage in a concert hall, where of course there ensues a much richer corporeal experience. Moreover, it is now becoming clear through scanning technologies that the various senses also share higher-order cerebral networks, or perceptual supramodalities that engage a crossover of sensory inputs from one sense to another and operate independently of any single one. In other words, as Richard Neutra suggested more than a half-century ago, the spatial understanding of a medieval cathedral is derived from not only vision but also the impact of our feet on the stone pavement and the reverberation of a distant cough. Auditory, visual, and tactile cues combine in every architectural experience, or as Neutra also noted, architecture is "omnisensorial."[52]

The multisensory nature of perception is very evident in the complex of senses that compose the somatosensory cortex. The word "somatic" comes from the Greek word *soma*, which means body, and the somatosensory cortex runs across the crown of the head at the anterior edge of the parietal lobe. Immediately in front of it, at the rear of the frontal lobe, is the motor cortex, which coordinates voluntary movement. Like the visual and auditory cortices, the somatosensory cortex can be divided into areas of specialized receptor neurons – regions dimensioned in proportion to the neural wiring of the body. Traditionally, people speak of five senses (physiologists often talk of more than twenty), but it is far more useful to view the somatosensory activities in themselves as a rich complex of interrelated sensory systems, not all of which are located in the somatosensory cortex. These include the homeostatic and visceral systems, musculoskeletal systems, proprioception, the vestibular system, and the other senses involved with touch.

The homeostatic and visceral systems, of course, continuously monitor and maintain our internal milieu by keeping track of all changes within the body, including the work of the trunk organs as well as hunger, thirst, sex, sleep, temperature, fatigue, and pain. They respond with neural and chemical messages (the latter carried by blood) to adjust or correct abnormalities or threats to the equilibrium of the system. Central to these activities is the hypothalamus, which is located below the thalamus and works closely with the pituitary gland at the bottom of the brain (see Figure 10.3). The hypothalamus oversees most somatic operations and produces its own peptides (oxytocin and vasopressin), which can affect the work of the pituitary gland, amygdala, hippocampus, olfactory system, and brainstem, as well as the cortex above. It also controls the human biological clock – the 24-hour or circadian rhythm – by regulating the secretion of melatonin. Other hormones implicated with emotional behavior pass into and through the hypothalamus, such as acetylcholine, dopamine, and serotonin. Dopamine, as we have seen, is much followed in research because of its connection with both pleasure and fear, while serotonin often affects the upswings and downswings of moods. The human brain is, in fact, a rich soup of chemicals controlling or modulating neural activity, and, with the scrutiny these chemicals are now receiving, it is likely that researchers will soon have something to say about their interaction with the built environment.

If the musculoskeletal system, with its bones, muscles, cartilage, tendons, and ligaments, provides the structure by which we stand and move through the world, proprioception is the sense by which we orient, position, and move our bodies in space. It comes about through a set of specialized neural receptors deep within the muscles, tendons, and joints, whose axons pass into the spinal cord and brain. Proprioception, especially when connected with movement, is sometimes called kinesthesia, and this latter term also emphasizes muscle memory and hand–eye coordination. Closely connected with these two systems is the vestibular system, a remarkable sensory organ near the auditory sensory complex that carries out a wide range of coordinated activities. It is connected to the eyes and ears, whose neurons respond to vestibular stimulation; it receives important input from the hands and fingers as well as the soles of the feet; it activates facial and jaw muscles; and it affects heart rates and blood pressure, muscle tone, the positioning of our limbs, respiration, and even immune responses. All of this is done simply to allow us to stand vertically and move through space with a rhythmic sense of balance.

The musculoskeletal, proprioceptive, and vestibular systems, with their particular set of biological rhythms, are extraordinarily sensitive to architectural enclosures. Johann Wolfgang von Goethe cited their importance two centuries ago when he noted the pleasant sensation induced by dancing and claimed that "we ought to be able to arouse similar sensations in a person whom we lead blindfold through a well-built house."[53] Our corporeal relation with architecture, of course, was repeatedly stressed by Wölfflin, as when he asserted that "we can appreciate the noble serenity of column" only because we understand gravity, that is, because we have all "collapsed to the ground when we no longer had the strength to resist the downward pull of our bodies."[54] Believing that all aesthetic experience arises from a knowledge of ourselves, he insisted that these principles form "the sole conditions under which our organic well-being appears possible."[55] Steer Rasmussen devoted an entire chapter to "Rhythm in Architecture," in which he admitted that there was "something mysterious" about its "stimulating effect," which he equated with music.[56] Richard Neutra, again, was poignant in discussing the gravitational forces that we experience within an architectural setting – forces that "are continually recorded and minutely felt *within our bodies*, within all the muscles we use in balancing ourselves." Such "inner pressures," he goes on to argue, "though they are in the majority not consciously perceived, produce feelings of comfort or discomfort, as the case may be."[57] Pallasmaa has summed up this point in a succinct way: "The body knows and remembers, architectural meaning derives from archaic responses and reactions remembered by the body and the senses."[58]

These musculoskeletal, proprioceptive, and vestibular systems again take on added complexity when combined with our sense of touch. Our skin is not only the oldest and largest of our regulatory organs, but it is essential to bodily comfort and maintenance of life. Because it is the earliest sense to develop in the human embryo, some had called touch "the mother of the senses," and of course it functions long before the eyes achieve visual competence.[59] Johann Gottfried Herder noted that "*sight reveals merely shapes,* but *touch alone reveals bodies,*" from which we have our basic understanding of the world: "A body that we have never recognized as a body by touching it, or the corpo-reality of which we have not been able to establish by means of its similarity to other objects," he goes on to argue, "would remain to us forever like the rings of Saturn or Jupiter, that is to say, a mere phe-nomenon, an *appearance.*"[60]

The skin, and its sense of touch, is the site of our most intimate communication with the world and is, at any age, the essence of our emotional well-being. Infants and adults need to be touched, and we often need to hold and feel an object in order to understand it. We can do so because of the incredible discrimination of our tactile senses and their capacity to evaluate weight, pressure, texture, temperature, hard-ness, and softness. Physiologically, there are five different types of nerves involved in the sense of touch, in addition to those responding to temperature and pain. The first is simply the hair that grows from our body, which is attached to a nerve at its base. Two other nerves close to the surface of the skin are the Meissner and Merkel receptors, which pinpoint the location of the stimulus. Two deeper nerve recep-tors are located in the dermis and detect vibration, magnitude, direc-tion, and the rate of change of tension in the skin. These nerves connect to a peripheral nerve bundle that sends the signal to the spinal cord, which then moves the stimulus up to the brainstem, thalamus, and somatosensory cortex. The cortex itself is functionally divided into zones with the largest areas (proportional to receptor density) given over to the face and hands. Once again, specific analyses are sent out from the primary somatosensory cortex to nearby areas more special-ized in their processing. All of this neurological activity takes place in as little time as it takes to flick away a fly.

In a purely tactile sense, we experience architecture in numerous ways, as many writers have discussed. In walking across a tiled floor or the gravel of a garden, our feet experience the texture and relative character of the material we engage – profoundly in some cases. In standing close to a window in cold weather we lose body heat and feel cold. A fire in a hearth on a holiday (no doubt tapping into deeply embedded tribal memories) will not only raise our thermal comfort but also our social and affective spirits. Conversely, the spectral range of a fluorescent light may disturb the nerve cells of the eye, which have not evolved for these particular spectra of light. We know the cool touch of materials like glass and metal, and the relative warmth of wood (both a product of heat transfer). A stair can be luxurious or onerous to climb in relation to our feet and legs; a handrail can be comfortable or awkward to the grasping hand. All of these are basic neurological reactions that reinforce the notion that the skin is but a neural extension of the brain, and its perceptions, as Neutra suggested, also carry with them judgments of whether we like a building or not.

Architects also sometimes speak of a plastic or tactile architecture, and from a neurological perspective this is an interesting statement. In one recent fMRI study of spatial working memory, for instance, a team of Italian researchers tested spatial representation with both visual and tactile cues. These two stimuli are, of course, first processed in their respective regions of the brain. Tactile-based stimulation activates the somatosensory cortex as well as areas of the insular, frontal, and parietal cortices. Vision begins in the occipital lobe and engages dozens of other areas as well. Yet in addition to these sensory networks, the researchers also found a larger supramodal or multisensory network that – for each visual or tactile perception – engages both sensory circuits.[61] In other words, tactile sensations stimulate areas of the visual cortex associated with visual imagery, and vice versa. We "feel" our visual images because, since our first days, we have acquired a library of tactile memories and this firsthand (so to speak) knowledge of the world contributes in a large way to our visual experience and understanding of things such as our built environment.

A more holistic understanding of hapticity and its various sensory modalities has other implications as well. First and foremost is the importance it lends to building materials and to the related sensory elements out of which a building is composed: among them light and shadow, color, texture, grain, repetition, contrast, coherence,

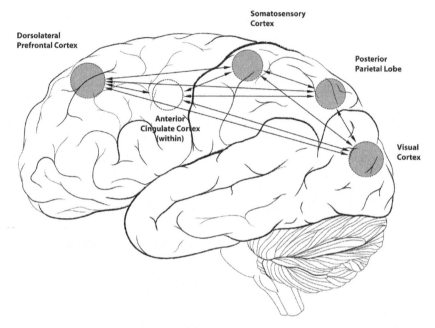

Figure 13.3   The supramodal network that is activated during spatial process-ing for either visual or tactile stimuli. Illustration by Amjad Alkoud

transparency, temperature, sound, scent, and site. Better architects have always exploited these effects and few would deny the powerful force that natural light, for instance, can bring to any architectural set-ting – above and beyond its physical comfort. A sensitive use of materi-als and light, it seems, has its own rewards, and it is interesting in this regard that such contemporary artists as Olafur Eliasson and Philippe Rahm – artists who have been attracted both to phenomenology and to the discoveries of neuroscience – place so much of their emphasis on these elements. The same lessons are there for architects, whose mate-rial fields and opportunities are, if anything, far more extensive in their range.

Perhaps equally interesting with regard to our haptic senses are such other implications as the relevance of scale, proportion, and geometry to design. Zeki, as a neuroaesthetician, was the first to step out on this issue by posing the question of whether there are in fact "universal aspects of form, entities through which one can define all forms, or ones which, when assembled together, can constitute any form."[62] If, for the physiologist, this question may turn to issues of whether there are certain brain cells that compose the "building blocks" of neurological processing, the architect has traditionally viewed scale and proportion as the essential articulation of a building's material form. Christopher Alexander has been one of the few architectural theorists in recent years to have emphasized these aspects of design, and it is interesting to follow the evolution of his thinking. Originally trained as a mathematician, his progression from design methodologies to a "pattern language" in the late 1960s and 1970s entailed a new emphasis on sociological and anthropological criteria of design. Behind these changes in outlook, however, lay his early interest in cognitive studies – an interest that came full circle with his recent multivolume study, *The Nature of Order* (2002), where the problems of scale, strong centers, good shapes, gradients, roughness, and orderly connectedness become his central focus.[63] Hence, his anthropological model transformed itself largely into a biological one, one now based in the perceptual or neurological dimensions of the architectural experience. Supporting him in this regard is the recent work of a number of scientists and architects pursuing biophilic design, led by Stephen R. Kellert and Judith H. Heerwagen.[64] The term "biophilia" was first advanced by Edward O. Wilson in 1984, and was defined as our "innate tendency to focus on life and lifelike processes."[65] The recent transposition of biophilia into architectural thought is an interesting one, in that neuroscience today seems to be not only validating our "innate" preference for living forms but also lending it a somewhat grander biological grounding. Beyond the admirable "greening" of architecture, it suggests issues of scale, lighting, views, refuge, order, and complexity—and beyond them what Steven Holl has termed the "re-assertion of the human body as the locus of experience."[66]

None of this is not to suggest a formulaic system for design or an attempt to narrow the field of technological innovation or design invention. In fact, the opposite is the case, because the brain, as science is now demonstrating, demands both novelty and highly varied environments. But if we accept the brain's propensity toward ambiguity and metaphors of life, and indeed the sensory-emotive grounding for these phenomena, then there remains for the architect a wide field of play – values that, in recent years, have been shunted aside by high-minded abstractions and abject formalism.

At this point, we have probably done little more than scratch the surface of what the near future holds, and the objective of this book is certainly not to suggest that neuroscience will offer any explicit panacea or theory to be fashionably embraced. A more well rounded and factual knowledge of ourselves is the principal value of this realm of science, and as we continue to gain a better biological understanding of how we interact with the world we will inevitably adjust our outlooks and build our own theories. What neuroscience and the broader field of cognitive investigations are once again reminding us is that we are still creatures imbued not only with aspirations but also with vestigial biological needs. If culture is the social edifice constructed on the footings of this heritage, it must therefore respect the primal nature of our existence.

Those writers discussed in the first half of this study are not just voices from the past but individuals who, in their own way, have thought a great deal about how the brain works and how important it is for us as designers to acknowledge the neurological complexity of our embodied condition. And the one red thread that characterizes the insights of an Alberti or a Neutra or a Zumthor is that the basis for their design lies not in some highly speculative system, but rather in our natural selves, or more specifically, in the analogies that we, as designers, extract from the workings of our bodies and brains. In this regard we have new and exuberant resources with extraordinary implications from which to draw at this very moment.

Epilogue

The Architect's Brain

*Today, our world is conveyed mostly by electronic screens, witnesses
to a world changing at every instant, belying stability.* (Rafael
Moneo)[1]

The intention of this study has been to explore a few of the creative
aspects of architectural thinking that have been given prominence by
the recent research in neuroscience. Yet there is another side of this
issue that follows from today's understanding of neural plasticity. As
we noted earlier, plasticity is the capacity of the brain to alter its neural
wiring as part of the learning process. And given the fact that as much
as 50 percent of the brain's neural circuitry is formed after birth, it is a
prodigious capacity indeed. Brain plasticity implies that with the right
effort and the right influences we can make ourselves smarter to some
extent, that we can enhance our creativity, and that the brain, as a living organ, neurologically changes over time. This transformation takes
place over the course of a lifetime, but even more so over the course of
generations as a host of environmental and cultural influences also
come into play. Obviously one of the suggestions of this book is that
the brain of the Renaissance architect or nineteenth-century architect
was configured quite differently from the brain of the twenty-first
century architect, for better or worse.

The artist Warren Neidich has come up with a term for this cerebral
capacity with respect to its equally engaging aesthetic implications,
which is "visual and cognitive ergonomics." He defines them as "the
tacit processes through which the aesthetic transformation of our perception, and our subsequent cognition of the physical world and its

changing nature, affects the way a particular set of stimuli is perceived and cognized."[2] His larger neurological argument is that if perceptual signals of a certain type (say, digital images rather than natural images) produce a strengthening of particular neural circuits during their firing, and if these circuits become intensified or made more efficient with each firing, then these "amplified maps," as it were, will have an advantage over the other maps in the brain's processing of memory and thought.[3] This advantage is especially strong in youthful brains, which have the greatest flexibility or plasticity with respect to environmental influences, and it is therefore in youth that generational differences are formed.

Such a neurological advantage, Neidich goes on to argue, is potentially problematic when we take into account the evolution of our culture's visual images over the last few generations – that is, from the pale radio slogans and black-and-white TV ads of Horkheimer and Adorno's prescient understanding of our "culture industry" to the highly seductive or "phatic" images (intensified images) of today's virtual and iPhone worlds.[4] These newer and ever more sophisticated images, carefully crafted by our commodity czars to excite and lure, "recurring over and over again, over and above their naturally occurring organic counterparts, will have a selective advantage for neurons and neural networks that code for them."[5] In the end, Neidich concludes, they have the powerful potential not only to "sculpt the brain" of each generation but also to "provide a formula through which commodity culture finds increasingly easy egress into the corporeality of the human nervous systems with its machinery for desire."[6]

Neidich's comments fall amid a broader discussion that has appeared over the last few decades with respect to the computer and its impact on education – a debate that now carries with it serious architectural implications. The educational theorist Jane Healy opened this debate as early as 1990 with her provocative book *Endangered Minds: Why Our Children Don't Think*, which dampened the educational expectations of the young digital age by pointing out that the human brain has at its disposal "two complementary methods of processing information": sequential and simultaneous. If the first is the left-brain skill that allows us to analyze mathematical equations or linguistic syntax, the latter, which is the favored right-brain mode of artists and other creative individuals, works differently:

This sort of thinking has been compared to a "ripple" effect, in which A elicits a wide network of connections with other sets of associations and ideas, often represented in images. The linkages may be well learned or spontaneous and unique, as in the process of first feeling, then "seeing," then articulating a metaphor.[7]

Healy goes on to note that good human thinking blends both realms: "Both halves of the brain, not simply the linear, analytic–verbal left hemisphere contribute to it. The more visual, intuitive right hemisphere probably provides much of the inspiration, while the left marches along in its dutiful role as timekeeper and realist."[8]

More recently, Mark Bauerlein's book, *The Dumbest Generation* (2008), chronicles not only the continually sagging reading scores of our internet-educated youth but also the fact that the nature of this digital medium – the eye engaged in rapid and sporadic scanning patterns down the scrolling internet page – actually inhibits or destroys the student's ability to read the more conventional printed page. One of his conclusions, based on a study by former Sun Microsystems engineer Jakob Nielson, is that the web is fundamentally "a consumer habitat, not an educational one."[9] Maggie Jackson has painted another bleak portrait of education in our cyber-centric age in *Distracted* (2008), which speaks extensively to the debilitating effects of the internet on the critical powers of focus and attention:

> As we cultivate lives of distraction, we are losing our capacity to create and preserve wisdom and slipping toward a time of ignorance that is paradoxically born amid an abundance of information and connectivity. Our tools transport us, our inventions are impressive, but our sense of perspective and shared vision shrivel.[10]

Another critic of the internet is Nicholas Carr, who wrote the attention-grabbing article for *The Atlantic*, "Is Google Making Us Stupid?" If the powers at Google, he offers, are attempting to perfect the search machine and relieve us of the tedium of knowing just about anything factual in the world, the down side is that we have become "decoders" of bits of information rather than readers with the opportunity to place this information within a context. In citing the work of the cognitive specialist Maryanne Wolf, he argues that we are essentially surrendering our ability to connect deep reading with deep thinking.[11] This loss of literacy has also to be squared with the neurological fact that there is no human gene for reading. This acquired skill, akin to learning a second language or developing exceptional proficiency with a violin, has to be mastered at an early age when that gaping divide (the Sylvian fissure) between the language and speech areas of the brain is most open to the formation of neural pathways. If they are not put in place during these years, the brain's structure is altered and this skill is impaired or rendered less efficient.

Still another aspect of our growing dependence on digital devices that has been much discussed in the past few years is the increasing detachment we feel toward our personal and physical surroundings. Healy again sounded an early clarion call with the view that "visual stimulation" in itself, such as presented in the electronic media, is not the neurological access point to nonverbal or creative reasoning: "Body movements, the ability to touch, feel, manipulate, and build sensory awareness of relationships in the physical world, are its main foundations."[12] Daniel H. Pink, in his book *A Whole New Mind* (2005), has constructed a broad argument around his belief that the left-brain skills of logic and analysis, the former "gatekeepers for entry into merito-cratic, middle-class society," are being superseded by the need for those right-brain talents of the designer or synthetic thinker – "the boundary crosser, the inventor, and the metaphor maker."[13] Steve Talbott, a former computer programmer, has written impassionedly on how the computer is distancing us from our social and personal selves, how the computer's logic, "necessary and valuable though it may be, sucks all of these flesh-and-blood concerns into a vortex of wonderfully effec-tive calculation." Fearing our intellectual and ethical decline as we submit glibly to the logical mindset of computational devices, he rec-ommends "a certain spirit of mischief and trickery from us, a willing-ness to fashion creative inner 'devices' that stand opposite the inner automatisms now resonating so powerfully with the external machin-ery of our lives."[14] Talbott's apprehension is highly reminiscent of the concerns voiced many years ago by the philosopher Hubert Dreyfus on the computer's effect:

> People have begun to think of themselves as objects able to fit into the inflexible calculation of disembodied machines: machines for which the human form-of-life must be analyzed into meaningless facts, rather than a field of concern organized by sensory-motor skills. Our risk is not the advent of super-intelligent computers, but of sub-intelligent human beings.[15]

One neurophysiologist who has weighed in on these issues in similarly disquieting terms is Rodolfo R. Llinás. His anxiety regarding the extent to which the digital world has taken over our lives extends along two fronts. First there is the inevitable global homogenization of thought and the banal likenesses of consumer societies everywhere, which he fears will eventually redefine the very concept of the self. Second, he is anxious that someday soon we may cease to desire to interact sensuously with the physical world. "Keep in mind," he says, "that the only reality that exists for us is already a virtual one – we are dreaming machines by nature! And so virtual reality can only feed on itself, with the risk that we can very easily bring about our own destruction."[16]

The Computer and Architecture

I have led with this purposefully provocative and foreboding note because I want to consider the computer and its use in architecture. Like nearly everyone, including most of the above critics, I am most appreciative of the extraordinary benefits of our digital age. Electronic connectivity, nanotechnologies, the wireless, globalization, the instantaneous sharing of the latest research – all have led to unparalleled intellectual gains and greatly accelerated advances along nearly every front of knowledge. The world today is radically different from that of just a few decades ago, and for the most part it is a better world.

The computer has also proved to be of great benefit to architects: not only relieving them of much of the tedium that formerly went into such things as specifications and working drawings but also in allowing more work to be accomplished in a shorter period of time. Moreover, the advent of the next-generation of Building-Information-Modeling or BIM systems with their promise of integrated building delivery (bringing together architects, engineers, owners, builders as a seamless team) will of course consolidate this transformation in the near future. It is not unduly optimistic to believe that these more efficient tools of the digital age will, in some ways, also bring with them a general enhancement of global qualitative standards, as already today it is not uncommon to see teams of designers and engineers involved with a particular project spread out over two or three continents.

But the computer, as we know, is also a design and modeling tool, and as such it should be considered like every other design tool. What does it really bring that is new to the design process in a creative sense in either a positive or negative way? What are its limits? Students now coming through school might not be aware that the computerization of architecture has been around in a serious way for less than two decades. For those of you whose education and design exercises are now centered entirely on the computer – you should also know that you are essentially the first such generation. No architects before you have been trained in quite the same way.

The computer as a tool for preparing construction documents first appeared in a few select firms in the early 1980s, but its widespread use, and particularly its evolution beyond basic CAD systems, really began in the 1990s. The office of Frank O. Gehry was one of the first to experiment with it in this way. In 1989 the office pondered how to prepare the working drawings for a fish sculpture for the Barcelona Olympics of 1992, and the designers decided to modify software related to aeronautical design. Gehry himself never worked with it; as a traditionally trained designer, he prefers to think with sketches, cardboard, and Elmer's glue. Nevertheless the modified software allowed him the freedom to ponder such designs as the Walt Disney Concert Hall (started in 1989) and the Guggenheim Museum in Bilbao (started in 1991), both of which have obviously achieved great success. Other new softwares were soon fashioned to dimension and detail complex surfaces, which in turn opened up fresh fields for design exploration. Thus, by the mid-1990s architects everywhere were exploring design strategies involving non-linearity, fractals, complexity theory, and field theory. The profession itself, at least on an iconic level, has since consolidated these gains with such designs as Toyo Ito's Sendai Mediatheque (1995–2001), UN Studio's Mercedes-Benz Museum (2001–6), and OMA's CCTV Headquarters (designed 2002). All of this formal innovation was made possible by the new generation of computer applications developed over a few short years.

The computerization of architecture has also had its many vocal champions, perhaps the most articulate of whom is William J. Mitchell. In his Star-Trek-inspired *e-topia: "URBAN LIFE, JIM – BUT NOT AS WE KNOW IT"* (1999) he set out the case for how the computer can and will revolutionize urban life, and among its "Lean and Green" possibilities are such features as dematerialization (lessening the need for physical construction), demobilization (reduced fuel consumption through telecommunications), and mass customization (non-standardized design). To illustrate just this last point, Mitchell argues that the "astonishing new kind of spatial and material poetry" exhibited in Gehry's Guggenheim Museum, for instance, appeals "to a more subtle and sophisticated rationality" – that is, to everyone except a few "unregenerate old Miesians."[17] More recently, in his book *Me++*, Mitchell mounts a much broader campaign on behalf of his belief that our millennial, ontological condition has morphed into one of cyborgnicity:

> So I am not Vitruvian man, enclosed within a single perfect circle, looking out at the world from my personal perspective coordinates and, simultaneously, providing the measure of all things. Nor am I, as architectural phenomenologists would have it, an autonomous, self-sufficient, biologically embodied subject encountering, objectifying, and responding to my immediate environment. I construct, and I am constructed, in a mutually recursive process that continually engages my fluid, permeable boundaries and my endlessly ramifying networks. I am a spatially extended cyborg.[18]

Mitchell undoubtedly opposes the comments of Dreyfus above, which were aimed critically at the various efforts to create computer models of Artificial Intelligence. This latter goal was first proffered in the 1950s when a group of computer scientists connected with the Rand Corporation and Carnegie Mellon University initiated a project to build a computer that could match the thinking power of the human brain. Within a decade the idea had mushroomed within dozens of doctoral programs and governmental research labs, programs that up until this time have more often than not foundered. Whereas the computer and its software have proved to be extraordinarily able in solving complicated quantifiable problems – everything from aircraft design and weather forecasting to non-linear analyses – it has, in mimicking human associational thought, proved to be altogether inadequate at the most rudimentary level.

The earlier efforts at Artificial Intelligence generally failed for a simple reason. The neural circuits of the brain do not function as a binary system of formal rules, akin to adding two plus two; the analogy of a computer with the human brain could not be a more false one. The brain is nonlinear (non-causal) in its circuitry, redundant in its potential pathways, and far more complex in its systemic organization than any software algorithms yet imagined. It is an organic system that has been honed by millions of years of supplementary overlays or biological refinement, following a geometric course of neural efficiency that would lead Darcy Thompson to a state of wonder. Much more so than even a decade ago, the most highly accomplished neuroscientists in the world today view the sophistication of the brain's associative powers with ever growing admiration. As one scientist has suggested, "if the brain were simple enough for us to understand it, we would be too simple to understand it."[19]

Let me again stress that software applications have now become a vital part of the design professions, and therefore their mastery should be an important goal of architectural education. But should the training of design students take place solely through the use of the computer? I think few would argue this case, but the direction of our architectural curricula is suggesting otherwise. It is now possible in many schools to enter a graduate program with a degree in another field and have little or no design training other than on the computer. At the same time, the numbers of non-specialized courses, such as might be offered in the humanities, has, over the years, been declining. My concerns are therefore threefold:

1   The computer, as the first tool of design, tends to have a leveling effect on presentational techniques and, arguably, design originality.
2   Computers tend to dematerialize design thinking and result in abstractions far removed from the world of human sensory experience.
3   Computer design tends to underutilize the innate capacities of the human brain for creative thinking.

And whereas older architects, who have been trained in traditional ways, can overcome these problems because of their experience, I would argue that younger architects who have never had such training are less likely to be able to do so.

Leveling Effect

Walk through the year-end reviews at any school of architecture and – if you are old enough to remember the presentations of a decade or two ago – you will notice several things. First, it is the rare student at the upper level who invests any hand talent in the design presentation. Second, sketches, study models, or finished models are rapidly becoming extinct. Third, the glossy paper on which nearly all presentations are printed is now standardized in width and quality, thanks to the limits of the printer in the computer lab. Fourth, and most seriously, all of the presentations are remarkably similar: both in graphic techniques, presentational atmospherics, and worse still, in the similarities of building design. This is also not just a local problem, because the portfolios of Asian applicants to our graduate programs are no different from those of North American, South American, or European applicants, which should not be surprising since all were crafted on the same laptops with the same software. And all of this leveling is taking place when we have, in many ways, the brightest generation of students ever to enter architectural programs.

Some will no doubt dispute these claims. One can argue that the model has been replaced by three-dimensional computer graphics, but are the two equally informative in a creative sense, particularly when the latter are often viewed on computer screens at minuscule scales? Is computer simulation really enhancing the student's powers of spatial thinking, or is it an abstract sectional manipulation achieved with very little effort, a formalistic exercise that at the same time detracts from other design concerns – such as the nature of materials or the craft of a good floor plan? What is the point of the enhanced realism of the latest software programs when the lush field of nature is still reduced to a few shades of green and the same gaseous cloud emerges in nearly every bird's-eye perspective? Who would deny that this photorealism has at the same time led to a homogeneity of approaches, forms, and materials – the unhappy byproduct of drop-down menus and limited design palettes? The formalist typology of Jean-Nicolas-Louis Durand, it seems, has been trumped tenfold by technology, but we still remain slaves to a few types. None of this is meant to deny that the computer is a tool that (like other tools, such as the pencil) has to be mastered early in the educational process. But would it not be better to delay its use in the design studio for a semester or two? And when it does become employed, should it not be used in conjunction with more conventional tools of design?

The leveling of design to a few "phatic" images is a more serious issue. Every generation of architectural students, to be sure, has had their preferred mentors, but something else seems to be occurring at the moment. The pool of the emulated now seems to have dwindled to a remarkably few architects, and the online images of their work, as Marshall McLuhan would appreciate, seem to be driving both presentational formats and design thinking. Perhaps it is just the easy accessibility to the most visited online "hits," but the creeping homogenization of forms, materials, and structure, if one may speak candidly, is a little uncanny. One could evoke here Jean Baudrillard's notion of hyper-reality, our society's undue enchantment with the simulation – if Neidich had not made precisely this point earlier.[20] As a profession, we seem to have become focused entirely on the image, and in the process are shunting aside all social, theoretical, and constructional interests. A few of the better students may rise above this level, but a surprisingly large number of students do not.

Abstraction

Not unconnected with this hyper-reality are the issues of dematerialization and abstraction in design. Is there any reason why the vast majority of computer designs by students employ glass as the principal exterior membrane? I think the reason is to be found not in the healthy appreciation of natural daylight in buildings or in the tremendous advances in glass technologies and their aesthetic possibilities, but rather in the limits of the tool itself. Computers are excellent media for selecting menu items and snapping lines, but, at the reduced scale at which students often work, the lines seem fated to remain scale-less lines on a darkened screen. But why, in the first place, do we unnecessarily narrow design thinking? Where is the conceptual menu for a spa's Alpine granite or a winery's rubble stone wall? In a not unexpected way, the abstractions of the computer aided design (CAD) systems have led to the underground-following of those few architects who purposely shun digital systems for design purposes, that is, of those who approach architecture simply with a coherent design philosophy, good materials, craftsmanship, and personal exploration. Peter Zumthor responds to today's trends by noting that design "starts from the premise of this physical, objective sensuousness of architecture, of its materials. To experience architecture in a concrete way means to touch, see, hear, and smell it. To discover and consciously work with these qualities – these are the themes of our teaching."[21] Rafael Moneo has even gone so far as to speak of investing design with something "lasting," almost a capricious idea in our computer age.[22]

If such approaches actually carry some sway with a few clients or corporate boards, it is because they are so far removed from the ephemeral forms of the digital world, and herein resides their sensuous appeal. There are no exotic cures needed to repair this mineral deficiency; the acquisition of a rich palette of material motives simply demands time and proper training. Travel and sketching, long a mainstay of architectural training, remains the quintessential way to see and feel firsthand what it means to understand architecture in a material and structural sense. History, theory, and a traditional grounding in the humanities can also bring depth to one's thinking. If neurological research says anything about this issue, it suggests the need for a discrete and highly varied environment: culturally, materially, and expressively. When faced with habituation (the replication of the same stimuli or materials over and over), the brain simply shuts down. A monotone environment, as so many computerized projects suggest, degrades the human condition.

Underutilization of the Brain

The popular understanding of the brain with analytical, logical, and language skills concentrated in the left side, while creative, emotional, and spatial activities are concentrated in the right, is of course a simplification. The primary areas for language and speech, as we have seen, are generally located in the left temporal and frontal lobes, while much of the processing of emotions, spatial thinking, and generalization take place in the right hemisphere. Nevertheless, the problem is a complex one.

What the scanning technologies are demonstrating is that the neural maps of our movements and thought processes tend to engage many areas of the brain at the same time and are rarely concentrated on just one side or another. It has long been assumed, for instance, that the left half of the brain with its linguistic and reasoning abilities was the more important one, even though Albert Einstein famously noted that he always thought mathematically not in words but in images. Thus scientists have for years debated whether mathematical intuition, for example, depended on analytical competence or visual-spatial powers. Such debates are now being answered. One functional magnetic resonance (fMRI) study has recently documented that exact arithmetic reasoning takes place in the left temporal lobes in the areas associated with linguistic skills, while approximate arithmetic thought dealing with such things as generalization and conceptualization takes place in the bilateral visual-spatial areas of the parietal lobes.[23] Another study with a positron emission tomography (PET) scan has shown that inductive reasoning activates mostly left-brain regions (frontal, temporal, and limbic areas), while deductive reasoning (the drawing of inferences from a larger principle) engages the frontal, temporal, and limbic areas of the right hemisphere.[24] These scanning images thus demonstrate that induction and deduction – in a classical sense, two contrary philosophical schools – are in fact two different neurological processes.

Antonio Damasio, through his own experiments, has said that the critical human ability to define a "self," that is, to represent the world through the modifications it causes the body proper, is located within "the brain's somatosensory complex, especially that of the right hemisphere in humans."[25] His team also followed the complex maps involved with the experience of emotions with PET scans, and one particular study involving the feeling of "joy" demonstrated significantly more activity in the right hemisphere than in the left.[26] Similarly, our uniquely human ability to keep time, as in music, takes place on the right side. We also saw earlier that the small area that flares up at the moment of creative (verbal) insight is located on the superior temporal gyrus of the right hemisphere, that is, it is an area that becomes active after the left half of the brain fails to solve the problem.[27] The explanation given by the scientists for this phenomenon – the right brain's aptitude for "coarse semantic coding" – is significant because another recent study has shown that while linguistic matters are generally limited to the left hemisphere, the "coarse semantic coding" of the right side springs into action in such high-level language tasks as comprehending a joke![28] Apparently the analytical areas of the brain are unable to perform this task.

It can therefore be said, with much qualification, that the left hemisphere of the brain tends to be concerned with analysis, language, and detail, while the right side seeks synthesis through the forces of intuition, emotion, spontaneity, and imagination. This is not a dramatic breakthrough, as we have generally known for some time that people have aptitudes, and that accountants, for instance, have a different way of "looking at things" than sculptors. If a few architects are able to develop both skills equally, most architects tend to have one or the other strength. As we have long known, the best architectural partnerships – like that of Adler and Sullivan – meld people with different talents.

This should also be true for architectural education. A well-rounded education should foster development in all areas of the brain for obvious reasons, not the least of which is that it will allow those with one propensity or the other to find their particular voice and develop their particular strength. But here, arguably, is where our emphasis on the computer as a tool for design is misplaced. Composing an elevation with a CAD program is not the same as sketching with a pencil. An exercise in spatial play on a computer screen is not the same thing as tearing cardboard and gluing together a study model. For one thing, the latter activities are slower and much more deliberative processes; for another, they almost certainly engage other areas of the brain. Drawing with a crayon is a tactile, mostly right-brain experience; clicking a mouse is a very different one. If some architects gently sway or hum while sketching on paper, it is the rare person who operates a mouse other than with swift jerky movements. Does this say something about the value of "human rhythm" and what parts of the brain are engaged?

V. S. Ramachandran tells the story of a seven-year old autistic child with incredible drawing skills. He ascribed her talent to the fact that with so many other areas of her brain shut down, the brain could allocate "all her attentional resources to the one module that's still functioning, her right parietal".[29] This veracity of this contention was supported by the rapid decline in the child's artistic gift as she grew older and her language skills on the left side began to develop. Ramachandran also cites neurological cases of patients with early dementia who, as their frontal and temporal lobes deteriorated, began to produce beautiful paintings and drawings with the right parietal lobe still intact. Oliver Sacks has noted the unusual musical abilities of children with Williams Syndrome, a unique form of mental retardation that combines intellectual strengths with severe deficits. Here the neuronal lack of development of the undersized occipital and parietal lobes is offset by the rich neuronal networks of the oversized temporal lobes, especially the planum temporale of the auditory cortex, which is critical for both speech and music.[30] It therefore seems – and this is a very important point – that the various parts of the brain indulge in a zero-sum game. "Use it or lose it" as the saying goes, or, in the case of the architect, develop the brain's full capacity for creative thinking or forever be condemned to work with limited neuronal circuits and lesser associative patterns. This is no longer educational theory or psychological speculation, but a biological fact.

If we want to continue to speak of architecture as a creative process, we have to take responsibility for training creative architects. An abundance of information about the brain, as this book has attempted to show, is now coming to light, and we should avail ourselves of it, even if much of it, including this chapter, should be taken in a provisional sense. We now have a better appreciation for how the brain works, how important it is for the brain to draw upon all of its specialized areas and potential strengths to foster creativity. If "coarse semantic coding" and "hyper-connectivity" are now deemed to be two of the linchpins of the creativie at, we should be able to find a way to draw out rather than inhibit these two powers. Aspects of architectural education, only a few years ago, did a fairly good job in recognizing the complexity of the human brain, and the necessity for design training to develop such resources. Things have changed, to be sure.

The computer, as it should once again be stressed, is now a vital part of the education of the architect because it is an invaluable organizational tool of production and in its own way can bring much to the design process. At the same time, its use should not be exclusive of other media if, indeed, it pejoratively affects the way we come to think about materials or design – that is, if it acts in its peculiar way as a "coefficient of friction" on our associative powers of creative thinking. Some, if not many, will contest this point, but I believe that neurological evidence is now amassing to support the contention. If we are going to err in an educational sense, for now I would rather err on the side of Pierre de Meuron, who recently commented:

> The computer is an important tool – no one could do without it – but for me it's only a tool and it doesn't replace thinking. It can make you disconnected and autistic, and that's why we always say, "Bring it out of the computer, print it up, use paper, use physicalities and models to understand and anticipate what this thing will be in the end: something physical, something real, something for people.[31]

Endnotes

Introduction

1 See Semir Zeki, *Inner Vision: An Exploration of Art and the Brain* (Oxford: Oxford University Press, 1999).

2 See John Onians, *Neuroarthistory: From Aristotle and Pliny to Baxandall and Zeki* (New Haven: Yale University Press, 2007). Onians promises at least two larger volumes to follow in the near future.

3 One of the outcomes of this collaboration was an interactive film *Neurotopographics*, which was shown at the Gimpel Fils Gallery in London in January 2008. More work is promised in this regard.

4 See the press release for the Association of Neuroesthetics at www.association-of-neuroesthetics.org.

5 Taken from the mission statement of the Academy of Neuroscience for Architecture, which can be found at their website http://www.anfarch.org.

Chapter 1

1 Leon Battista Alberti, *On the Art of Building in Ten Books*, trans. Joseph Rykwert, Neil Leach, and Robert Tavernor (Cambridge, MA: MIT Press, 1988), p. 5. For an extensive discussion of the Latin meaning of Vitruvius's words, see Indra Kagis McEwen, *Vitruvius: Writing the Body of Architecture* (Cambridge, MA: MIT Press, 2003).

2 On the life and work of Alberti, see Franco Borsi, *Leon Battista Alberti: The Complete Works*, trans. Rudolf G. Carpanini (New York: Electa, 1986); Joan Gadol, *Leon Battista Alberti: Universal Man of the Early Renaissance* (Chicago: University of Chicago Press, 1969). See also Liane Lefaivre, *Leon Battista Alberti's Hypnerotomachia Poliphili: Re-cognizing*

the Architectural Body in the Early Italian Renaissance (Cambridge, MA: MIT Press, 1997).

3   Leon Battista Alberti, *On Painting and On Sculpture*, ed. and trans. Cecil Grayson (London: Phaidon, 1972), p. 95.

4   Ibid., p. 33.

5   Ibid.

6   Ibid., p. 39.

7   Ibid., p. 55.

8   Ibid., p. 103.

9   Ibid., p. 79.

10 Ibid., p. 95.

11 Vitruvius, *Ten Books on Architecture*, trans. Ingrid D. Rowland, Commentary and Illustrations by Thomas Noble Howe (Cambridge: Cambridge University Press, 1999), Bk 3:1.2.

12 Alberti, *On the Art of Building*, Bk. 9:5, p. 301.

13 Ibid., Bk. 3:12, p. 81.

14 Ibid., Bk. 6:12, p. 180; Bk. 3:7, p. 71; Bk. 3:12, p. 81.

15 Ibid., Bk. 3:12; pp. 79, 219.

16 Ibid., Bk. 5:17, p. 146; Bk. 9:3, p. 296.

17 Ibid. Prol., p. 5.

18 Ibid., Bk. 1:1, p. 7.

19 Ibid., Bk. 1:9, p. 23.

20 Ibid., Bk. 6:5, p. 163.

21 Vitruvius, *Ten Books on Architecture*, Bk. 3:1.1

22 Alberti, *On the Art of Building*, Bk. 6:2, p. 156.

23 De natura deorum, trans. by H. Rackham (Cambridge, MA: Harvard University Press, 1979). 1:28.79.

24 Alberti, *On the Art of Building*, Bk. 6:2, p. 156.

25 Ibid., Bk. 6:4, p. 158.

26 Ibid., Bk. 6:6, p. 164.

27 Ibid., Bk. 6:13, p. 183.

28 Ibid., Bk. 8:9, p. 287.

29 Ibid., Bk. 7:1, p. 191.

30 Ibid., Bk. 7:16, p. 240.

31 This is the summary of Thomas Noble Howe's commentary on Book Four of, Vitruvius's *Ten Books on Architecture*, p. 211.

32 Alberti, *On the Art of Building*, Bk. 9:5, p. 302.

33 Ibid.

34 Cicero, *Orator*, trans. H. M. Hubbell (Cambridge, MA: Harvard University Press, 1971), 24:81.

35 Alberti, *On the Art of Building*, Bk. 9:5, p. 303.

36 Vitruvius, *Ten Books on Architecture*, Bk. 1:2.4, p. 25.

37 Cicero, *De natura*, 2:27.69.
38 Alberti, *On the Art of Building*, Bk. 9:8, p. 312.
39 Vitruvius, *Ten Books on Architecture*, Bk. 3:3.13, p. 50.
40 Ibid., see Bk. 3:3.13, 3.5.4, 4:4.2–3, among other places.
41 *Filarete's Treatise on Architecture: Being the Treatise by Antonio di Piero Averlino, Known as Filarete*, trans. John R. Spencer, 2 vols (New Haven: Yale University Press, 1965), Bk. 1, Folio 6r, p. 12.
42 Ibid., Bk. 7, Folio 49r, p. 85.
43 Ibid., Bk. 2, Folio 7v–8r, pp. 15–16.
44 Ibid., Bk. 2, Folio, 8r, p. 16.
45 Ibid., Bk. 8, Folio 56v, p. 97; Bk. 8, 55r, p. 94.
46 Ibid., Bk. 1, 2v, p. 6.
47 For a discussion of these three manuscripts, see Richard J. Betts, "On the Chronology of Francesco di Giorgio's Treatises: New Evidence from an Unpublished Manuscript," *The Journal of the Society of Architectural Historians* (March 1977), vol. 36 no. 1, pp. 3–14. See also Joseph Rykwert's discussion of Francesco di Giorgio in *The Dancing Column: On Order in Architecture* (Cambridge, MA: MIT Press, 1996).
48 Ibid., p. 8. Cited from Spencer Codex and trans. Betts.
49 For biographies of his multi-faceted thought, see the writings of Martin Kemp, especially *Leonardo da Vinci: The Marvellous Works of Nature and Man* (Oxford: Oxford University Press, 2006) and *Leonardo da Vinci: Experience, Experiment and Design* (Princeton: Princeton University Press, 2006).
50 See Erwin Panofsky, *The Codex Huygens and Leonardo da Vinci's Art Theory: The Pierpont Morgan Library Codex M.A. 1139* (Westwood, CT: Greenwood Press, 1940). See also Carlo Pedretti's discussion of the codex in *The Literary Works of Leonardo da Vinci*, vol. 1, commentary by Carlo Pedretti, (Berkeley: University of California Press, 1977), pp. 48–75.
51 See Plate 5 in the Panofsky text, or Plates 8 in the Pedretti text.
52 Kemp, *Experience*, p. 87.
53 Ibid., p. 104.
54 See Pedretti *The Literary Works*, p. 54.
55 Kemp, *Experience*, p. 124.
56 Luca Pacioli, *De Divina Proportione*. Translation cited from Rudolf Wittkower, *Architectural Principles in the Age of Humanism* (London: Academy Editions, 1973), p. 15.
57 Kemp, *The Marvellous Works*, p. 185.
58 Ibid., pp. 207, 240.
59 Michelangelo, Letter to unknown Cardinal, December 1550, no. 358, in *The Letters of Michelangelo*, trans. E. H. Ramsden, 1537–63 (Stanford: Stanford University Press, 1963), p. 129. The addressee of the letter has

been variously named as Cardinal Ridolfo Pio da Carpi or Cardinal Marcello Cervini. Even the date of the letter is uncertain, and it has been assigned to 1550 and 1560.

60 Palladio, *The Four Books of Architecture*, trans. Isaac Ware (New York: Dover, 1965; orig. 1738), p. 1.

Chapter 2

1   Claude Perrault, *Les Dix livres d'architecture de Vitruve*, 1684 edn. (Paris: Pierre Mardaga, 1984), p. 79n.16.

2   On the life and ideas of Claude Perrault, see Wolfgang Herrmann's classic study, *The Theory of Claude Perrault* (London: A. Zwemmer, 1973).

3   René Descartes, *Rules for the Direction of the Mind* (1628), in *The Philosophical Writings of Descartes*, trans. John Cottingham, Robert Stoothoff, and Dugald Murdoch (Cambridge: Cambridge University Press, 1985), 1: 13.

4   On the history of the construction of the Louvre see Robert W. Berger, *The Palace of the Sun: The Louvre of Louis XIV* (University Park: Pennsylvania State University, 1993).

5   Claude Perrault, *Les Dix livres*, p. 79n.16.

6   On the quarrel, see Hippolyte Rigault, *Histoire de la Querrelle des Anciens et des Modernes* (Paris: Hachette, 1856).

7   The best discussion of Blondel's theory in English is found in Herrmann's *Theory of Claude Perrault*.

8   See Claude Perrault, *Voyage à Bordeaux* (Paris: Renouard, 1909).

9   Vitruvius *On Architecture*, trans. Frank Granger (Cambridge, MA: Harvard University Press, 1970), Bk 3:3.8, pp. 174–5.

10 Claude Perrault, *Ordonnance for the Five Kinds of Columns after the Method of the Ancients*, trans. Indra Kagis McEwen (Santa Monica: Getty Publication Programs, 1993).

11 Vitruvius *On Architecture*, Bk. 4:1.8, p. 207.

12 Perrault, *Ordonnance*, p. 49.

13 Ibid., p. 51.

14 On Laugier, see Wolfgang Herrmann, *Laugier and Eighteenth Century French Theory* (London: Zwemmer, 1962).

15 Marc-Antoine Laugier, *Essay on Architecture*, trans. Wolfgang Herrmann (London: Hennessey & Ingalls, 1977), p. 2.

16 Ibid., p. 4.

17 See Jean-Jacques Rousseau, "Has the Restoration of the Sciences and Arts Tended to Purify Morals?" (1750), in *The First and Second*

Discourse, trans. Roger D. Masters and Judith R. Masters (New York: St. Martin's Press, 1964).

18 Laugier, *Essay on Architecture*, p. 16.

19 Julien-David Le Roy, *The Ruins of the Most Beautiful Monuments of Greece* (1770 edition), trans. David Britt (Los Angeles: Getty Publication Programs, 2004). The introduction by Robin Middleton provides a good initiation into both the Greco-Roman debate and the thought of Le Roy.

20 Julien-David Le Roy, *Les Ruines des plus beaux monuments de la Grece* (Paris: Guerin & Delatour, 1758), Part 2, p. ii (omitted in 1770 edn.). See J. J. Winckelmann, *Reflections on the Imitation of Greek Works in Painting and Sculpture*, trans. Elfriede Heyer and Roger C. Norton (La Salle, IL: Open Court, 1987).

21 Julien-David Le Roy, *Les Ruines*, Part 2, p. vi.

22 Julien-David Le Roy, *Histoire de la disposition et des formes differentes que les chrétiens ont données à leur temples, depuis le Règne de Constantin la Grand jusqu'à nous* (Paris: Desaind & Saillant, 1764), p. 50. Translated by David Britt; the passage is repeated in Le Roy *The Ruins*, p. 369.

23 Ibid., p. 55; trans. Britt, p. 370.

24 Ibid., p. 59; trans. Britt, p. 372.

25 Ibid., p. 63; trans. Britt, p. 373.

26 Le Roy, (1770 edn.), *The Ruins*, pp. 367–86.

Chapter 3

1 Edmund Burke, *A Philosophical Inquiry into the Origin of Our Ideas of the Sublime and Beautiful*, in *The Works of Edmund Burke* (London: G. Bell & Sons, 1913), 1:158.

2 John Locke, *An Essay Concerning Human Understanding*, ed. Alexander Campbell Fraser (New York: Dover, 1959), 1:121–4.

3 See "On the Association of Ideas," Ibid., pp. 527–35.

4 Allan Ramsay, "A Dialogue on Taste" (1755), in *The Investigator* (London: 1762), p. 33.

5 David Hume, "On the Standard of Taste," in *Four Dissertations* (Bristol: Thoemmes Press, 1995), pp. 208–9.

6 Ibid., pp. 214–15.

7 Edmund Burke, *A Philosophical Inquiry*, pp. 85, 53.

8 See Joseph Addison, the *Spectator* (London: George Routledge & Sons, n.d.), 412.

9 Burke, *A Philosophical Inquiry*, p. 74.

10   Ibid., p. 100.

11   Ibid., pp. 103–5.

12   Ibid., p. 108.

13   Ibid.

14   Ibid., p. 121.

15   Ibid., p. 153.

16   Ibid.

17   For a brief history of this movement, see my *Modern Architectural Theory: A Historical Survey, 1673–1968* (New York: Cambridge University Press, 2005), pp. 51–63.

18   William Gilpin, *An Essay on Prints: Containing Remarks on the Principles of Picturesque Beauty* (London, 1768), pp. 1–2.

19   See Joshua Reynolds, *Discourses on Art*, ed. Robert R. Wark (New Haven: Yale University Press, 1959), 13th discourse, p. 240.

20   Uvedale Price, *Essays on the Picturesque as Compared with the Sublime and the Beautiful; and, on the Use of Studying Pictures for the Purpose of Improving Real Landscape* (London: Mawman, 1810; orig. 1794), 1: 22.

21   Ibid., 1. 87–8.

22   Richard Payne Knight, *An Analytical Inquiry into the Principles of Taste*, 2nd edn. (London: Mews-Gate and J. White, 1805), p. 196.

23   Ibid., p. 54.

24   Ibid., p. 99.

25   Ibid., p. 146.

26   Ibid., p. 196.

27   Ibid., p. 83.

28   Ibid., pp. 426–7.

29   Ibid., p. 469.

30   See Robert Fleming, *Robert Adam and His Circle in Edinburgh and Rome* (London: John Murray, 1962), p. 303.

31   Preface, *The Works in Architecture of Robert and James Adam, Esquires (1773–78)*, ed. Robert Oresko (London: Academy Editions, 1975), pp. 45–6n.

32   Uvedale Price, "An Essay on Architecture and Buildings as connected with Scenery" (1798), in *Essays on the Picturesque*, 2: 212.

33   Ibid., p. 260.

34   Knight, *An Analytical Inquiry*, p. 160, 223.

35   Ibid., p. 215.

36   Ibid., pp. 220–1.

37   Ibid., p. 225.

38   Ibid., p. 172.

Chapter 4

1 The classic study of Kant's ideas is Ernst Cassirer, *Kant's Life and Thought*, trans. James Haden (New Haven: Yale University Press, 1981; orig. 1918).

2 Immanuel Kant, Preface to the second edition, *Critique of Pure Reason*, trans. Norman Kemp Smith (New York: St. Martin's Press, 1965), p. 22.

3 Immanuel Kant, *Critique of Judgement*, trans. J. H. Bernard (New York: Hafner Press, 1951), p. 34.

4 See John H. Zammito's discussion of this term in *The Genesis of Kant's Critique of Judgment* (Chicago: University of Chicago Press, 1992), pp. 89–105, 266–7.

5 Stephan Körner, *Kant* (New Haven: Yale University Press, 1955), p. 181.

6 Cassirer, *Kant's Life and Thought*, p. 287.

7 Kant, *Critique of Judgement*, p. 61.

8 Cassirer, *Kant's Life and Thought*, p. 312.

9 Kant, *Critique of Judgement*, p. 73.

10 Ibid., p. 37.

11 Ibid., p. 175.

12 Ibid., p. 180.

13 August Schlegel, *August Schlegels Vorlesungen über schöne Litteratur und Kunst*, Part One, 1801–2 (Heilbronn, 1884; reprint Nendeln: Krause, 1968), p. 160.

14 Ibid., p. 165.

15 Ibid., p. 168.

16 Cicero, *De oratore*, 3.180.

17 August Schlegel, *August Schlegels Vorlesungen über schöne Litteratur und Kunst*, p. 179.

18 Friedrich Wilhelm Joseph Schelling, *The Philosophy of Art*, ed. and trans. Douglas W. Stott (Minneapolis: University Press, 1989), p. 166.

19 Ibid., p. 168.

20 Ibid., p. 173.

21 Ibid., p. 165.

22 Arthur Schopenhauer, *On the Fourfold Root of the Principle of Sufficient Reason: A Philosophical Essay*, trans. E. F. J. Payne (La Salle, IL: Open Court, 1974), p. 77.

23 Ibid., p. 78

24 Ibid., p. 79.

25 Arthur Schopenhauer, *The World as Will and Representation*, trans. E. F. J. Payne (New York: Dover Publications, 1969), §43, p. 214.

26 Ibid. pp. 214–15. "Therefore the beauty of a building is certainly to be found in the evident and obvious suitability of every part, not to the outward arbitrary purpose of man (to the extent the world belongs to practical architecture), but directly to the stability of the whole. The position, size, and form of every part must have so necessary a relation to this stability that if it were possible to remove some part, the whole would inevitably collapse."

27 Ibid., p. 214.

28 Ibid.

29 Ibid., p. 215.

Chapter 5

1 For an overview of Schinkel's life and career see Bary Bergdoll, *Karl Friedrich Schinkel: An Architecture for Prussia* (New York: Rizzoli, 1994).

2 Goerd Peschken (ed.), *Das architektonische Lehrbuch* (Berlin: Deutscher Kunstverlag, 1979), p. 22. Peschken regards these comments as Schinkel's first effort to write a book on architecture, and assigns it to 1804 or to the next few years.

3 Ibid.

4 Ibid., p. 28. Schinkel's comments were made in response to Aloys Hirt's *Die Baukunst nach den Grundsätzen der Alten* (1809).

5 Ibid., p. 148.

6 Ibid., p. 58.

7 Ibid., p. 49.

8 Ibid., p. 45.

9 Ibid., p. 59.

10 Ibid., p. 150.

11 For a good summary of Bötticher's life and ideas in English, see Mitchell Schwarzer, "Ontology and Representation in Karl Bötticher's Theory of Tectonics," *Journal of the Society of Architectural Historians* (September 1993), vol. 52, no. 3, pp. 267–80. See also Kenneth Frampton's treatment of Bötticher in *Studies in Tectonic Culture: The Poetics of Construction in Nineteenth and Twentieth Century Architecture* (Cambridge, MA: MIT Press, 1995), pp. 81–4.

12 Karl Bötticher, "Entwickelung der Formen der hellenischen Tektonik," *Allgemeine Bauzeitung* (1840), vol. 5, p. 316.

13 Ibid., p. 317.

14 Ibid., p. 328.

15 Karl Bötticher, *Die Tektonik der Hellenen* (Potsdam: Ferdinand Riegel, 1852), vol. 1, p. xiv.

16 Ibid., pp. xiv–xv.

17 Ibid., p. 28.

18 On the life and practice of Semper, see my *Gottfried Semper: Architect of the Nineteenth Century* (New Haven: Yale University Press, 1996).

19 Gottfried Semper, letter to Eduard Vieweg, September 23, 1843, Semper Archiv, ETH-Hönggerberg.

20 It was Wolfgang Herrmann who uncovered the date of Semper's book request. See his "Semper and the Archaeologist Bötticher," in *Gottfried Semper: In Search of Architecture* (Cambridge, MA: MIT Press, 1984), pp. 249–52.

21 Cited from Herrmann, "Semper and the Archaeologist Bötticher," p. 141. Semper's remarks were apparently deleted by the editor in the published version of the text.

22 See Harry Francis Mallgrave, "Gottfried Semper, London Lecture of Autumn 1854: 'On Architectural Symbols'," *Res 9: Anthropology and Aesthetics* (Spring 1985), p. 61.

23 Ibid., p. 63.

24 Gottfried Semper, *Style in the Technical and Tectonic Arts; or, Practical Aesthetics*, trans. Harry Francis Mallgrave and Michael Robinson (Los Angeles: Getty Publications, 2004), p. 342.

25 Ibid.

26 Ibid., p. 343.

27 Ibid., p. 728.

28 Ibid., p. 646.

29 Ibid., p. 783.

30 Ibid., p. 646.

31 Ibid., p. 732.

32 Gottfried Semper, the manuscript "The Attributes of Formal Beauty" (c.1856/1859), in Herrmann, *Gottfried Semper*, p. 219.

33 Semper, *Style*, p. 249.

34 Ibid., pp. 438–9n.85.

35 See my discussion of the third volume in Mallgrave, *Gottfried Semper*, pp. 302–8.

36 Gottfried Semper, "On Architectural Styles" (1869), in *The Four Elements of Architecture and Other Writings*, trans. Harry Francis Mallgrave and Wolfgang Herrmann (New York: Cambridge University Press, 1989), p. 284.

37 For a discussion of Semper's influence in Chicago, see Roula Geraniotis's informative essay, "German Architectural Theory and Practice in Chicago,

1850–1900," *Winterthur Portfolio* (1986) *vol.* 21, no. 4 pp. 293–306. See also my *Modern Architectural Theory: A Historical Survey, 1673–1968* (New York: Cambridge University Press, 2005), pp. 164–6, 195–220.

Chapter 6

1 Heinrich Wölfflin, "Prolegomena to a Psychology of Architecture," in Robert Vischer, Conrad Fiedler, Heinrich Wölfflin, Adolf Göller, Adolf Hildebrand, and August Schmarsow, *Empathy, Form, and Space: Problems in German Aesthetics 1873–1893*, trans. Harry Francis Mallgrave and Eleftherios Ikonomou (Santa Monica: Getty Publication Programs, 1994), p. 149.

2 Friedrich Theodor Vischer, *Aesthetik; oder, Wissenschaft des Schönen*, ed. Robert Vischer, 2nd edn. (Munich: Meyer & Jessen, 1922–3), vol. 3, sec. 559.

3 Friedrich Theodor Vischer, "Kritik meiner Äesthetik," in *Kritische Gänge* (Stuttgart: Cotta, 1866), 5: 143. Vischer at this later date was also influenced by Hermann Lotze's *Microcosmos* (1856–64).

4 Ibid., cited from 2nd edn. (Munich: Meyer & Jessen, 1922–3), 4: 316–22.

5 Karl Albert Scherner, *Das Leben des Traums* (Berlin: Heinrich Schindler, 1861), p. 207.

6 Robert Vischer, "On the Optical Sense of Form: A Contribution to Aesthetics," in Vischer, et al. *Empathy, Form, and Space*, p. 92. The text was originally published as *Über das optische Formgefühl: Ein Beitrag zur Aesthetik* (Leipzig: Herrmann Credner, 1873).

7 Ibid., p. 95

8 Ibid., p. 105.

9 Ibid., p. 104.

10 Ibid., p. 117.

11 Robert Vischer, "Der ästhetische Akt und die reine Form," in *Drei Schriften zum ästhetischen Formproblem* (Halle: Max Niemeyer, 1927), p. 52.

12 Robert Vischer, "On the Optical Sense of Form: A Contribution to Aesthetics," in Vischer, et al., *Empathy, Form, and Space*, p. 99.

13 On its influence on Endell and van de Velde, see my *Modern Architectural Theory: A Historical Survey, 1673–1968* (New York: Cambridge University Press, 2005), pp. 211–13.

14 Heinrich Wolfflin, "Prolegomena to a Psychology of Architecture," in Vischer et al., *Empathy, Form, and Space*, p. 149. The text was originally published as *Prolegomena zu einer Psychologie der Architektur* (Munich: Kgl. Hof- & Univeresitäts-Buchdruckerei, 1886).

15 Ibid., p. 151.
16 Ibid., p. 159.
17 Ibid., p. 152.
18 Ibid., p. 179.
19 Ibid., p. 182.
20 See Heinrich Wölfflin, *Renaissance and Baroque*, trans. Kathrin Simon (Ithaca: Cornell University Press, 1966). See especially the section "The Causes of the Change in Style," pp. 71–88.
21 Adolf Göller, "What is the Cause of Perpetual Style Change?" in Vischer et al., *Empathy, Form, and Space*, p. 198. The essay "Was ist die Ursache der immerwährenden Stilveränderung in der Architektur?" appeared in Göller's book *Zur Aesthetik der Architektur: Vorträge und Studien* (Stuttgart: Konrad Wittwer, 1887), pp. 1–48.
22 Ibid., p. 195.
23 Ibid., p. 202.
24 Adolf Göller, "Wie entsteht die Schönheit der Maassverhältnisse und das Stilgefühl?" in *Zur Aesthetik der Architektur*, p. 54.
25 Adolf Göller, *Die Entstehung der architektonischen Stilformen: Eine Geschichte der Baukunst nach dem Werden und Wandern der Formgedanken* (Stuttgart: Konrad Wittwer, 1888), p. 448.
26 Cornelius Gurlitt, "Göller's ästhetische Lehre," *Deutsche Bauzeitung* (December 17, 1887), vol. 21, pp. 602–4, 606–7.

Chapter 7

1 Kurt Koffka, "On the Structure of the Unconscious," in *The Unconscious: A Symposium* (New York: Alfred A. Knopf, 1928), p. 65.
2 See Adolf Zeising, *Neue Lehre von den Proportionen des menschlichen Körpers (1854), Aesthetische Forschungen* (1855); Eduard Hanslick, *The Beautiful in Music: A Contribution to the Revisal of Musical Aesthetics* (1854, trans. into Eng.1891); Conrad Fiedler, *Über die Beurtheilung von Werken der bildenden Kunst* (1876), "Bemerkungen über Wesen und Geschichte der Baukunst" (1878); Robert Zimmermann, *Aesthetik* (1958–65); Gustav Fechner, *Elemente der Psychophysik* (1860); Hermann Lotze, *Microkosmos* (1857–64), *Geschichte der Aesthetik in Deutschland* (1868).
3 Helmholtz's book was translated into English by Alexander J. Ellis. See *On the Sensations of Tone as a Physiological Basis for the Theory of Music* (New York: Dover, 1954).
4 See Wilhelm Wundt, *Principles of Physiological Psychology*, trans. Edward Bradford Titchener (1904), in "Classics in the History of Psychology,"

an internet resource developed by Christopher D. Green, York University, Toronto, Ontario, Introduction, p. 2.

5   See Eleftherios Ikonomou's discussion of Stumpf in relation to the later theories of August Schmarsow in *Empathy, Form, and Space: Problems in German Aesthetics 1873–1893*, trans. Harry Francis Mallgrave and Eleftherios Ikonomou (Santa Monica: Getty Publication Programs, 1994), p. 60.

6   The term "Gestalt" was first popularized by Christian von Ehrenfels in a paper he wrote in 1890. For a comprehensive treatment of the intellectual context of Gestalt theory, see Mitchell G. Ash, *Gestalt Psychology in German Culture, 1890–1967: Holism and the Quest for Objectivity* (New York: Cambridge University Press, 1995).

7   Max Wertheimer, "Experimentelle Studien über das Sehen von Bewegung," *Zeitschrift für Psychologie* (1912), 61, pp.161–265.

8   Kurt Koffka, *Principles of Gestalt Psychology* (New York: Harcourt, Brace and Company: 1935), p. 53.

9   Ibid., p. 110.

10   Wolfgang Köhler, *Gestalt Psychology: An Introduction to New Concepts in Modern Psychology* (New York: Liveright Publishing Corporation, 1947; orig.1929), p. 139.

11   Erich M. von Hornbostel, "The Unity of the Senses," trans. Elizabeth Koffka and Warren Vinton, in *Psyche* (1927), vol. 7, no.28, p. 87.

12   Kurt Goldstein, *The Organism: A Holistic Approach to Biology Derived from Pathological Data in Man* (New York: Zone Books: 2000; orig. 1934), p. 214.

13   Koffka, *Principles of Gestalt Psychology*, p. 67.

14   Köhler, *Gestalt Psychology*, p. 103.

15   Wolfgang Köhler, *Dynamics in Psychology* (New York: Washington Square Press, 1965), pp. 61–2.

16   Koffka, "On the Structure of the Unconscious," p. 58.

17   Ibid., p. 65.

18   Koffka, *Principles of Gestalt Psychology*, p. 51.

19   See, for instance, George Lakoff and Mark Johnson, *Philosophy in the Flesh: The Embodied Mind and its Challenge to Western Thought* (New York: Basic Books, 1999), p. 13.

20   Wolfgang Köhler, *Die physischen Gestalten in Ruhe und im stationären Zustand* (Braunschweig, 1920), p. 193. Cited from Koffka, *Principles of Gestalt Psychology*, p. 62.

21   Köhler, *Gestalt Psychology*, 61.

22   Wolfgang Köhler, "The New Psychology and Physics" (1930), in Wolfgang Köhler, *The Selected Papers of Wolfgang Köhler* ed. Mary Henle (New York: Liveright, 1971), p. 240.

23 Wolfgang Köhler, "An Old Pseudoproblem" (1929), in Köhler, *The Selected Papers*, p. 138.

24 Köhler, *Dynamics in Psychology*, p. 115.

25 See Goldstein, *The Organism*, p. 307. For his critique of isomorphism, see p. 301.

26 See R. B. Tootel, M. S. Silverman, E. Switkes, and R. L. De Valois, "Deoxyglucose Analysis of Retinoptic Organization in Primate Cortex," *Science* (1982), vol. 218, pp. 902–4.

27 Rudolf Arnheim, *Art and Visual Perception: A Psychology of the Creative Eye* (Berkeley: University of California Press, 1974, orig. 1954), p. 445.

28 Ibid., p. 450.

29 Ibid.

30 Ibid., p. 454.

31 Rudolf Arnheim, *Visual Thinking* (Berkeley: University of California Press, 1969), p. 13.

32 Ibid., 19.

33 Ibid., p. 27, 37.

34 Ibid., p. 233.

35 Merlin Donald, *Origins of the Modern Mind: Three Stages in the Evolution of Culture* and Cognition (Cambridge, MA: Harvard University Press, 1991), p. 167.

36 In particular, Arnheim makes known his debt to Theodor Lipps's *Raumaesthetik und geometrisch-optische Täuschungen* (Leipzig: J. A. Barth, 1893–7).

37 Rudolf Arnheim, *The Dynamics of Architectural Form* (Berkeley: University of California Press, 1977), p. 2.

38 Ibid., p. 163.

39 Ibid., p. 179.

40 Ibid., pp. 183–8.

41 Ibid., p. 116.

42 Ibid., p. 120.

43 Ibid.

44 Ibid., p. 208.

45 Ibid.

46 Ibid., p. 209.

47 Ibid., p. 212.

48 Ibid., pp. 212–13.

Chapter 8

1 Richard Neutra, *Survival through Design* (London: Oxford University Press, 1954), p. 4

2   On Hayek's life and ideas, see Alan Ebenstein, *Friedrich Hayek: A Biography* (New York: Palgrave, 2001).

3   Friedrich Hayek, *The Sensory Order: An Inquiry into the Foundations of Theoretical Psychology* (Chicago: University of Chicago Press, 1976; orig. 1952), 8.46.

4   Ibid., 2.48.

5   Ibid., 1.21.

6   Friedrich Hayek, in Walter Weimer and David Palermo (eds), *Cognition and Symbolic Processes*, vol. 2 (Hillsdale, NJ: Lawrence Erlbaum associates, 1982), pp. 287–8; cited from Ebenstein, *Friedrich Hayek*, p. 150.

7   Hayek, *The Sensory Order*, 5.8.

8   Ibid., 5.17.

9   Ibid., 5.42.

10   Ibid., 5.41.

11   Ibid., 6.37.

12   Ibid., 6.47

13   Ibid., 2.3.

14   Ibid., 2.9, 2.11.

15   Ibid., 3.74.

16   Ibid., 7.15.

17   D. O. Hebb, *The Organization of Behavior: A Neuropsychological Theory* (New York: John Wiley & Sons, 1949).

18   Hayek, *The Sensory Order*, Preface, p. v.iii.

19   Hebb, *The Organization of Behavior*, p. 19.

20   Ibid., p. 58.

21   Ibid., p. 60.

22   Ibid., p. 62.

23   Ibid., p. 144.

24   Ibid., p. 166.

25   Neutra, *Survival through Design*, p. 3.

26   Ibid., p. 117.

27   Ibid., p. 245.

28   On the life and work of Neutra, see Thomas S. Hines, *Richard Neutra and the Search for Modern Architecture* (New York: Oxford University Press, 1982).

29   Neutra, *Survival through Design*, p. 118.

30   Ibid., p. 123.

31   Ibid., p. 137.

32   Ibid., p. 132.

33   Ibid., p. 142.

34   Ibid., p. 83.

35   Ibid., p. 229.

36   Ibid., pp. 59–60.
37   Ibid., pp. 129–30.
38   Ibid. p. 352.
39   It is perhaps a little more of a coincidence that its appearance roughly coincided with Amos H. Hawley's *Human Ecology: A Theory of Community Structure* (1950). Both books testify to how valuable research becomes lost from one generation to the next.

Chapter 9

1   Maurice Merleau-Ponty, *The Visible and the Invisible*, ed. Claude Lefort, trans. Alphonso Lingis (Evanston: Northwestern University Press, 1968), p. 248.
2   Maurice Merleau-Ponty, *The Structure of Behavior*, trans. Alden L. Fisher (Boston: Beacon Press, 1963; orig. 1942), p. 136.
3   Ibid., p. 156.
4   Maurice Merleau-Ponty, *Phenomenology of Perception*, trans. Colin Smith (London: Routledge & Kegan Paul, 1962; orig. 1945), p. 441.
5   Ibid., p. 326.
6   Ibid., p. 9.
7   Ibid., pp. 48–9.
8   Ibid., p. 61.
9   Ibid., p. 139.
10   Ibid., p. 106.
11   Ibid., p. 98.
12   Ibid., p. 136.
13   Ibid., p. 217.
14   Ibid., p. 258.
15   Ibid., p. 235.
16   Ibid., p. 456. Cited from *Pilote de guerre*, pp. 171–6.
17   This is the title, for instance, of Alphonse De Waelhens's "Foreword" to the second French edition of *Le Structure du comportement*.
18   Merleau-Ponty, *The Visible and the Invisible*, p. 133.
19   Ibid., p. 138.
20   Ibid., p. 123.
21   Ibid., p. 248.
22   Ibid., pp. 248–9.
23   Ibid., p. 152.
24   Steen Eiler Rasmussen, *Experiencing Architecture* (Cambridge, MA: MIT Press, 1964; orig. 1959), Preface.
25   Ibid., p. 36.

26   Ibid., p. 37.
27   Ibid., 48.
28   Ibid., p. 33.
29   ibid., p. 187.
30   Ibid., p. 17.
31   Ibid., p. 59.
32   Ibid., p. 70.
33   Christian Norberg-Schulz, *Intentions in Architecture* (Cambridge, MA: MIT Press, 1965; orig. 1963), p. 7.
34   Christian Norberg-Schulz, *Genius Loci: Towards a Phenomenology of Architecture* (New York: Rizzoli, 1980), p. 5.
35   Joseph Rykwert, *On Adam's House in Paradise: The Idea of the Primitive Hut in Architectural History* (Cambridge, MA: MIT Press, 1972).
36   With regard to his earlier writings, see especially "Meaning and Building" (1960) and "A Sitting Position – A Question of Method" (1965), both are in Rykwert's *The Necessity of Artifice* (New York: Rizzoli, 1982). See also Joseph Rykwert, *The Dancing Column: On Order in Architecture* (Cambridge, MA: MIT Press, 1996).
37   Dalibor Vesely, *Architecture in the Age of Divided Representation: The Question of Creativity in the Shadow of Production* (Cambridge, MA: MIT Press, 2004).
38   Kenneth Frampton, "On Reading Heidegger," *Oppositions* 4 (October 1974).
39   Ibid., n.p.
40   Kenneth Frampton, "Towards a Critical Regionalism: Six Points for an Architecture of Resistance," in Hal Foster (ed.), *The Anti-Aesthetic: Essays on Postmodern Culture* (Seattle: Bay Press, 1983).
41   Ibid., p. 25.
42   Ibid., p. 28.
43   Ibid.
44   Kenneth Frampton, *Studies in Tectonic Culture: The Poetics of Construction in Nineteenth and Twentieth Century Architecture* (Cambridge, MA: MIT Press, 1995).
45   On Pallasmaa's intellectual development see his interview with Peter MacKeith in Juhani Pallasmaa, *Encounters: Architectural Essays* (Helsinki: Rakennusieto Oy, 2005), pp. 6–21.
46   Pallasmaa, *Encounters*, p. 57.
47   Ibid., p. 87.
48   Ibid., p. 89.
49   Ibid., p. 90.
50   Ibid., p. 96.
51   Ibid., p. 189.

52 Ibid., p. 301, 305.

53 Juhani Pallasmaa, "An Architecture of the Seven Senses," *a+u*, Architecture and Urbanism, special issue, Steven Holl, Juhani Pallasmaa, and Alberto Pérez-Gómez (eds), *Questions of Perception: Phenomenology of Architecture* (July 1994), p. 29.

54 Ibid., p. 34.

55 Ibid.

56 Ibid., p. 35.

57 Ibid., p. 36.

58 Juhani Pallasmaa, *The Eyes of the Skin: Architecture and the Senses* (Chichester: Wiley-Academy, 2005).

Chapter 10

1 The title of Francis Crick's book *The Astonishing Hypothesis: The Scientific Search for the Soul* (New York: Touchstone, 1994).

2 György Buzsáki, *Rhythms of the Brain* (Oxford: Oxford University Press, 2006), pp. 34–53.

3 Bernard J. Baars, *In the Theater of Consciousness: The Workplace of the Mind* (Oxford: Oxford University Press, 1997), p. 6.

4 Norman Bryson, Introduction to Warren Neidich, *Blow-Up: Photography, Cinema and the Brain* (New York: Distributed Art Publishers, 2003), p. 14.

5 On the idea of binding, see especially Rodolfo R. Llinás, *The I of the Vortex* (Cambridge, MA: MIT Press, 2001).

6 Buzsáki, *Rhythms of the Brain*, p. 11.

7 Llinás, *The I of the Vortex*, p. 94.

8 Christof Koch, *The Quest for Consciousness: A Neurobiological Approach* (Englewood, Co: Roberts and Company Publishers, 2004), pp. 89–90.

9 Anthony Damasio, *Looking for Spinoza: Joy, Sorrow, and the Feeling Brain* (Orlando: Harvest Book, 2003), pp. 62, 74, 125.

10 Rita Carter, *Mapping the Mind* (Berkeley: University of California Press, 1998), p. 54.

11 See Jean-Pierre Changeux, *The Physiology of Truth: Neuroscience and Human Knowledge*, trans. M. B. DeBevoise (Cambridge, MA: Belknap Press, 2004), pp. 205–6.

12 See T. Ebert, C. Pantev, C. Wienbruch, B. Rockstroh, and E. Taub, "Increased Cortical Representation of the Fingers of the Left Hand in String Players," *Science* (1995), vol. 270, pp. 305–7.

13 Susan Greenfield, *The Private Life of the Brain: Emotions, Consciousness, and the Secret of the Self* (New York: John Wiley & Sons, 2000), pp. 13–14.
14 Neidich, *Blow-Up: Photography, Cinema and the Brain*, pp. 26, 78.
15 See Merlin Donald, *Origins of the Modern Mind: Three Stages in the Evolution of Culture and Cognition* (Cambridge, MA: Harvard University Press, 1991), pp. 2–3.

Chapter 11

1   Semir Zeki, "Artistic Creativity and the Brain," *Science* (July 6, 2001), vol. 293 no. 5527, p. 52.
2   For a general account of vision, see Semir Zeki, *A Vision of the Brain* (Oxford: Blackwell Scientific Publications, 1993).
3   See David H. Hubel and Torsten N. Wiesel, *Brain and Visual Perception: The Story of a 25-Year Collaboration* (Oxford: Oxford University Press, 2005).
4   See especially Robert L Solso, *The Psychology of Art and the Evolution of the Conscious Brain* (Cambridge, MA: MIT Press, 2003), pp. 133–67.
5   The term was first put forth by Semir Zeki in 1974 in a paper entitled "Functional Specialization in the Visual Cortex of the Rhesus Monkey," *Nature*, vol. 274, pp. 423–8.
6   See Semir Zeki, "The Disunity of Consciousness," *Trends in Cognitive Sciences* (May 2003), vol. 7, no. 5, pp. 214–18.
7   Jean-Pierre Changeux, *Neuronal Man: The Biology of the Mind*, trans. Laurence Garey (New York: Pantheon books, 1985), p. 277. See also Rodolfo Llinás and D. Paré, "The Brain as a Closed System Modulated by the Senses," and Wolf Singer, "The Binding Problem of Neural Networks," in Rodolfo Llinás and Patricia S. Churchland, *The Mind–Brain Continuum: Sensory Processes* (Cambridge, MA: MIT Press, 1996).
8   Semir Zeki, "Art and the Brain," *Journal of Consciousness Studies: Controversies in Science & the Humanities* (June/July 1999), vol. 6, nos. 6–7, p. 77.
9   Ibid., p. 79.
10 Ibid., pp. 79–80.
11 Zeki provides a detail explanation of this theory in *A Vision of the Brain*, pp. 246–55.
12 Semir Zeki, "The Neurology of Ambiguity," *Consciousness and Cognition* (March 2004), 13 (1). Cited from *Science Direct*, http://www.science direct.com, p. 6.
13 Semir Zeki, *Inner Vision: An Exploration of Art and the Brain* (Oxford: Oxford University Press, 1999), p. 202.
14 Zeki, "Art and the Brain," pp. 89 and 113.

15 Zeki, *Inner Vision*, pp. 99–100.

16 Ibid., pp. 109–16.

17 Ibid., p. 104.

18 Ibid., pp. 39–42.

19 Ibid., p. 115. Zeki cites Mondrian, in a letter to van Doesburg: "Following the high-handed manner in which you have used the diagonal, all further collaboration between us has become impossible."

20 Ibid., pp. 105–8.

21 See, for instanced, John Hyman, "Art and Neuroscience," Interdisciplines: Art and Cognition Workshops, at http://www.interdisciplines.org/artcognition/papers/15. See also Amy Ione, "An Inquiry into Paul Cézanne: The Rome of the Artist in Studies of Perception and Consciousness," *Journal of Consciousness Studies* (2000), vol. 7, nos. 8–9, pp. 57–74.

22 The best description of this is found in his essay "The Neurology of Ambiguity," cited from Mark Turner, *The Artful Mind: Cognitive Science and the Riddle of Human Creativity* (Oxford: Oxford University Press, 2006), pp. 247–8, 261–2.

23 Ibid., p. 246.

24 Ibid., p. 245.

25 Zeki, *Inner Vision*, p. 25.

26 Ibid., pp. 22–9.

27 Richard Payne Knight, *An Analytical Inquiry into the Principles of Taste*, 2nd edn. (London: Mews-Gate and J. White, 1805), p. 469.

28 See in particular Juhani Pallasmaa, "Immateriality and Transparency: Technique and Expression in Glass Architecture" (2003), in *Encounters: Architectural Essays*, ed. Peter Mackeith (Helsinki: Rakennustieto Oy, 2005), pp. 197–209.

29 Rudolf Arnheim, *The Dynamics of Architectural Form* (Berkeley: University of California Press, 1977), pp. 183–8, 116.

30 Ibid., pp. 163, 179.

31 Ibid., pp. 87–91.

32 Robert Venturi, *Complexity and Contradiction in Architecture* (New York: Museum of Modern Art, 1966), p. 27.

33 Ibid., p. 31.

34 Frank Lloyd Wright, Introduction to *Ausgefürhte Bauten und Entwürfe von Frank Lloyd Wright*," in *Frank Lloyd Wright: Collected Writings, 1894–1930*, ed. Bruce Brooks Pfeiffer (New York: Rizzoli, 1992), 1: 113.

35 Frank Lloyd Wright, "In the Cause of Architecture" (1908), Ibid, 1: 94.

36 Ibid., p. 88.

37 Frank Lloyd Wright, *The Natural House* (New York: Horizon Press, 1954), p. 38. See also David Leatherbarrow's essay, "Sitting in the City,

or The Body in the World," in George Dodds and Robert Tavernor (eds), *Body and Building: Essays on the Changing Relation of Body and Architecture* (Cambridge, MA: MIT Press, 2002), pp. 268–88.

38   Neil Levine, *The Architecture of Frank Lloyd Wright* (Princeton: Princeton University Press, 1996), p. 33.

39   Ibid.

40   Ibid., p. 57.

41   Ibid.

42   Marc'Antonio Barbaro was the brother of Daniel Barbaro, the long-time patron and mentor of Palladio.

43   Jacob Burckhardt, *The Architecture of the Italian Renaissance*, trans. James Palmes, revised and edited by Peter Murray (Chicago: University of Chicago Press, 1985), p. 102.

44   Rudolf Wittkower, *Architectural Principles in the Age of Humanism* (London: Academy Editions, 1962), pp. 95–6.

45   Ibid., pp. 93–5.

46   James S. Ackerman, *Palladio* (Hamondsworth: Penguin, 1977), p. 130.

47   Deborah Howard, "Venice between East and West: Marc'Antonio Barbaro and Palladio's Church of the Redentore," *Journal of the Society of Architectural Historians* (September 2003), vol. 62, no. 3, pp. 306–25.

48   Leonardo Benevolo, *The Architecture of the Renaissance* (Boulder: Westview Press, 1978) 1: 525.

49   Ibid., 1:527.

50   Staale Sinding-Larsen, "Palladio's Redentore, a Compromise in Composition," *The Art Bulletin* (December 1965), vol. 47, no. 4, p. 421.

51   Ibid, p. 423.

52   Zeki, *Inner Vision*, p. 25.

Chapter 12

1   Frascari, Marco. *Monsters of Architecture: Anthropomorphism in Architectural Theory* (Savage, MD: Rowman & Littlefield Publishers, 1991), p. 1.

2   Barbara Maria Stafford, *Echo Objects: The Cognitive Work of Images* (Chicago: University of Chicago Press, 2007), pp. 3, 76.

3   Heinrich Wölfflin, "Prolegomena to a Psychology of Architecture," in Robert Vischer, Conrad Fiedler, Heinrich Wölfflin, Adolf Göller, Adolf Hildebrand, and August Schmarsow, *Empathy, Form, and Space: Problems in German Aesthetics 1873–1893*, trans. Harry Francis Mallgrave and Eleftherios Ikonomou (Santa Monica: Getty Publication Programs, 1994), p. 152.

4 August Schmarsow, "The Essence of Architectural Creation," in Vischer et al., *Empathy, Form, and Space*, pp. 286–7.

5 V. S. Ramachandran, *A Brief Tour of Human Consciousness: From Impostor Poodles to Purple Numbers* (New York: Pi Press, 2004), pp. 2–3.

6 György Buzsáki and Andreas Draguhn, "Neuronal Oscillations in Cortical Networks," *Science* (June 25, 2004), vol. 304, no. 5679. Cited from Academic Search Premier, http://web.ebscohost, p. 2.

7 See especially György Buzsáki, *Rhythms of the Brain* (Oxford: Oxford University Press, 2006).

8 Jean-Pierre Changeux, *Neuronal Man: The Biology of Mind*, trans. Laurence Carey (New York: Pantheon Books, 1985). The French edition, *L'Homme Neuronal*, appeared in 1983. See his extensive discussion with Paul Ricoeur on the metaphysics of this issue in *What Makes us Think? A Neuroscientist and a Philosopher Argue about Ethics, Human Nature, and the Brain* (Princeton: Princeton University Press, 2000).

9 See Eric R. Kandel, *In Search of Memory: The Emergence of a New Science of Mind* (New York: Norton, 2006).

10 Joaquín M. Fuster, *Memory in the Cerebral Cortex: An Empirical Approach to Neural Networks in the Human and Nonhuman Primate* (Cambridge, MA: MIT Press, 1995), pp. 2, 35.

11 Ibid., pp. 21, 35.

12 Gerald M. Edelman, "Building a Picture of the Brain," *Daedalus* (Spring 1998), vol. 127, no. 2. Cited from OCLC first Search, http://firstsearch.oclc.org, p. 8.

13 Joseph LeDoux, *Synaptic Self: How Our Brains Become Who We Are* (New York: Penguin, 2002), p. 107.

14 Buzsáki, *Rhythms of the Brain*, p. 278.

15 Francis Crick and Christof Koch, "Towards a Neurobiological Theory of Consciousness," *Seminars in Neuroscience* (1990), vol. 2, pp. 263–75; Francis Crick, *The Astonishing Hypothesis: A Scientific Search for the Soul* (New York: Simon & Schuster, 1993); Christof Koch, *The Quest for Consciousness: A Neurobiological Approach* (Englewood, CO: Roberts and Company, 2004).

16 Crick, *The Astonishing Hypothesis*, p. 259.

17 Koch, *The Quest for Consciousness*, p. 16.

18 Ibid., p. 233. Cited from a joint paper of 1995, "Are We Aware of Neural Activity in Primary Visual Cortex?"

19 Ibid., pp. 304, 90–1.

20 Ibid., p. 305.

21 Ibid., p. 308.

22 See Gerald M. Edelman and Vernon Mountcastle, *The Mindful Brain: Cortical Organization and the Group-Selective Theory of Higher Brain*

Function (Cambridge, MA: MIT Press, 1978); Gerald M. Edelman, *Neural Darwinism: The Theory of Neuronal Group Selection* (New York: Basic Books, 1987); *Topobiology: An Introduction to Molecular Embryology* (New York: Basic Books, 1988); *The Remembered Present: A Biological Theory of Consciousness* (New York: Basic Books, 1989).

23   See Gerald M. Edelman, *Bright Air, Brilliant Fire: On the Matter of the Mind* (New York: Basic Books, 1992); (with Giulio Tononi) *A Universe of Consciousness: How Matter Becomes Imagination* (New York: Basic Books, 2000); *Wider Than the Sky: The Phenomenal Gift of Consciousness* (New Haven: Yale University Press, 2004); and *Second Nature: Brain Science and Human Knowledge* (New Haven: Yale University Press, 2006).

24   For perhaps his clearest explanation of these principles, see Edelman, *The Remembered Present*, pp. 40–5.

25   Edelman, *A Universe of Consciousness*, p. 63.

26   See in particular Semir Zeki and Andreas Bartels, "Toward a Theory of Visual Consciousness," *Consciousness and Cognition* (1999), 8, pp. 225–59, and Semir Zeki, "The Disunity of Consciousness," *Trends in Cognitive Sciences* (May 2003), vol. 7, no. 5, pp. 214–18.

27   John Kounios, Jennifer L. Frymiare, Edward M. Bowden, Jessica I. Fleck, Karuna Subramaniam, Todd B. Parris, and Mark Jung-Beeman, "The Prepared Mind: Neural Activity Prior to Problem Presentation Predicts Subsequent Solution by Sudden Insight," *Association for Psychological Science* (2006), vol. 17, no.10, p. 883. For a broader discussion of this experiment and several related ones, see Jonah Lehrer, "The Eureka Hunt; Why Do Good Ideas Come to Us When They Do?," *The New Yorker* (July 28, 2008), vol. 84, no. 22.

28   Ibid., p. 888. See also Mark Jung-Beeman, Edward M. Bowden, Jason Haberman, Jennifer L. Frymiare, Stella Arambel-Liu, Richard Greenblatt, Paul J. Reber, and John Kounios, "Neural Activity When People Solve Verbal Problems with Insight," *PLoS Biology* (April 2004), vol. 2, no. 4, pp. 505–6.

29   See Frank Barron and David M. Harrington, "Creativity, Intelligence, and Personality," *Annual Review of Psychology* (1981), vol. 32, pp. 439–76, p. 442.

30   Juhani Pallasmaa, Interview with Peter MacKeith, in *Encounters: Architectural Essays* (Helsinki: Rakennustieto Oy, 2005), p. 9.

31   Steven Pinker, *How the Mind Works* (New York: W. W. Norton & Company, 1997), p. 361.

32   See Gregory Berns, "Neuroscience Sheds New Light on Creativity," at http://www.fastcompany.com. Adapted from his book *Iconoclast* (Cambridge, MA: Harvard Business Press, 2008).

33   Kenneth M. Heilman, Stephen E. Nadeau, and David O. Beversdorf, "Creative Innovation: Possible Brain Mechanisms," *Neurocase* (2003), vol. 9, no. 5, p. 375.

34   As reported by Jonah Lehrer in Lehrer, "The Eureka Hunt".

35   Ramachandran, *A Brief Tour of Human Consciousness*, p. 68.

36   Ibid. p. 71.

37   Ibid., p. 72.

38   Ibid., p. 75.

39   Marco Frascari, "Architectural Synaesthesia: A Hypothesis on the Makeup of Scarpa's Modernist Architectural Drawings," at http://art3idea.psu.edu/synesthesia, p. 7.

40   Ibid., p. 3.

41   Rudolf Arnheim, *The Dynamics of Architectural Form* (Berkeley: University of California Press, 2007), p. 209.

42   Pinker, *How the Mind Works*, p. 352.

43   Ibid., pp. 355–6.

44   George Lakoff and Mark Johnson, *Metaphors We Live By* (Chicago: University of Chicago Press, 2003; orig. 1980), Afterword, p. 243.

45   Ibid., p. 8.

46   Ibid., p. 46.

47   Mark Johnson, *The Body in the Mind: The Bodily Basis of Meaning, Imagination, and Reason* (Chicago: University of Chicago Press, 1989), p. 171.

48   George Lakoff and Mark Johnson, *Philosophy in the Flesh: The Embodied Mind and its Challenge to Western Thought* (New York: Basic Books, 1999), p. 13.

49   Lakoff and Johnson, *Metaphors We Live By*, Afterword, p. 256.

50   Lakoff and Johnson, *Philosophy in the Flesh*, p. 20.

51   Ibid., pp. 22–3.

52   Modell's two studies of the 1990s are *Other Times, Other Realities* (Cambridge, MA: Harvard University Press, 1990) and *The Private Self* (Cambridge, MA: Harvard University Press, 1993).

53   Arnold H. Modell, *Imagination and the Meaningful Brain* (Cambridge, MA: MIT Press, 2003), p. xii.

54   Ibid. p. 70.

55   Ibid., pp. 82–3.

56   Edelman is quite familiar with the work of Modell and Lackoff and Johnson, as various of his citations show.

57   Edelman, *Second Nature*, p. 58.

58   Ibid., pp. 58–9.

59   See, for instances, two images of such huts published by Juhani Pallasmaa in "The Two Languages of Architecture," in *Encounters*, p. 42.

60   See Alberto Pérez-Gómez's comments on Vitruvius, in "The Space of Architecture: Meaning as Presence and Representation," in Steven Holl, Juhani Pallasmaa, and Alberto Pérez-Gómez, *Questions of Perception: Phenomenology of Architecture* (San Francisco: William Stout Publishers, 2006; originally published as special issue of *a + u*, July 1994), pp. 9–10.

61   See Indra Kagis McEwen, *Vitruvius: Writing the Body of Architecture* (Cambridge, MA: MIT Press, 2003), pp. 5–13.

62   John Onians, *Bearers of Meaning: The Classical Orders in Antiquity, the Middle Ages, and the Renaissance* (Princeton: Princeton University Press, 1988), p. 8. Onians updated and expanded this thesis for a neurological perspective in "Greek Temple and Greek Brain," in George Dodds and Robert Tavernor (eds), *Body and Building: Essays on the Changing Relation of Body and Architecture* (Cambridge, MA: MIT Press, 2002), pp. 44–63.

63   Joseph Rykwert, *The Dancing Column: On Order in Architecture* (Cambridge, MA: MIT Press, 1996), p. 373.

64   See Jean-Nicolas-Louis Durand, *Précis of the Lectures of Architecture* (Los Angeles: Getty Publication Programs, 2000).

65   Alberto Pérez-Gómez, *Architecture and the Crisis of Modern Science* (Cambridge, MA: MIT Press, 1983), p. 6.

66   Gottfried Semper, particularly in *Science, Industry, and Art* (1852), struggled with the incompatible demands of science and art and in the end came down forcefully on the side of the latter.

67   See my introduction to *Otto Wagner: Modern Architecture, A Guidebook for His Students to This Field of Art*, (Santa Monica: Getty Publication Programs, 1988), pp. 33–9.

68   Charles Jencks, *The Language of Post-Modern Architecture* (New York: Rizzoli, 1977), pp. 15–19.

69   Paul Ricoeur, *The Rule of Metaphor: Multi-disciplinary Studies of the Creation of Meaning in Language*, trans. Robert Czerny (Toronto: University of Toronto Press, 1977), pp. 3–7.

70   Rudolf Arnheim, *The Dynamics of Architectural Form* (Berkeley: University of California Press, 1977), pp. 207–8. Arnheim was citing Alfred Lorenzer and his critique of the "intentional and consciously applied symbolism" of Ledoux and Vaudoyer.

71   Jencks, *The Language of Post-Modern Architecture*, pp. 97–101.

72   Arnheim, *The Dynamics of Architectural Form*, p. 207.

73   Hideaki Kawabata and Semir Zeki, "Neural Correlates of Beauty," *Journal of Neurophysiology* (2004), vol. 91, pp. 1699–1705.

74   Chun Siong Soon, Marcel, Hans-Jochen Heinze, and John-Dylan Haynes, "Unconscious Determinants of Free Decisions in the Human Brain," *Nature Neuroscience* (May 2008), vol. 11, no. 5, pp. 543–5.

75 Peter Zumthor, *Thinking Architecture*, trans. Maureen Oberli-Turner and Catherine Schelbert (Basel: Birkhäuser, 2006), p. 7.

76 See Juhani Pallasmaa, "The Two Languages of Architecture: Elements of a Bio-Cultural Approach to Architecture," in *Encounters*, pp. 26–7.

77 Steven Holl, "Questions of Perception – Phenomenology of Architecture," in Holl, Pallasmaa, and Pérez-Gómez, *Questions of Perception*, p. 41.

78 Vittorio Gregotti, "Mimesis," *Casabella* (April 1983), no. 490, pp. 12–13.

79 See Erich Auerbach, *Mimesis: The Representation of Reality in Western Literature*, trans. Willard R. Trask (Princeton: Princeton University Press, 1953).

80 Vittorio Gregotti, "Exercise of Detailing," *Casabella* (June 1983), no. 492, pp. 10–11.

81 Marco Frascari, "The *Particolareggiamento* in the Narration of Architecture," *Journal of Architectural Education* (Autumn 1989) vol. 43, no. 1, p. 10.

82 Ibid., p. 11.

83 Alberto Pérez-Gómez, "The Space of Architecture: Meaning as Presence and Representation," in Holl, Pallasmaa, and Pérez-Gómez, *Questions of Perception*, p. 14.

84 Ibid., 24.

85 Rykwert, *The Dancing Column*, pp. 388–9.

86 Dalibor Vesely, *Architecture in the Age of Divided Representation: The Question of Creativity in the Shadow of Production* (Cambridge, MA: MIT Press, 2004), p. 366.

87 Dalibor Vesely, "The Architectonics of Embodiment," in Dodds and Tavernor, *Body and Building*, pp. 33–4.

88 Merlin Donald, *Origins of the Modern Mind: Three Stages in the Evolution of Culture* and Cognition (Cambridge, MA: Harvard University Press, 1991), pp. 168–200.

Chapter 13

1 Juhani Pallasmaa, "Hapticity and Time: Notes on Fragile Architecture" (2000), in *Encounters: Architectural Essays* (Helsinki: Rakennustieto Oy, 2005), p. 323.

2 Peter Zumthor, *Thinking Architecture* (Basel: Birkhäuser, 2006), p. 77.

3 Jean Piaget and Bärbel Inhelder, *The Child's Conception of Space* (London: Routledge and K. Paul, 1956), p. 18.

4 James J. Gibson, *The Senses Considered as Perceptual Systems* (Boston: Houghton Mifflin, 1966), p. 102.

5   Juhani Pallasmaa, "Hapticity and Time: Notes on Fragile Architecture," p. 323. Steven Holl speaks of detailing as "The Haptic Realm," in Steven Holl, "Questions of Perception – Phenomenology of Architecture," in Steven Holl, Juhani Pallasmaa, and Alberto Pérez-Gómez, *Questions of Perception: Phenomenology of Architecture* (San Francisco: William Stout Publishers, 2006; originally published as special issue of *a + u*, July 1994), pp. 90–112. See also Máire Eithne O'Neill, "Corporeal Experience: A Haptic Way of Knowing," *Journal of Architectural Education* (September 2001), vol. 55, no. 1, pp. 3–12; and Kamiel van Kreij, "Sensory Intensification in Architecture," Technical University Delft, at www.mielio.nl.

6   Semir Zeki, "Artistic Creativity and the Brain," *Science* (July 6, 2001), vol. 293, no. 5527, p. 51.

7   Semir Zeki, "Neural Concept Formation and Art: Dante, Michelangelo, Wagner," in Rose, F. Clifford, *Neurology of the Arts: Painting, Music, Literature* (London: Imperial College Press, 2004), p. 19.

8   Zumthor, *Thinking Architecture*, pp. 31–2.

9   Steven Holl, "Phenomena and Idea," *GA Architect 11: Steven Holl*, ed. Yukio Futagawa (1993), pp. 12, 16–17.

10   Joseph LeDoux, *Synaptic Self: How Our Brains Become Who We Are* (New York: Penguin, 2002), p. 206.

11   See Susan Greenfield, *The Private Life of the Brain: Emotions, Consciousness, and the Secret of the Self* (New York: John Wiley & Sons, 2000), p. 154.

12   See Antonio R. Damasio, Thomas J. Grabowski, Antoine Bechara, Hanna Damasio, Laura L. B. Ponto, Josef Parvizi, and Richard D. Hichwa, "Subcortical and Cortical Brain Activity During the Feeling of Self-generated Emotions," *Nature Neuroscience* (2000), vol. 3, no. 10, p. 1051.

13   Antonio Damasio, *Looking for Spinoza: Joy, Sorrow, and the Feeling Brain* (Orlando: Harvest Books, 2003), p. 85.

14   Ibid., pp. 59, 96–101.

15   Ibid., p. 106.

16   Greenfield, *The Private Life of the Brain*, pp. 3–4.

17   Diane Ackerman, *An Alchemy of Mind: The Marvel and Mystery of the Brain* (New York: Scribner, 2004), p. 193.

18   See John P. Eberhard, *Architecture and the Brain: A New Knowledge Base from Neuroscience* (Ostberg: Atlanta, 2007). The relation of mental depression and the blighted urban environment has long been noted. For a recent study, see S. Galea, J. Ahern, S. Rudenstine, Z. Wallace, and D. Vlahov, "Urban Built Environment and Depression: A Multilevel Analysis," *Journal of Epidemiology & Community Health* (October 2005), vol. 59, no. 10, pp. 822–7.

19   Damasio, *Looking* for *Spinoza*, p. 165.

20   Jaak Panksepp, *Affective Neuroscience: The Foundations of Human and Animal Emotions* (Oxford: Oxford University Press, 1998), p. 48.

21   See Jaak Panksepp, "Emotional Endophenotypes in Evolutionary Psychiatry," *Progress in Neuro-Psychopharacology and Biological Psychiatry* (July 2006), vol. 30, no. 5, pp. 774–84.

22   Edmund Burke, *A Philosophical Inquiry into the Origin of Our Ideas of the Sublime and Beautiful*, in *The Works of Edmund Burke* (London: G. Bell & sons, 1913), 1, pp. 67–8.

23   Uvedale Price, *Essays on the Picturesque as Compared with the Sublime and the Beautiful; and, on the Use of Studying Pictures for the Purpose of Improving Real Landscape* (London: Mawman, 1810; orig. 1794), 1, p. 22; Richard Payne Knight, *An Analytical Inquiry into the Principles of Taste*, 2nd edn. (London: Mews-Gate and J. White, 1805), p. 469.

24   Kenneth M. Heilman, *Creativity and the Brain* (New York: Psychology Press, 2005), p. 70.

25   Jaak Panksepp, "On the Embodied Neural Nature of Core Emotional Affects," *Journal of Consciousness Studies* (2005), vol. 12, nos. 8–10, p. 170.

26   Jaak Panksepp, "Affective Consciousness: Core Emotional Feelings in Animals and Humans," *Consciousness and Cognition* (2005), 14 p. 47.

27   Ibid.

28   Panksepp, "Emotional Endophenotypes in Evolutionary Psychiatry," pp. 77.

29   Douglas F. Watt, "Consciousness, Emotional Self-Regulation and the Brain: Review Article," *Journal of Consciousness Studies* (2004), vol. 11, no. 9, pp. 77–8.

30   Jaak Panksepp and Günther Bernatzky, "Emotional Sounds and the Brain: The Neuro-affective Foundations of Musical Appreciation," *Behavioural Processes* (2002), vol. 60, p. 134.

31   Anne J. Blood and Robert J. Zatorre, "Intensely Pleasurable Responses to Music Correlated with Activity in Brain Regions Implicated in Reward and Emotion," *Proceedings of the National Academy of Science* (September 25, 2001), vol. 98, no. 20, p. 11818.

32   Robert J. Zatorre, "Music, the Food of Neuroscience," *Nature* (March 17, 2005), vol. 434, p. 314.

33   See Christian Gazer and Gottfried Schlaug, "Brain Structures Differ between Musicians and Non-Musicians," *Journal of Neuroscience* (2003), vol. 23, no. 27, pp. 9240–5; and Siobhan Hutchinson, Leslie Hui-Lin Lee, Nadine Gaab, and Gottfried Schlaug, "Cerebellar Volume of Musicians," *Cerebral Cortex* (2003), vol. 13, pp. 943–9.

34   See the fMRI study carried out by Devarajan Sridaran, Daniel J. Levitin, Chris H. Chaft, Jonathan Berger, and Vinod Menon, "Neural Dynamics

of Event Segmentation in Music: Converging Evidence for Dissociable Ventral and Dorsal Networks," *Neuron* (August 2, 2007), vol. 55, no. 3, pp. 521–32.

35   See the conclusions of the team of physicians led by Michael Miller, as reported in "Joyful Music May Promote Heart Health, according to University of Maryland School of Medicine Study," in University of Maryland Medical Center, at http://www.umm.edu/news/releases/music-cardiovascular.htm.

36   V. B. Penhune, R. J. Zatorre, and A. C. Evans, "Cerebellar Contributions to Motor Timing: A PET Study of Auditory and Visual Rhythms Reproduction," *Journal of Cognitive Neuroscience* (1998), vol. 10, no. 6, pp. 752–65.

37   Gottfried Semper, *Style in the Technical and Tectonic Arts; or, Practical Aesthetics*, trans. Harry Francis Mallgrave and Michael Robinson (Los Angeles: Getty Publication Programs, 2004), p. 82. See also the manuscript "The Attributes of Formal Beauty" (c.1856/1859), in Wolfgang Herrmann, *Gottfried Semper: In Search of Architecture* (Cambridge, MA: MIT Press, 1984), p. 219.

38   Wolfgang Köhler, *Gestalt Psychology* (New York: H. Liveright, 1937), p. 230. "But these terms are applicable not only to auditory facts but also to visually perceived developments. Hence, when such dynamic traits occur in the inner life of a person, they can be most adequately represented in his behavior as heard and seen by others."

39   See Merlin Donald, *Origins of the Modern Mind: Three Stages in the Evolution of Culture* and Cognition (Cambridge, MA: Harvard University Press, 1991), p. 186.

40   See G. Rizzolatti and L. Craighero, "The Mirror-Neuron System," *Annual Review in Neuroscience* (2004), vol. 27, pp. 169–92.

41   V. S. Ramachandran, *A Brief Tour of Human Consciousness: From Impostor Poodles to Purple Numbers* (New York: Pi Press, 2004), pp. 37–8.

42   Heinrich Wölfflin, "Prolegomena to a Psychology of Architecture," in *Empathy, Form, and Space* (Santa Monica: Getty Publication Programs, 1994), pp. 149–90. See Chapter Six of this book for discussion.

43   See J. O'Keefe and J. Dostrovsky, "The Hippocampus as a Spatial Map. Preliminary Evidence from Unit Activity in the Freely-Moving Rat," *Brain Res* (1971), vol. 34, no. 171–5. See also John O'Keefe and Lynn Nadel, *The Hippocampus as a Cognitive Map* (Oxford: Clarendon Press, 1978).

44   See J. B. Ranke, Jr., "Head Direction Cells in the Deep Cell Layer of Dorsal Postsubiculum in Freely Moving Rats," in *Electrical Activity of the Archicortex*, ed. G. Buzsáki and C. H. Vanderwolf (Budapest: Akademiai Kiado, 1985), pp. 217–20.

45 Torkel Hafting, Marianne Fyhn, Sturla Molden, May-Britt Moser, and Edvard I. Moser, "Microstructure of a Spatial Map in the Entorhinal Cortex," *Nature* (August 11, 2005), vol. 436, p. 801.

46 Ibid. A New Zealand psychologist, David K. Bilkey, has recently suggested a "Field Density Model" of how these various spatial regions interact, one that postulates a group of "geometry cells." See his "Space and Context in the Temporal Cortex," *Hippocampus* (2007), vol. 17, p. 814.

47 Gabriele Janzen and Miranda van Turennout, "Selective Neural Representation of Objects Relevant for Navigation," *Nature Neuroscience* (June 2004), vol. 7, no. 6, pp. 673–8.

48 See Hugo J. Spiers and Eleanor A. Maguire, "A 'Landmark' Study of the Neural Basis of Navigation," *Nature Neuroscience* (June 2004), vol. 7, no. 6, p. 572.

49 Hugo J. Spiers and Eleanor A. Maguire, "A Navigational Guidance System in the Human Brain," *Hippocampus* (2007), vol. 17, pp. 624–5.

50 See Russell A. Epstein, J. Steven Higgins, and Sharon L. Thompson-Schill, "Learning Places from Views: Variation in Scene Processing as a Function of Experience and Navigational Ability," *Journal of Cognitive Neuroscience* (2005), vol. 17, no.1, pp. 73–83; Nicole Etchamendy and Veronique D. Bohbot, "Spontaneous Navigational Strategies and Performance in the Virtual Town," *Hippocampus* (2007), vol. 17, no. 8, pp. 595–9.

51 See Eve A. Edelstein, "Mapping Memory of Space & Place," Report on the 2005 Workshop on Neuroscience & Health Care Architecture, at www.anfarch.org. The project was funded by the Academy of Neuroscience for Architecture.

52 Richard Neutra, *Survival through Design* (New York: Oxford University Press, 1954), pp. 139, 198.

53 Johann Wolfgang von Goethe, "Palladio, Architecture" (1795), in *Goethe on Art*, ed. and trans. John Gage (London: Scolar Press, 1980), p. 197.

54 Wölfflin, "Prolegomena toward a Psychology of Architecture," in *Empathy, Form, and Space*, p. 151.

55 Ibid., p. 158.

56 Steer Eiler Rasmussen, *Experiencing Architecture* (Cambridge, MA: MIT Press, 1962), pp. 134–5.

57 Neutra, *Survival through Design*, pp. 152–3. See also pp. 199–200.

58 Juhani Pallasmaa, *The Eyes of the Skin: Architecture and the Senses* (Chichester: John Wiley & Sons, 2005), p. 60.

59 Ashley Montagu, *Touching: The Human Significance of the Skin* (New York: Columbia University Press, 1971), p. 1.

60 Johann Gottfried Herder, *Sculpture: Some Observations on Shape and Form from Pygmalion's Creative Dream*, ed. and trans. Jason Gaiger (Chicago: University of Chicago Press, 2002), pp. 35–6.

61   E. Ricciardi, D. Bonnino, C. Gentile, L. Sani, P. Pietrini, and T. Vecchi, "Neural Correlates of Spatial Working Memory in Humans: A Functional Magnetic Resonance Imaging Study Comparing Visual and Tactile Processes," *Neuroscience* (2006), vol. 139, p. 347. See also Pietro Pietrini, Maura L. Furey, Emiliano Ricciardi, M. Ida Gobbini, W-H. Carolyn Wu, Leonardo Cohen, Mario Guazzelli, James V. Haxby, "Beyond Sensory Images: Object-Based Representation in Human Ventral Pathway," *Proceedings of the National Academy of Sciences* (April 13, 2004), vol. 101, no. 15, pp. 5658–63. I thank Matthew Blewitt for the first citation.

62   Semir Zeki, *Inner Vision: An Exploration of Art and the Brain* (Oxford: Oxford University Press, 1999), p. 99.

63   Christopher Alexander, *The Nature of Order: An Essay on the Art of Building and the Nature of the Universe*, 4 vols. (Berkeley: The Center for Environmental Structure, 2002). See also the work of Nikos A. Salingaros, *A Theory of Architecture* (Solingen: UMBAU-VERLAG, 2006), and *Principles of Urban Structure* (Delft: Techne, 2005).

64   See especially Stephen R. Kellert, Judith H. Heerwagen, and Martin L. Mador, *Biophilic Design: The Theory, Science, and Practice of Bring Buildings to Life* (New York: John Wiley & Sons, 2008).

65   Edward O. Wilson, *Biophilia* (Cambridge, MA: Harvard University Press, 1984), p. 1.

66   Steven Holl, "Questions of Perception – Phenomenology of Architecture," in Holl, Pallasmaa and Pérez-Gómez, *Questions of Perception*, p. 116.

Epilogue

1   Rafael Moneo, *The Freedom of the Architect*, Raoul Wallenberg Lecture (Ann Arbor: University of Michigan, 2002), p. 13.

2   Warren Neidich, "Visual and Cognitive Ergonomics: Formulating a Model through which Neurobiology and Aesthetics are Linked," in *Blow-Up: Photography, Cinema and the Brain* (New York: Distributed Art Publishers, 2003), p. 27.

3   Ibid., "Blow-Up," p. 81.

4   Horkheimer and Adorno's term "culture industry" refers to the tendency of capitalist mass culture to produce standardized cultural forms or pleasurable products to dull the masses into conformity and passivity. See Max Horkheimer and Theodor W. Adorno, *Dialectic of Enlightenment*, trans. John Cumming (New York: Continuum, 1999; orig. 1947), pp. 120–67. Paul Virilio has defined the phatic image as "a targeted image that forces you to look and holds you your attention." See his *The Vision*

Machine, trans. Julie Rose (Bloomington: Indiana University Press, 1994; orig. 1988), p. 14.

5   Neidich, "The Sculpted Brain," in *Blow-Up*, p. 140.

6   Ibid., p. 141.

7   Jane Healy, *Endangered Minds: Why Children Don't Think – and What we Can Do About It* (New York: Touchstone, 1999; orig 1990), p. 322.

8   Ibid., p. 323.

9   Mark Bauerlein, *The Dumbest Generation: How the Digital Age Stupefies Young Americans and Jeopardizes Our Future* (New York: Tarcher/Penguin, 2008), p. 149.

10 Maggie Jackson, *Distracted: The Erosion of Attention and the Coming Dark Age* (Amherst, NY: Prometheus Books, 2008), p. 16.

11 Nicholas Carr, "Is Google Making Us Stupid: What the Internet is Doing to Our Brains," *The Atlantic* (July/August 2008), available at http://theatlantic.com/doc/200807/google. He refers to Maryanne Wolf's book *Proust and the Squid: The Story and Science of the Reading Brain* (New York: Harper, 2007).

12 Healy, *Endangered Minds*, p. 342.

13 Daniel H. Pink, *A Whole New Mind: Moving from the Information Age to the Conceptual Age* (New York: Rivershead Books, 2005), p. 29, 130.

14 Steve Talbott, *Devices of the Soul: Battling for Our Selves in the Age of Machines* (Sebastopol, CA: O'Reilly & Assoc., 2007), pp. 11–12.

15 Hubert Dreyfus, *What Computers Still Can't Do* (Cambridge, MA: MIT Press, 1992), p. 280. The book first appeared under a slightly different title in 1972, and in a revised edition in 1979.

16 Rodolfo R. Llinás, *I of the Vortex: From Neurons to Self* (Cambridge, MA: MIT Press, 2002), p. 259.

17 William J. Mitchell, *e-topia: "URBAN LIFE JIM – BUT NOT AS WE KNOW IT"* (Cambridge, MA: MIT Press, 1999), P. 152.

18 William J. Mitchell, *Me++: THE CYBORG SELF AND THE NETWORKED CITY* (Cambridge, MA: MIT Press, 2003), p. 39.

19 György Buzsáki, *Rhythms of the Brain* (Oxford: Oxford University Press, 2006), p. vii. Burzáki attributes this statement to Ken Hill.

20 See Jean Baudrillard's *Symbolic Exchange and Death* (1976).

21 Peter Zumthor, *Thinking Architecture* (Basel: Birkhäuser, 2006), p. 66.

22 See Rafael Moneo, "The Idea of Lasting," *Perspecta 24: The Yale Architectural Journal* (1988), pp. 154–5.

23 S. Dehaene, E. Spelki, P. Pinel, R. Stanescu, and S. Tsivkin, "Sources of Mathematical Thinking: Behavioral and Brain-Imaging Evidence, *Science* (May 7, 1999), vol. 284, p. 970.

24   Lawrence M. Parsons and Daniel Osherson, "New Evidence for Distinct Right and Left Brain Systems for Deductive versus Probabilistic Reasoning, *Cerebral Cortex* (October 2001), vol. 11, pp. 954–65.

25   Antonio Damasio, *Descartes' Error: Emotion, Reason, and the Human Brain* (New York: Penguin, 2005), p. 231.

26   Antonio Damasio, *Looking for Spinoza: Joy Sorrow, and the Feeling Brain* (Orlando: Harvest Book, 2003), p. 99.

27   John Kounios, Jennifer L. Frymiare, Edward M. Bowden, Jessica I. Fleck, Karuna Subramaniam, Todd B. Parris, and Mark Jung-Beeman, "The Prepared Mind: Neural Activity Prior to Problem Presentation Predicts Subsequent Solution by Sudden Insight," *Association for Psychological Science*, vol. 17, no. 10, p. 883.

28   Seana Coulson and Ying Choon Wu, "Right Hemisphere Activation of Joke-Related Information: An Event-Related Brain Potential Study," *Journal of Cognitive Neuroscience* (2005), vol. 17, no. 3, pp. 494–506.

29   V. S. Ramachandran, *A Brief Tour of Human Consciousness: From Impostor Poodles to Purple Numbers* (New York: Pi Press, 2004), p. 53.

30   Oliver Sacks, *Musicophilia: Tales of Music and the Brain* (New York: Knopf, 2008), p. 329.

31   Alastair Gordon, "Credit Swiss," Interview with Pierre de Meuron and Jacques Herzog, in *WSJ. The Magazine from the Wall Street Journal* (Winter 2008), p. 27.

Bibliography

Ackerman, Diane, *A Natural History of the Senses* (New York: Vintage Books, 1990).

Ackerman, Diane, *An Alchemy of Mind: The Marvel and Mystery of the Brain* (New York: Scribner, 2004).

Ackerman, James S., *Palladio* (Hamondsworth: Penguin, 1977).

Alberti, Leon Battista, *On Painting and On Sculpture*, ed. and trans. Cecil Grayson (London: Phaidon, 1972).

Alberti, Leon Battista, *On the Art of Building in Ten Books*, trans. Joseph Rykwert, Neil Leach, and Robert Tavernor (Cambridge: MIT Press, 1988).

Alexander, Christopher, *The Nature of Order: An Essay on the Art of Building and the Nature of the Universe*, 4 vols (Berkeley: The Center for Environmental Structure, 2002).

Alexander, Christopher, Sara Ishikawa, and Murray Silverstein, *A Pattern Language: Towns, Buildings, Construction* (New York: Oxford University Press, 1977).

Arnheim, Rudolf, *Art and Visual Perception: A Psychology of the Creative Eye* (Berkeley: University of California Press, 1974; orig. 1954).

Arnheim, Rudolf, *Visual Thinking* (Berkeley: University of California Press, 1969).

Arnheim, Rudolf, *The Dynamics of Architectural Form* (Berkeley: University of California Press, 2007).

Ash, Mitchell G., *Gestalt Psychology in German Culture, 1890–1967: Holism and the Quest for Objectivity* (New York: Cambridge University Press, 1995).

Baars, Bernard J., *In the Theater of Consciousness: The Workplace of the Mind* (Oxford: Oxford University Press, 1997).

Barron, Frank and David M. Harrington, "Creativity, Intelligence, and Personality," *Annual Review of Psychology*, vol. 32, pp. 439–76 (1981).

Baudrillard, Jean, *Symbolic Exchange and Death* (London: Thousand Oaks, 1993).

Bauerlein, Mark, *The Dumbest Generation: How the Digital Age Stupefies Young Americans and Jeopardizes Our Future* (New York: Tarcher/ Penguin, 2008).

Bergdoll, Barry, *Karl Friedrich Schinkel: An Architecture for Prussia* (New York: Rizzoli, 1994).

Berger, Robert. W., *The Palace of the Sun: The Louvre of Louis XIV* (University Park: Pennsylvania State University, 1993).

Berns, Gregory, "Neuroscience Sheds New Light on Creativity," at http:// www.fastcompany.com.

Bilkey, David K., "Space and Context in the Temporal Cortex," *Hippocampus,* vol. 17, pp. 813–25 (2007).

Blood, Anne J. and Robert J. Zatorre, "Intensely Pleasurable Responses to Music Correlated with Activity in Brain Regions Implicated in Reward and Emotion," *Proceedings of the National Academy of Science,* vol. 98, no. 20 (September 25, 2001).

Borsi, Franco, *Leon Battista Alberti: The Complete Works,* trans. Rudolf G. Carpanini (New York: Electa, 1986).

Bötticher, Karl, "Entwickelung der Formen der hellenischen Tektonik," *Allgemeine Bauzeitung* vol. 5 (1840).

Bötticher, Karl, *Die Tektonik der Hellenen* (Potsdam: Ferdinand Riegel, 1852).

Burckhardt, Jacob, *The Architecture of the Italian Renaissance,* trans. James Palmes, revised and edited by Peter Murray (Chicago: University of Chicago Press, 1985).

Burke, Edmund, *A Philosophical Inquiry into the Origin of Our Ideas of the Sublime and Beautiful,* in *The Works of Edmund Burke* (London: G. Bell & Sons, 1913).

Buzsáki, György, *Rhythms of the Brain* (Oxford: Oxford University Press, 2006).

Buzsáki, György and Andreas Draguhn, "Neuronal Oscillations in Cortical Networks," *Science,* vol. 304, no. 5679 (June 25, 2004).

Carr, Nicholas, "Is Google Making Us Stupid: What the Internet is Doing to Our Brains," *The Atlantic* (July/August 2008).

Carter, Rita, *Mapping the Mind* (Berkeley: University of California Press, 1998).

Cassirer, Ernst, *Kant's Life and Thought,* trans. James Haden (New Haven: Yale University Press, 1981; orig. 1918).

Changeux, Jean-Pierre, *Neuronal Man: The Biology of the Mind,* trans. by Laurence Garey (New York: Pantheon Books, 1985).

Changeux, Jean-Pierre, *The Physiology of Truth: Neuroscience and Human Knowledge,* trans. by M. B. DeBevoise (Cambridge, MA: Belknap Press, 2004).

Changeux, Jean-Pierre and Ricoeur, Paul, *What Makes us Think? A Neuroscientist and a Philosopher Argue about Ethics, Human Nature, and the Brain* (Princeton: Princeton University Press, 2000).

Cicero. *Orator*, trans. H. M. Hubbell (Cambridge, MA: Harvard University Press, 1971).

Cicero, *De Natura Deorum*, trans. H. Rackham (Cambridge, MA: Harvard University Press, 1979).

Coulson, Seana and Ying Choon Wu, "Right Hemisphere Activation of Joke-Related Information: An Event-Related Brain Potential Study," *Journal of Cognitive Neuroscience*, vol. 17, no. 3, pp. 494–506. (2005).

Crick, Francis, *The Astonishing Hypothesis: The Scientific Search for the Soul* (New York: Touchstone, 1994).

Crick, Francis and Christof Koch, "Towards a Neurobiological Theory of Consciousness," *Seminars in Neuroscience*, vol. 2, pp. 263–75 (1990).

Damasio, Antonio, *Descartes' Error: Emotion, Reason, and the Human Brain* (New York: Penguin, 1994).

Damasio, Antonio, *The Feeling of What Happens: Body and Emotion in the Making of Consciousness* (Orlando: Harvest Books, 2000).

Damasio, Antonio, *Looking for Spinoza: Joy, Sorrow, and the Feeling Brain* (Orlando: Harvest Books, 2003).

Damasio, Antonio R., Thomas J. Grabowski, Antoine Bechara, Hanna Damasio, Laura L. B. Ponto, Josef Parvizi, and Richard Hichwa, "Subcortical and Cortical Brain Activity during the Feeling of Self-Generated Emotions," *Nature Neuroscience*, vol. 3, pp. 1049–56 (2000).

Dehaene, S., E. Spelki, P. Pinel, R. Stanescu, and S. Tsivkin, "Sources of Mathematical Thinking: Behavioral and Brain-Imaging Evidence," *Science*, vol. 284 (May 7, 1999).

Descartes, René, *Rules for the Direction of the Mind* (1628), in *The Philosophical Writings of Descartes*, trans. John Cottingham, Robert Stoothoff, and Dugald Murdoch, 3 vols. (Cambridge: Cambridge University Press, 1985).

Donald, Merlin, *Origins of the Modern Mind: Three Stages in the Evolution of Culture and Cognition* (Cambridge, MA: Harvard University Press, 1991).

Dreyfus, Hubert, *What Computers Still Can't Do* (Cambridge, MA: MIT Press, 1992).

Durand, Jean-Nicolas-Louis, *Précis of the Lectures of Architecture* (Los Angeles: Getty Publication Programs, 2000).

Ebenstein, Alan, *Friedrich Hayek: A Biography* (New York: Palgrave, 2001).

Eberhard, John P., *Architecture and the Brain: A New Knowledge Base from Neuroscience* (Ostberg: Atlanta, 2007).

Ebert, T., C. Pantev, C. Wienbruch, B. Rockstroh, and E. Taub, "Increased Cortical Representation of the Fingers of the Left Hand in String Players," *Science*, vol. 270, pp. 305–7 (1995).

Edelman, Gerald M., *Neural Darwinism: The Theory of Neuronal Group Selection* (New York: Basic Books, 1987).

Edelman, Gerald M., *The Remembered Present: A Biological Theory of Consciousness* (New York: Basic Books, 1989).

Edelman, Gerald M., *Bright Air; Brilliant Fire: On the Matter of the Mind* (New York: Basic Books, 1992).

Edelman, Gerald M., "Building a Picture of the Brain," *Daedalus*, vol. 127, no. 2 (Spring 1998).

Edelman, Gerald M., *Wider Than the Sky: The Phenomenal Gift of Consciousness* (New Haven: Yale University Press, 2005).

Edelman, Gerald M., *Second Nature: Brain Science and Human Knowledge* (New Haven: Yale University Press, 2006).

Edelman, Gerald M. and Giulio Tononi, *A Universe of Consciousness: How Matter Becomes Imagination* (New York: Basic Books, 2000).

Edelstein, Eve A. "Mapping Memory of Space & Place," Report on the 2005 Workshop on Neuroscience & Health Care Architecture, at www.anfarch. org.

Epstein, Russell A.; J. Steven Higgins, and Sharon L. Thompson-Schill, "Learning Places from Views: Variation in Scene Processing as a Function of Experience and Navigational Ability," *Journal of Cognitive Neuroscience*, vol. 17, no.1 (2005).

Etchamendy, Nicole and Veronique D. Bohbot, "Spontaneous Navigational Strategies and Performance in the Virtual Town," *Hippocampus* vol. 17, pp. 595–9 (2007).

Filarete (Antonia di Piero Avertino), *Filarete's Treatise on Architecture: Being the Treatise by Antonio di Piero Averlino, Known as Filarete*, trans. John R. Spencer, 2 vols (New Haven: Yale University Press, 1965).

Frampton, Kenneth, "On Reading Heidegger," *Oppositions* 4 (October 1974).

Frampton, Kenneth, "Towards a Critical Regionalism: Six Points for an Architecture of Resistance," in Hal Foster (ed.), *The Anti-Aesthetic: Essays on Postmodern Culture* (Seattle: Bay Press, 1983).

Frampton, Kenneth, *Studies in Tectonic Culture: The Poetics of Construction in Nineteenth and Twentieth Century Architecture* (Cambridge, MA: MIT Press, 1995).

Frascari, Marco, "The *Particolareggiamento* in the Narration of Architecture," *Journal of Architectural Education*, vol. 43, no. 1 (Autumn 1989).

Frascari, Marco, *Monsters of Architecture: Anthropomorphism in Architectural Theory* (Savage, MD: Rowman & Littlefield Publishers, 1991).

Frascari, Marco, "Architectural Synaesthesia: A Hypothesis on the Makeup of Scarpa's Modernist Architectural Drawings," at http://art3idea.psu.edu/ synesthesia.

Fuster, Joaquín M., *Memory in the Cerebral Cortex: An Empirical Approach to Neural Networks in the Human and Nonhuman Primate* (Cambridge, MA: MIT Press, 1995).

Gadol, Joan, *Leon Battista Alberti: Universal Man of the Early Renaissance* (Chicago: University of Chicago Press, 1969).

Galea, S., J, Ahern, S. Rudenstine, Z. Wallace, D. Vlahov, "Urban Built Environment and Depression: A Multilevel Analysis," *Journal of Epidemiology & Community Health*, vol. 59, no. 10, pp. 822–7 (October 2005).

Gazer, Christian and Gottfried Schlaug, "Brain Structures Differ between Musicians and Non-Musicians," *Journal of Neuroscience*, vol. 23, no. 27, pp. 9240–5 (2003).

Geraniotis, Roula, "German Architectural Theory and Practice in Chicago, 1850–1900," *Winterthur Portfolio* vol. 21, no. 4 pp. 293–306 (1986).

Gibson, James, *The Senses Considered as Perceptual Systems* (Boston: Houghton Mifflin, 1966).

Goethe, Johann Wolfgang, "Palladio, Architecture" (1795), in *Goethe on Art*, ed. and trans. John Gage (London: Scolar Press, 1980).

Goldstein, Kurt, *The Organism: A Holistic Approach to Biology Derived from Pathological Data in Man* (New York: Zone Books, 2000; orig. 1934).

Göller, Adolf, *Zur Aesthetik der Architektur: Vorträge und Studien* (Stuttgart: Konrad Wittwer, 1887).

Göller, Adolf, *Die Entstehung der architektonischen Stilformen: Eine Geschichte der Baukunst nach dem Werden und Wandern der Formgedanken* (Stuttgart: Konrad Wittwer, 1888).

Göller, Adolf, "What is the Cause of Perpetual Style Change?" in *Empathy, Form, and Space: Problems in German Aesthetics 1873–1893*, trans. Harry Francis Mallgrave and Eleftherios Ikonomou (Santa Monica: Getty Publication Programs, 1994).

Gombrich, Ernst, *Art and Illusion: A Study in the Pscyhology of Pictorial Representation* (Princeton: Bollingen, 1961).

Gombrich, Ernst, *Sense of Order: The Sense of Order: A Study in the Psychology of Decorative Art* (Ithaca: Cornell University Press, 1979).

Gordon, Alastair, "Credit Swiss," Interview with Pierre de Meuron and Jacques Herzog, in *WSJ. The Magazine from the Wall Street Journal* (Winter 2008), pp. 26–7.

Greenfield, Susan, *The Private Life of the Brain: Emotions, Consciousness, and the Secret of the Self* (New York: John Wiley & Sons, 2000).

Gregotti, Vittorio, "Mimesis," *Casabella*, no. 490, pp. 12–13 (April 1983).

Gurlitt, Cornelius, "Göller's ästhetische Lehre," *Deutsche Bauzeitung* 21, pp. 602–4, 606–7 (December 17, 1887).

Hafting, Torkel, Marianne Fyhn, Sturla Molden, May-Britt Moser, and Edvard I. Moser, "Microstructure of a Spatial Map in the Entorhinal Cortex," *Nature*, vol. 436 (August 11, 2005).

Hayek, Friedrich, *The Sensory Order: An Inquiry into the Foundations of Theoretical Psychology* (Chicago: University of Chicago Press, 1976; orig. 1952).

Healy, Jane, *Endangered Minds: Why Our Children Don't Think – and What We Can Do About It* (New York: Touchstone, 1999; orig 1990).

Hebb, D. O., *The Organization of Behavior: A Neuropsychological Theory* (New York: John Wiley & Sons, 1949).

Heilman, Kenneth M., Stephen E. Nadeau, and David O. Beversdorf, "Creative Innovation: Possible Brain Mechanisms," *Neurocase*, vol. 9, no.5, p. 375 (2003).

Heilman, Kenneth M., *Creativity and the Brain* (New York: Psychology Press, 2005).

Herder, Johann Gottfried, *Sculpture: Some Observations on Shape and Form from Pygmalion's Creative Dream*, ed. and trans. Jason Gaiger (Chicago: University of Chicago Press, 2002).

Herrmann, Wolfgang, *Laugier and Eighteenth Century French Theory* (London: Zwemmer, 1962).

Herrmann, Wolfgang, *The Theory of Claude Perrault* (London: A. Zwemmer, 1973).

Herrmann, Wolfgang, *Gottfried Semper: In Search of Architecture* (Cambridge, MA: MIT Press, 1984).

Herrmann, Wolfgang, *In What Style Should We Build?: The German Debate on Architectural Style* (Santa Monica: Getty Publication Programs, 1992).

Hines, Thomas S., *Richard Neutra and the Search for Modern Architecture* (New York: Oxford University Press, 1982).

Holl, Steven, Juhani Pallasmaa, Alberto Pérez-Gómez, *Questions of Perception: Phenomenology of Architecture* (San Francisco: William Stout Publishers, 2006; originally published as special issue of *a + u*, July 1994).

Horbostel, Erich M., "The Unity of the Senses," trans. by Elizabeth Koffka and Warren Vinton, *Psyche*, vol. 7, no. 28 (1927).

Horkheimer, Max and Adorno, Theodor W., *Dialectic of Enlightenment*, trans. John Cumming (New York: Continuum, 1999; orig. 1947).

Howard, Deborah, "Venice between East and West: Marc'Antonio Barbaro and Palladio's Church of the Redentore," *Journal of the Society of Architectural Historians*, vol. 62, no. 3, pp. 306–25 (September 2003).

Hubel, David H. and Torsten N. Wiesel, *Brain and Visual Perception: The Story of a 25-Year Collaboration* (Oxford: Oxford University Press, 2005).

Hutchinson, Siobhan, Leslie Hui-Lin Lee, Nadine Gaab, and Gottfried Schlaug, "Cerebellar Volume of Musicians," *Cerebral Cortex*, vol. 13, pp. 943–9 (2003).

Hyman, John, "Art and Neuroscience," Interdisciplines: Art and Cognition Workshops, at http://www.interdisciplines.org/artcognition/papers/15.

Ione, Amy, "An Inquiry into Paul Cézanne: The Rome of the Artist in Studies of Perception and Consciousness," *Journal of Consciousness Studies*, vol. 7, nos. 8–9, pp. 57–74 (2000).

Jackson, Maggie, *Distracted: The Erosion of Attention and the Coming Dark Age* (Amherst, NY: Prometheus Books, 2008).

Janzen, Gabriele and Miranda van Turennout, "Selective Neural Representation of Objects Relevant for Navigation," *Nature Neuroscience*, vol. 7, no. 6, pp. 673–8 (June 2004).

Jencks, Charles, *The Language of Post-Modern Architecture* (New York: Rizzoli, 1977).

Johnson, Mark, *The Body in the Mind: The Bodily Basis of Meaning, Imagination, and Reason* (Chicago: University of Chicago Press, 1989).

Johnson, Mark H. (ed.), *Brain Development and Cognition* (Oxford: Blackwell, 1993).

Kandel, Eric R., *In Search of Memory: The Emergence of a New Science of Mind* (New York: Norton, 2006).

Kant, Immanuel, *Critique of Judgment*, trans. J. H. Bernard (New York: Hafner Press, 1951).

Kant, Immanuel, *Critique of Pure Reason*, trans. Norman Kemp Smith (New York: St. Martin's Press, 1965).

Kawabata, Hideaki and Semir Zeki, "Neural Correlates of Beauty," *Journal of Neurophysiology*, vol. 91, pp. 1699–1705 (2004).

Kemp, Martin, *Leonardo da Vinci: Experience, Experiment and Design* (Princeton: Princeton University Press, 2006).

Kemp, Martin, *Leonardo da Vinci: The Marvellous Works of Nature and Man* (Oxford: Oxford University Press, 2006).

Knight, Richard Payne, *An Analytical Inquiry into the Principles of Taste*, 2nd edn. (London: Mews-Gate and J. White, 1805).

Koch, Christof, *The Quest for Consciousness: A Neurobiological Approach* (Englewood, CO: Roberts and Company Publishers, 2004).

Koffka, Kurt, "On the Structure of the Unconscious," in *The Unconscious: A Symposium* (New York: Alfred A. Knopf, 1928).

Koffka, Kurt, *Principles of Gestalt Psychology* (New York: Harcourt, Brace and Company: 1935).

Köhler, Wolfgang, *Gestalt Psychology* (New York: H. Liveright, 1937).

Köhler, Wolfgang, *Dynamics in Psychology* (New York: Washington Square Press, 1965).

Köhler, Wolfgang, *The Selected Papers of Wolfgang Köhler* (New York: Liveright, 1971).

Körner, Stephan, *Kant* (New Haven: Yale University Press, 1955).

Kounios, John, Jennifer L. Frymiare, Edward M. Bowden, Jessica I. Fleck, Karuna Subramaniam, Todd B. Parris, and Mark Jung-Beeman, "The Prepared Mind: Neural Activity Prior to Problem Presentation Predicts Subsequent Solution by Sudden Insight," *Association for Psychological Science*, vol. 17, no. 10 (2006).

Kreij, Kamiel van "Sensory Intensification in Architecture," Technical University Delft, at www.mielio.nl.

Lakoff, George and Mark Johnson, *Metaphors We Live By* (Chicago: University of Chicago Press, 2003; orig. 1980).

Lakoff, George and Mark Johnson, *Philosophy in the Flesh: The Embodied Mind and its Challenge to Western Thought* (New York: Basic Books, 1999).

Laugier, Marc-Antoin, *Essay on Architecture*, trans. by Wolfgang Herrmann (London: Hennessey & Ingalls, 1977).

Leatherbarrow, David and Mohsen Mostafavi, *Surface Architecture* (Cambridge, MA: MIT Press, 2002).

LeDoux, Joseph, *Synaptic Self: How Our Brains Become Who We Are* (New York: Penguin, 2002).

Lefaivre, Liane, *Leon Battista Alberti's Hypnerotomachia Poliphili: Re-cognizing the Architectural Body in the Early Italian Renaissance* (Cambridge, MA: MIT Press, 1997).

Lehrer, Jonah, "The Eureka Hunt; Why do Good Ideas Come To Us When They Do?," *The New Yorker*, vol. 84, no. 22 (July 28, 2008).

Leonardo da Vinci, *The Literary Works of Leonardo Da Vinci*, commentary by Carlo Pedretti, vol. 1 (Berkeley: University of California Press, 1977).

Le Roy, Julien-David, *Les ruines des plus beaux monuments de la Grece* (Paris: Guerin & Delatour, 1758).

Le Roy, Julien-David, *Histoire de la disposition et des formes differentes que les chrétiens ont données à leur temples, depuis le Règne de Constantin la Grand jusqu'à nous* (Paris: Desaind & Saillant, 1764).

Le Roy, Julien-David, *The Ruins of the Most Beautiful Monuments of Greece* (1770 edn.), trans. by David Britt (Los Angeles: Getty Publication Programs, 2004).

Levine, Neil, *The Architecture of Frank Lloyd Wright* (Princeton: Princeton University Press, 1996).

Llinás, Rodolfo R., *The I of the Vortex* (Cambridge, MA: MIT Press, 2001).

Llinás, Rodolfo R. and Patricia S. Churchland, *The Mind–Brain Continuum: Sensory Processes* (Cambridge, MA: MIT Press, 1996).

McEwen, Indra Kagis, *Vitruvius: Writing the Body of Architecture* (Cambridge, MA: MIT Press, 2003).

Malnar, Joy Monice and Frank Vodvarka, *Sensory Design* (Minneapolis: University of Minnesota Press, 2004).

Mallgrave, Harry Francis, "Gottfried Semper, London Lecture of Autumn 1854: 'On Architectural Symbols'," *Res 9: Anthropology and Aesthetics* (Spring 1985).

Mallgrave, Harry Francis, *Gottfried Semper: Architect of the Nineteenth Century* (New Haven: Yale University Press, 1996).

Mallgrave, Harry Francis, *Modern Architectural Theory: A Historical Survey, 1673–1968* (New York: Cambridge University Press, 2005).

Merleau-Ponty, Maurice, *The Structure of Behavior*, trans. Alden L. Fisher (Boston: Beacon Press, 1963; orig. 1942).

Merleau–Ponty, Maurice, *Phenomenology of Perception*, trans. Colin Smith (London: Routledge & Kegan Paul, 1962; orig. 1945).

Merleau-Ponty, Maurice, *The Visible and the Invisible*, ed. Claude Lefort, trans. Alphonso Lingis (Evanston: Northwestern University Press, 1968).

Michelangelo, *The Letters of Michelangelo, 1537–1563*, trans. by E. H. Ramsden (Stanford: Stanford University Press, 1963).

Miller, Michael, cited in "Joyful Music May Promote Heart Health, according to University of Maryland School of Medicine Study," in University of Maryland Medical Center, at http://www.umm.edu/news/releases/music-cardiovascular.htm.

Mitchell, William J., *e-topia: "URBAN LIFE JIM – BUT NOT AS WE KNOW IT"* (Cambridge, MA: MIT Press, 1999).

Mitchell, William J., *Me++: THE CYBORG SELF AND THE NETWORKED CITY* (Cambridge, MA: MIT Press, 2003).

Modell, Arnold H., *The Private Self* (Cambridge, MA: Harvard University Press, 1993).

Modell, Arnold H., *Imagination and the Meaningful Brain* (Cambridge, MA: MIT Press, 2003).

Moneo, Rafael, "The Idea of Lasting," *Perspecta 24: The Yale Architectural Journal* (1988), pp. 154–5.

Moneo, Rafael, *The Freedom of the Architect*, Raoul Wallenberg Lecture (Ann Arbor: University of Michigan, 2002).

Montagu, Ashley, *Touching: The Human Significance of the Skin* (New York: Columbia University Press, 1971).

Monval, Jean, *Soufflot, Sa vie. Son oeuvre. Son esthétique* (Paris: Alphonse Lemerre, 1918).

Mostafavi, Mohsen and David Leatherbarrow, *On Weathering: The Life of Buildings in Time* (Cambridge, MA: MIT Press, 1993).

Neidich, Warren. *Blow-Up: Photography, Cinema and the Brain* (New York: Distributed Art Publishers, 2003).

Neutra, Richard, *Survival through Design* (New York: Oxford University Press, 1954).

O'Keefe, John and J. Dostrovsky, "The Hippocampus as a Spatial Map. Preliminary Evidence from Unit Activity in the Freely-Moving Rat," *Brain Res*, vol. 34, no. 1, pp. 171–5 (1971).

O'Neill, Máire Eithne, "Corporeal Experience: A Haptic Way of Knowing," *Journal of Architectural Education*, vol. 55, no. 1, pp. 3–12 (September 2001).

Onians, John, *Bearers of Meaning: The Classical Orders in Antiquity, the Middle Ages, and the Renaissance* (Princeton: Princeton University Press, 1988).

Onians, John, "Greek Temple and Greek Brain," in George Dodds and Robert Tavernor (eds.), *Body and Building: Essays on the Changing Relation of Body and Architecture* (Cambridge, MA: MIT Press, 2002).

Onians, John, *Neuroarthistory: From Aristotle and Pliny to Baxandall and Zeki* (New Haven: Yale University Press, 2007).

Oppenheimer, Todd, "The Computer Delusion" *The Atlantic* (July 1997).

Palladio, *The Four Books of Architecture*, trans. Isaac Ware (1738), (New York: Dover, 1965).

Pallasmaa, Juhani, *Encounters: Architectural Essays*, ed. Peter Mackeith (Helsinki: Rakennustieto Oy, 2005).

Pallasmaa, Juhani, *The Eyes of the Skin: Architecture and the Senses* (Chichester: John Wiley & Sons, 2005).

Panofsky, Erwin, *The Codex Huygens and Leonardo da Vinci's Art Theory: The Pierpont Morgan Library Codex M.A. 1139* (Westwood, CT: Greenwood Press, 1940).

Panksepp, Jaak, *Affective Neuroscience: The Foundations of Human and Animal Emotions* (Oxford: Oxford University Press, 1998).

Panksepp, Jaak. "On the Embodied Neural Nature of Core Emotional Affects," *Journal of Consciousness Studies*, vol. 12, nos. 8–10 (2005).

Panksepp, Jaak. "Emotional Endophenotypes in Evolutionary Psychiatry," *Progress in Neuro-Psychopharacology and Biological Psychiatry*, vol. 30, no. 5, pp. 774–84 (July 2006).

Panksepp, Jaak and Günther Bernatzky, "Emotional Sounds and the Brain: The Neuro-Affective Foundations of Musical Appreciation," *Behavioural Processes, vol.* 60 (2002).

Penhune, V. B, R. J. Zatorre, and A. C. Evans, "Cerebellar Contributions to Motor Timing: A PET Study of Auditory and Visual Rhythms Reproduction," *Journal of Cognitive Neuroscience*, vol. 10, no. 6, pp. 752–65 (1998).

Pérez-Gómez, Alberto, *Architecture and the Crisis of Modern Science* (Cambridge, MA: MIT Press, 1983).

Perrault, Claude, *Voyage à Bordeaux* (Paris: Renouard, 1909).

Perrault, Claude, *Les Dix livres d'architecture de Vitruve*, 1684 edn. (Paris: Pierre Mardaga, 1984).

Perrault, Claude, *Ordonnance for the Five Kinds of Columns after the Method of the Ancients*, trans. Indra Kagis McEwen (Santa Monica: Getty Publication Programs, 1993).

Piaget, Jean and Inhelder, Bärbel, *The Child's Conception of Space* (London: Routledge and K. Paul, 1956).

Pietrini, Pietro, Maura Furey, Emiliano Ricciardi, M. Ida Gobbini, W.-H. Carolyn Wu, Leonardo Cohen, Mario Guazzelli, and James V. Haxby, "Beyond Sensory Images: Object-Based Representation in Human

Ventral Pathway," *Proceedings of the National Academy of Sciences*, vol. 101, no. 15, pp. 5658–63 (April 13, 2004).

Pink, Daniel H., *A Whole New Mind: Moving from the Information Age to the Conceptual Age* (New York: Riverhead Books, 2005).

Pinker, Steven, *How the Mind Works* (New York: W. W. Norton & Company, 1997).

Price, Uvedale, *Essays on the Picturesque as Compared with the Sublime and the Beautiful; and, on the Use of Studying Pictures for the Purpose of Improving Real Landscape* (London: Mawman, 1810; orig. 1794).

Ramachandran, V. S., *A Brief Tour of Human Consciousness: From Impostor Poodles to Purple Numbers* (New York: Pi Press, 2004).

Ranke, Jr., J. B., "Head Direction Cells in the Deep Cell Layer of Dorsal Postsubiculum in Freely Moving Rats," in *Electrical Activity of the Archicortex*, Akademiai Kiado, Budapest, pp. 217–20.

Rasmussen, Steer Eiler, *Experiencing Architecture* (Cambridge, MA: MIT Press, 1962).

Ricciardi, E., D. Bonnino, C. Gentile, L. Sani, P. Pietrini, and T. Vecchi, "Neural Correlates of Spatial Working Memory in Humans: A Functional Magnetic Resonance Imaging Study Comparing Visual and Tactile Processes," *Neuroscience*, vol. 139 (2006).

Ricoeur, Paul, *The Rule of Metaphor: Multi-disciplinary Studies of the Creation of Meaning in Language*, trans. Robert Czerny (Toronto: University of Toronto Press, 1977).

Rigault, Hippolyte, *Histoire de la Querrelle des Anciens et des Modernes* (Paris: Hachette, 1856).

Rizzolatti, G. and L. Craighero, "The Mirror-Neuron System," *Annual Review in Neuroscience*, vol. 27: 169–92 (2004).

Rousseau, Jean-Jacques, "Has the Restoration of the Sciences and Arts Tended to Purify Morals?" (1750), in *The First and Second Discourse*, trans. Roger D. Masters and Judith R. Masters (New York: St. Martin's Press, 1964).

Rykwert, Joseph, *Adam's House in Paradise: The Idea of the Primitive Hut in Architectural History* (Cambridge, MA: MIT Press, 1972).

Rykwert, Joseph, *The Dancing Column: On Order in Architecture* (Cambridge, MA: MIT Press, 1996).

Rykwert, Joseph, *The Necessity of Artifice* (New York: Rizzoli, 1982).

Sacks, Oliver, *Musicophilia: Tales of Music and the Brain* (New York: Knopf, 2008).

Salingaros, Nikos A., *A Theory of Architecture* (Solingen: UMBAU-VERLAG, 2006).

Schelling, Friedrich Wilhelm Joseph, *The Philosophy of Art*, ed. and trans. Douglas W. Stott (Minneapolis: University Press, 1989).

Schelling, Friedrich Wilhelm Joseph, *System of Transcendental Idealism (1800)*, trans. Peter Heath (Charlottesville: University Press of Virginia, 1993).

Schinkel, Karl Friedrich, Peschken Goerd (ed.), *Das architektonische Lehrbuch* (Berlin: Deutscher Kunstverlag, 1979).

Schlegel, August, *August Schlegel's Vorlesungen über schöne Literatur und Kunst*, 1801–2 (Heilbronn, 1884; reprint Nendeln: Krause, 1968).

Schmarsow, August, "The Essence of Architectural Creation," in *Empathy, Form, and Space: Problems in German Aesthetics 1873–1893*, trans. Harry Francis Mallgrave and Eleftherios Ikonomou (Santa Monica: Getty Publication Programs, 1994).

Schopenhauer, Arthur, *The World as Will and Representation*, trans. E. F. J. Payne (New York: Dover Publications, 1969).

Schopenhauer, Arthur, *On the Fourfold Root of the Principle of Sufficient Reason*, trans. by E. F. J. Payne (La Salle, IL: Open Court, 1974).

Schwarzer, Mitchell, "Ontology and Representation in Karl Bötticher's Theory of Tectonics," *Journal of the Society of Architectural Historians*, vol. 52, no.3, pp. 267–80 (September 1993).

Semper, Gottfried, *The Four Elements of Architecture and Other Writings*, trans. Harry Francis Mallgrave and Wolfgang Herrmann (New York: Cambridge University Press, 1989).

Semper, Gottfried, *Style in the Technical and Tectonic Arts; or, Practical Aesthetics*, trans. Harry Francis Mallgrave and Michael Robinson (Los Angeles: Getty Publication Programs, 2004).

Sinding-Larsen, Staale, "Palladio's Redentore, a Compromise in Composition," *The Art Bulletin*, vol. 47, no. 4, pp. 419–37 (December 1965).

Siong Soon, Chun, Marcel Hans-Jochen Heinze, and John-Dylan Haynes, "Unconscious Determinants of Free Decisions in the Human Brain," *Nature Neuroscience*, vol. 11, no. 5, pp. 543–5 (May 2008).

Snokin (ed.), Michael, *Karl Friedrich Schinkel: A Universal Man* (New Haven: Yale University Press, 1991).

Solso, Robert L., *The Psychology of Art and the Evolution of the Conscious Brain* (Cambridge, MA: MIT Press, 2003).

Soufflot, Jacques-Germian, "Mémoire pour servir de solution à cette question: savoir si dans l'art de l'architecture le goût est préférable à la science des règles ou la sciences des règles au goût," in *Nouvelles archives statisques, historiques et littéraires de départment du Rhône* (Lyons: Barret, 1843).

Soufflot, Jacques-Germain, "Mémoire sur les proportions de l'architecture," in Michel Petzet, *Soufflots Sainte-Geneviève und der französische Kirchenbau des 18. Jahrhunderts* (Berlin: Walter de Gruyter, 1961).

Spiers, Hugo J. and Eleanor A. Maguire, "A 'Landmark' Study of the Neural Basis of Navigation," *Nature Neuroscience*, vol. 7, no. 6 (June 2004).

Spiers, Hugo J. and Eleanor A. Maguire, "A Navigational Guidance System in the Human Brain," *Hippocampus*, vol. 17, no. 8, pp. 624–5 (2007).

Sridaran, Devarajan, Daniel J. Levitin, Chris H. Chaft, Jonathan Berger, and Vinod Menon, "Neural Dynamics of Event Segmentation in Music: Converging Evidence for Dissociable Ventral and Dorsal Networks," *Neuron*, vol. 55, no. 3, pp. 521–32 (August 2, 2007).

Stafford, Barbara Maria, *Echo Objects: The Cognitive Work of Images* (Chicago: University of Chicago Press, 2007).

Talbott, Steve, *Devices of the Soul: Battling for Our Selves in the Age of Machines* (Sebastopol, CA: O'Reilly & Assoc., 2007).

Tootel, R. B., M. S. Silverman, E. Switkes, and R. L. De Valois, "Deoxyglucose Analysis of Retinoptic Organization in Primate Cortex," *Science*, vol. 218, pp. 902–4 (1982).

Turner, Mark, *The Artful Mind: Cognitive Science and the Riddle of Human Creativity* (Oxford: Oxford University Press, 2006).

Vesely, Dalibor, "The Architectonics of Embodiment," in *Body and Building: Essays on the Changing Relation of Body and Architecture* (Cambridge, MA: MIT Press, 2002).

Vesely, Dalibor, *Architecture in the Age of Divided Representation: The Question of Creativity in the Shadow of Production* (Cambridge, MA: MIT Press, 2004).

Virilio, Paul, *The Vision Machine*, trans. Julie Rose (Bloomington: Indiana University Press, 1994; orig. 1988).

Vischer, Friedrich Theodor, "Kritik meiner Äesthetik," in *Kritische Gänge*, vol. 5 (Stuttgart: Cotta, 1866).

Vischer, Friedrich Theodor, *Aesthetik; oder, Wissenschaft des Schönen*, ed. Robert Vischer, vol. 3, 2nd edn. (Munich: Meyer & Jessen, 1922–3).

Vischer, Robert, "Der ästhetische Akt und die reine Form," in *Drei Schriften zum ästhetischen Formproblem* (Halle: Max Niemeyer, 1927).

Vischer, Robert, "On the Optical Sense of Form: A Contribution to Aesthetics," in *Empathy, Form, and Space: Problems in German Aesthetics 1873–1893*, trans. Harry Francis Mallgrave and Eleftherios Ikonomou (Santa Monica: Getty Publication Programs, 1994).

Vitruvius, *Ten Books on Architecture*, trans. Ingrid D. Rowland, Commentary and Illustrations by Thomas Noble Howe (Cambridge: Cambridge University Press, 1999).

Wagner, Otto, *Otto Wagner: Modern Architecture, A Guidebook for His Students to This Field of Art*, trans. Harry Francis Mallgrave (Santa Monica: Getty Publication Programs, 1988).

Watt, Douglas F., "Consciousness, Emotional Self-Regulation and the Brain: Review Article," *Journal of Consciousness Studies*, vol. 11, no. 9, pp. 77–8 (2004).

Wertheimer, Max, "Experimentelle Studien über das Sehen von Bewegung," *Zeitschrift für Psychologie*, vol. 61, pp. 161–265 (1912).

Winckelmann, J. J., *Reflections on the Imitation of Greek Works in Painting and Sculpture*, trans. Elfriede Heyer and Roger C. Norton (La Salle, IL: Open Court, 1987).

Wittkower, Rudolf, *Architectural Principles in the Age of Humanism* (London: Academy Editions, 1962).

Wölfflin, Heinrich, "Prolegomena to a Psychology of Architecture," in *Empathy, Form, and Space: Problems in German Aesthetics 1873–1893*, trans. Harry Francis Mallgrave and Eleftherios Ikonomou (Santa Monica: Getty Publication Programs, 1994).

Wright, Frank Lloyd, *Frank Lloyd Wright: Collected Writings, 1894–1930*, ed. Bruce Brooks Pfeiffer (New York: Rizzoli, 1992).

Wundt, Wilhelm, *Principles of Physiological Psychology*, trans. Edward Bradford Titchener (1904), in "Classics in the History of Psychology," An internet resource developed by Christopher D. Green, York University, Toronto, Ontario.

Zammito, John H., *The Genesis of Kant's Critique of Judgment* (Chicago: University of Chicago Press, 1992).

Zatorre, Robert, "Music, the Food of Neuroscience," *Nature*, vol. 434 (March 17, 2005).

Zeki, Semir, "Functional Specialization in the Visual Cortex of the Rhesus Monkey," *Nature*, vol. 274, pp. 423–8 (1974).

Zeki, Semir, "Art and the Brain," *Journal of Consciousness Studies: Controversies in Science & the Humanities*, vol. 6, nos. 6–7, pp. 76–96 (June/July 1999).

Zeki, Semir, "Artistic Creativity and the Brain," *Science*, vol. 293, no. 5527, pp. 51–2 (June 7, 2001).

Zeki, Semir, "The Disunity of Consciousness," *Trends in Cognitive Sciences*, vol .7, no. 5, pp. 214–18 (May 2003).

Zeki, Semir, *Inner Vision: An Exploration of Art and the Brain* (Oxford: Oxford University Press, 1999).

Zeki, Semir, "Neural Concept Formation and Art: Dante, Michelangelo, Wagner, in Rose, F. Clifford, *Neurology of the Arts: Painting, Music, Literature* (London: Imperial College Press, 2004).

Zeki, Semir, "The Neurology of Ambiguity," *Consciousness and Cognition*, vol. 13, no. 1, pp. 173–96 (March 2004).

Zeki, Semir and Andreas Bartels, "Toward a Theory of Visual Consciousness," *Consciousness and Cognition*, vol. 8, pp. 225–59 (1999).

Zeki, Semir, *A Vision of the Brain* (Oxford: Blackwell Scientific Publications, 1993).

Zukowsky, John (ed.), *Karl Friedrich Schinkel: The Drama of Architecture* (Chicago: Art Institute of Chicago, 1994).

Zumthor, Peter, *Atmospheres: Architectural Environments – Surrounding Objects* (Basel: Birkhäuser, 2006).

Zumthor, Peter, *Thinking Architecture*, trans. Maureen Oberli-Turner and Catherine Schelbert (Basel: Birkhäuser, 2006).

Index